COMBAT LOVE

A Story of Leaving, Longing, and Searching for Home

COMBAT L♡VE

ALISYN CAMEROTA

RARE BIRD
LOS ANGELES, CALIF.

RARE BIRD

THIS IS A GENUINE RARE BIRD BOOK

Rare Bird Books
6044 North Figueroa Street
Los Angeles, CA 90042
rarebirdbooks.com

For more information, address:
Rare Bird Books Subsidiary Rights Department
6044 North Figueroa Street
Los Angeles, CA 90042

Thanks to Tom Hearn, Doug McLearen, Fran Pelzman Liscio, and Bobby Grossman
for their killer Shrapnel photos

Set in Minion
Printed in the United States

10 9 8 7 6 5 4 3 2 1

Library of Congress Cataloging-in-Publication Data available upon request

Contents

For my mother

com.bat/ˈkämˌbat/ *noun—1. fighting, battle, conflict.*
verb—take action to reduce or prevent something bad or undesirable.

Author's Note

The decision to write a memoir is not an easy one, especially when your day job requires you to stay out of every story you broadcast to the world. TV news anchors are trained to keep their own histories and feelings under wraps. Besides, why open the painful pages of your diary to the public? Why crack that emotional can of worms? As anyone who has ever made it to the other side of survival mode knows, it's nice to pretend that all's well and always has been.

Writing this book gave me a chance to return to the imperfect past, to find the scattered pieces and try to make sense of them, putting them together to make a whole. To make me whole. The story of my becoming a TV reporter begins with a fervent childhood desire to be seen and heard. It turns out that being a TV reporter was exactly what that little girl needed to feel valued. It took the adult woman longer to figure out how to have a whole and happy life.

I've been told by bosses that my special sauce as a journalist is an ability to connect, whether I'm interviewing a crime victim or the criminal. I'm not faking this. I *do* feel a connection. I often relate to victims and perpetrators, to drug addicts and their desperate families, to cheaters and the cheated. I've known different forms of desperation too.

In journalism school, we're taught to be impartial. *Check your biases at the door.* But of course, we do bring our own life experiences to the story. And some stories can hit very close to home. I often wish I could say to an interview subject: "I recognize you. I've been there." But that's not in my job description.

There are a lot of great books out there about being a journalist. This isn't one of them. I won't be writing about my sit-downs with Donald Trump or Hilary Clinton or Joe Biden. This isn't a behind-the-scenes look at CNN or a tell-all about my time at FOX. (I should probably have mentioned this before you bought the book but thank you!) This is a story about love, loss, and relationships. It's a story about sex, drugs, and punk rock. Mostly, it's the story of a lifelong search for that elusive place called home. So, come to think of it, I guess it is about being a journalist.

I have a great auditory memory for words, lyrics, jokes, and stories. I often remember conversations word for word. But as I wrestled with how to write this memoir, I didn't want to rely solely on my own recall. So, I turned to letters, photographs, and diaries I kept during that time. I also went back and interviewed every primary person in this story (well, those who were still alive) to confirm the accuracy of my version of events. I cross-checked my chronology with newspaper clippings, concert posters, ticket stubs, and other original sources. For privacy reasons, I've changed all of my family's names, and almost all of my friends' names—except for the people too famous to tamper with, (i.e., Shrapnel, Mailer). The name "Peter Reefer" is a composite character, a stand-in for various friends who were always around, too many to name.

Every note, diary entry, and letter is virtually verbatim.

I wrote this book for a couple reasons. The first is deeply personal. Being the mom of three teenagers, who are the same age as I was in much of this book, I wanted to make sense of the white space between shelter and risk, nurture and neglect, parenting and personal freedom. The second is that I've come to believe that sharing our stories of struggle is empowering—for the storyteller and the listener.

So, even though I've spent decades trying to play by the important journalistic rule of not making myself the story, I think it might be helpful for viewers and readers, particularly in these divided times, to know that even your trusty, neutral news anchor also has a backstory of pain and struggle, survival and hope.

Preface

Confession: I don't love breaking news. I know that's weird for a newscaster to say. And sure, breaking news is fine when I'm in a climate-controlled studio getting developing details fed to me through my earpiece and teleprompter. But being out in a sweaty or snowy field, running-and-gunning to beat the rest of the scrum, is hard as hell. I've never been one of those newshounds who gets an endorphin high from the initial inkling of a situation unfolding. I prefer to let a story slow-bake, giving me time to gather my thoughts and get my head around the arc before I start broadcasting bits and pieces of scant information to the world.

Some breaking news sends an expected jolt.

"OK, we're coming to you right out of the break!" My producer is breathless. Through the plastic device nestled in the cradle of my ear, he relays the latest info. "Largest auto recall in history. Some thirty-four million vehicles. Multiple plaintiffs filing lawsuits." His stilted syntax tells me he's reading a newswire alert. His planned rundown has just blown up, and he's scrambling during our three-minute commercial break. "Here's what you need to know, the Takata airbags are the problem and it's really scary stuff. I've just read a few of the affidavits, and apparently, when these airbags deploy in a crash, shrapnel explodes everywhere."

Shrapnel everywhere.

You'd be surprised how often I have to say the word "shrapnel" for my job. An auto recall, a battle in Ukraine, a mass shooting. Of course, I can't tell anyone that, for me, the word carries a positive connotation. Naturally, I can't let a fond expression cross my face. Even all these decades later, every time I say "shrapnel," I wonder who out there caught it. Maybe Frankie happened to be in front of a TV and gave a knowing nod. Maybe Beez was waiting at a doctor's office and smiled at the screen.

Most breaking news makes me anxious. I get nervous about jumping on a plane and jetting off to a foreign location with no return date. That's the job of a journalist. At the first sign of a crisis, we start mobilizing, calling around for airline seats, grabbing our passports and go-bags with enough CLIF Bars and face powder to last for the unknown duration of the emergency.

Confession #2: I'm bad at the go-bag. I routinely land at a location only to discover I've forgotten to pack vital necessities like a laptop charger and pants. Because, on some level, I'm trying to apply the brakes to breaking news. I guess the trips to unfamiliar places in my teenage years took their toll. I prefer to stay put. I like knowing when I'll be home.

By definition, breaking news is disturbing: terror attacks, plane crashes, school shootings. There's an aloneness to these emergencies. Yes, I have the support of a team of incredibly talented producers, but when it comes to accurately making sense of it on-air, the responsibility is mine alone.

As my taxi speeds to the airport, I'm extra jittery. A ticker tape of questions scrolls through my head: *What time will I land? Will I miss my connection? How long will it take to drive 200 miles? Where will I sleep? Will the pouring rain ruin my hair? Should I stop to buy a brush and blow dryer?* But those thoughts are better than the ones vying to invade: the bloody scene, the parents waiting for word, the children who will never come home. What if *I* never come home?

I race through security with seconds to spare before takeoff. No time to grab a sandwich or a couple spare pairs of underwear. I run to the gate and down the jetway onto the plane.

And there they are. Unexpected, yet so familiar.

Scattered about the cabin, I see the faces of old friends. There's my former cohost from another station, whom I haven't seen in years. And my old intern, who's now a local reporter. And the same three network correspondents I've crossed paths with in Paris and Nova Scotia and Orlando. They point. We laugh. I say, "Ah, we meet again," because it feels like we've been here so many times. And the next thing I know, the anchor from a rival morning show, who I don't really know but feel like I do because we see each other's faces every morning, starts showing me pictures of his toddler, and, on some level, we're old friends, though we've never met. We share a knowledge of what it's taken for both of us to get here and how hard the days ahead will be in the broiling Texas sun or the freezing Brussels rain. How we'll have to remain cool and composed while saying gut-wrenching things.

We also know that neither of us knows when we'll have our next meal or get some sleep or see our loved ones. He says that the story we're about to cover is awful, that he has a ten-year-old kid, just like the parents we will interview. I squeeze his arm because our breaking news bond allows that kind of intimacy, even between virtual strangers. Regardless of what network we work for, we're all part of a close-knit news family. I've made a lifelong practice of turning friends, and sometimes strangers, into family. Growing up without siblings and trying to navigate life's turbulence with distant and distracted parents turned on my searchlights to find "family" wherever I could. These surrogate families mean more to me than they'll ever know.

A cameraman I used to work with had a favorite phrase about our common TV practice of showing up at the scene of a disaster, getting subjects to spill their guts, then leaving:

"Fly in, wreck a few lives, fly out."

I never saw it that way. I always believed that on balance, our presence at a disaster was helpful, not hurtful. But I took his point that we demand a lot of a community. We ask cops to share their files and give us leads. We convince victims to go on camera, open their homes to us, and bare their souls. Our questions in sit-down interviews require a concentration of sadness and intimacy, during which it can feel like no one has ever listened more closely or connected more deeply. It can feel like we've become best friends; sometimes it can even feel like love (I still have a half-dozen letters from one enamored bank robber I interviewed in prison). Then we journalists unhook our microphones, pack up our light kits and camera bags, and head off on our merry way. If I'm being completely candid, I'm always relieved to board that plane out and head away from the trauma. We get to leave; the devastated community is left behind.

For a long time, I thought those were the only two choices.

PART ONE

leave /lēv/ *verb. 1. to go away from; 2. to allow to remain.*
leav.ing /ˈlivɪŋ/ *noun. 1. something that is left; 2. residue.*

PART ONE

The First to Flee

My story begins in front of a TV screen. I don't mean on camera. I mean literally sitting in front of a television. From the moment I got home from elementary school to just before dinner, I sat in what we called our "TV room," which also served as a tiny guest room with a pullout sofa, big turquoise desk, red twist pile carpet, and my beloved twenty-three-inch color Zenith. I was by myself but never alone, thanks to Keith Partridge, Marcia Brady, Eddie Munster, Wilma Flintstone, Gilligan and his pals, et al. Reruns, original episodes, it didn't matter. I just wanted the company of my TV friends. My mother remembers hearing a novel sound coming from the TV room one day when I was a toddler. I couldn't speak in full sentences yet, but there I was, chortling away over some hilarious hijinks on *I Love Lucy*. At five years old, I sent a letter to David Cassidy (a.k.a. Keith Partridge) inviting him to my birthday party.

I watched TV the way other kids played sports. I was *invested*. By six, I could sing every theme song and had memorized the names in the credits. I guffawed along with laugh tracks, which I assumed was the laughter of other viewers at home in their own TV rooms. I wanted them to hear my voice too. So, I got off the sofa, kneeled next to the Zenith—its screen hot from overuse—then flattened my cheek against the static-prone metal speaker, and laughed extra heartily into it to make sure my enjoyment was being broadcast to the world.

Around that same time, at five or six years old, an invisible cameraman started following me around. He hovered over me (in a manner suspiciously similar to the cartoon character The Great Gazoo from *The Flintstones*), capturing newsworthy moments in my life when nobody else seemed to be paying attention.

Did you catch that? I asked his aerial presence.

I sure did, he assured me.

Back then, I didn't know that someday I would appear on television, but I knew I was already on assignment, ears perked, searching for answers. I stood in front of my mother in our narrow kitchen as she tended to a bubbling pot of tomato gravy, the smell of parsley permeating the steamy air.

"Who do you love more?" I asked. "Me or Dad?"

She'd heard this one before. "Well," she said, dunking a wooden spoon into the cauldron of boiling water to stir the macaroni. "I love you both."

"I know. But who do you love *the most*?" I hung by her side, waiting as she fished out a pasta shell for me to determine if it was al dente and ready to be drained.

Mom stared into the steam. "I love you both, in different ways."

That was not the right answer. The right answer was that she loved me the most in the world, the way I felt about her. It's strange how even a young child can sense when something is not quite right, when someone is distant, or if some part is missing, even though that person is standing right next to her. Somehow my six-year-old radar picked up this distant signal, which compelled me to check in constantly and bring her back. Maybe a bear hug or sunshower of kisses could have broken my spell of neediness, assured me I wasn't alone, and assuaged my brewing anxiety, but those weren't remedies my parents used. Words were the salve my mother preferred.

"Alisyn, you are my only child, and I was meant to have you," she finally said. "I didn't care if you were a boy or a girl. I asked God for a child that was healthy and smart. And I knew from the first week you were born that you were exactly the right child for me."

Even that didn't satisfy me. Mom was my favorite companion, and I believed I was hers—the two of us side-by-side in the produce section of ShopRite, at the counter to pick up Dad's dry cleaning, in our vegetable garden tugging out weeds. Mom brought me to her late-night rehearsals for every high school musical she ever directed. When I was three, she cast me as a munchkin in *The Wizard of Oz* so I could be with her rather than with a babysitter. I couldn't imagine a life without her but feared she might disappear.

In truth, it was Dad who was slowly vanishing, even when he was sitting on our satiny green sofa, the color of a dollar bill. Every night before dinner, I watched him set his martini glass on the coffee table under the framed print of Don Quixote. Dad stirred the clear liquid with his pointer finger, unsettling three cloudy onions lolling at the bottom. He took a sip, then stared into the long shafts of late-afternoon sun streaming into the living room. Dust particles hung in the sunbeams, suspended and drifting.

On those evenings, the living room was heavy with a hollow quiet that made my stomach ache. But then the needle made its scratchy landing, and I held my breath, clasping my hands, ready for the music to lift the mood. Starting very young, I understood the power of music. Music as an escape, music as medicine, music as guidance. I looked to lyrics as mystical affirmations from music gods that carried wisdom and direction for my life. I memorized songs quickly, even when I didn't understand the words, and sang them as if looking out into a packed house: *"Will Come In, bee-yen venu. Welcome…Happy to see you!"*

"It's *Willkommen*," Dad said.

"Leave your troubles outside!" I ordered Dad. "So-life eez disappointing? Forget it! In here, life eez beautiful…Zee girls are beautiful…Even zee orchestra is beautiful!"

Dad laughed his deep laugh and moved his head to the *Cabaret* soundtrack to let me know he was playing along, then flicked open his shiny silver lighter, sparking the blue flame, holding it to his cigarette, breathing in deeply, exhaling swirls of gray smoke into the fading gold light.

Some nights, it was *Cabaret*. Some nights *Man of La Mancha*, the lyrics of which I also sang with gusto. *"That one man, scorned and covered with scars, still strove, with his last ounce of courage, to reach the unreachable star!"* The songs were always about being somewhere else, a foreign land, far away from a living room in New Jersey.

After dinner, Dad actually vanished—upstairs to the TV room to watch *Mission Impossible* or *It Takes a Thief* or just to sleep. Dad's after-dinner routine demanded quiet.

"Dad has a headache," Mom explained. Even on the nights I was allowed to sit by his side to watch TV, I knew not to engage in chitchat. I sensed Dad preferred things left unspoken, and a child learns how to leave questions unasked. Most nights, I happily stayed downstairs with Mom. We would settle in on our side of the sofa, the opposite from Dad's, to read whatever book she had selected that week. *Little House in the Big Woods, Alice in Wonderland, A Wrinkle in Time, The Phantom Tollbooth.*

"I wonder if you're ready for *Huckleberry Finn*," Mom mused, tapping her index finger gently against her lips. "Though we should probably start with *Tom Sawyer.*"

When we finished a book, she crossed it off her handwritten list, then we walked hand in hand to the public library, one block from our home, in search of our next story. Under the honeyed glow of the lamp, Mom turned to the first page of our latest selection and ran her long slender finger over the words.

"*My Ántonia.* By Willa Cather. Let's see when this book was written." She flipped the page. "Copyright 1918. So, then fifty-five years ago. OK, Pumpkin, are you ready?"

I nodded.

She turned another page and pointed to a quote in italics. "*Optima dies... prima fugit*–Virgil." She paused.

"What does that mean?"

"It's Latin. It means the best days are the first to flee."

I squeezed my arm through Mom's, making sure she couldn't go anywhere, and rested my head on her shoulder, breathing in the sweet smell of her green apple shampoo. She stroked my braids.

"What happens if you die?" I said.

"I'm not going to die."

"I know. But what if you do?"

"Well, then, Gram and Poppy would take care of you."

That wasn't the right answer, either. The right answer was that I would die too. Only later did I realize she never said Dad would take care of me—and only later did I realize I never expected him to. I wrapped my arms more tightly around her. Sometimes, as I drifted to sleep, she'd close the book and sing.

"You are my sunshine, my only sunshine. You make me happy when skies are blue. You'll never know dear, how much I love you. Please don't take my sunshine away."

International Man of Mystery

On paper, my parents' marriage made sense. Both were raised in the Italian immigrant stronghold of South Philadelphia, in stifling row houses, with Rosary-clutching relatives. My mother, Catherine Graziana, was a Grace Kelly look-alike. My father, Antonio Camerota, while not movie-star handsome, had bright green eyes and plenty of savoir faire. Both were academic stars. My father attended an invitation-only all-boys high school and later the Army Language School, graduating first in his class. My mother attended a large public high school, graduating first in her class and earning a full scholarship to the University of Pennsylvania.

But Dad wasn't Mom's first choice.

In college, my mother had fallen in love with a nuclear physics major, and on her twenty-first birthday, they got engaged. Her fiancé was Jewish, which was enough to make my Roman Catholic grandmother take to bed with a cold compress on her head while aunts and uncles launched an intense how-could-you-do-this-to-your-mother campaign. After three months of gnawing guilt, my mother broke off her engagement.

A year later, when she brought home my father, a not-quite-divorced man eight years her senior, my grandparents kept quiet. At least Antonio was Catholic, they said. My father was also cosmopolitan. He spoke six languages. He showed up in his Porsche wearing a jacket and tie, and spoke fluent Italian to my grandfather's cousin visiting from Italy—something my Philadelphia-born grandparents could not do. My father was also skilled in the popular Italian art of *la bella figura*—projecting a polished appearance to make a good impression, a concept he simultaneously scoffed at and practiced.

Mom wasn't materialistic. She didn't care about the Porsche, but she did think it symbolized the life of adventure she would have with my father. When they got married, Mom had never been west of Philadelphia or east of her summer spot, Wildwood, New Jersey. She'd never been on an airplane.

My parents moved two hours north of Philadelphia to the tiny town of Shrewsbury, New Jersey, named after the town in England known for being Darwin's birthplace. They bought a home on the main thoroughfare: a four-lane highway, Route 35, or Broad Street to locals. Our house was set ten stone steps above street level and painted bright white with shiny black shutters. It was made of poured concrete, which gave it a distinctively sturdy look. My parents particularly liked the property: one long acre on which my father planted a big vegetable garden, an herb garden, and several stone fruit trees. They added an above-ground pool.

Shrewsbury was just two square miles with roughly three thousand people; a solidly middle-class small town filled with modest split-levels and ranch houses, wild honeysuckle bushes, and sidewalks for bikes with banana seats. Our house was exactly seven miles away from the ocean. Half a block away was the Allen House, one of the oldest buildings in New Jersey, the scene of a Continental troop massacre by Loyalist soldiers in 1779. Down the street was Christ Church, which still held a hole in its steeple from musket fire.

My parents picked Shrewsbury because of its proximity to Monmouth Regional, a new high school in the next town over where they'd both landed teaching positions. Dad became a Russian teacher and head of the language department; Mom became an English and drama teacher. It was not lost on my mother that the seventy-five-mile drive from Philly to Shrewsbury could serve as a buffer between her and her parents. At twenty-two, she didn't know a single other young woman who had dared to move that far from home and leave her family behind. And my mother was fine with that.

Some people joked that my father might be a spy. Maybe it was his impeccable *la bella figura* that kept you from seeing under his surface. Or his mysterious way of not answering questions. Or the way he held his martini glass like James Bond. Maybe it was because he spoke fluent Italian, French, Spanish, German, and Russian. Even a little Chinese. After graduating from the Army Language School, Dad had spent a year stationed in Germany during the Korean War and was tasked with interrogating border crossers in their native languages. At least that's what he told us.

The day before I was born, Dad left his teaching job and took a new position with Scholastic Publishing as their language specialist in charge of European editions. Scholastic was impressed with Dad's linguistic brilliance, but the job turned out to be less substantial than advertised. Several years later, when the position of Vice President opened, Dad was passed over in favor of the boss's son. Dad was crushed. His mood darkened. He started opting out of dinner parties with friends and birthday parties with relatives. He began roaming the Diamond District in midtown Manhattan, admiring the gems and fantasizing about getting away from it all—the commute, the boss, the concrete jungle.

To appease him, Scholastic offered to send Dad on a business trip to Rome and said he could bring us along. Mom's face lit up. *Italy!* We'd be going on a plane! I had a recurring dream in which I could fly up the basement stairs in my nightgown, but I couldn't imagine what it would feel like to truly be in the clouds. Mom and I hurried to the library to check out books on teaching Italian to children. Dad went ahead to Rome for two weeks while Mom and I sat on the sofa practicing Italian. Mom made up funny phrases for me to repeat. "*Perche e una banana nella vasca da bagno?*" she asked. Why is a banana in the bathtub? I collapsed in giggles. Some nights I was too excited to fall asleep.

The morning before our flight, Dad called from Rome. I watched Mom's face drain. She hung up and looked down at the rug for many long seconds before telling me. The trip was off. Something about bedbugs in the mattresses and Dad quitting his job. I begged her to call him back. I was only six but already believed I had the persuasive power to convince someone to change his mind. But Dad was gone. The hotel couldn't find him. I went to my room, tripped over my open suitcase, and threw myself on my bed. Downstairs, I heard Mom on the phone, struggling through long pauses to explain to Gram and Poppy, my grandparents, that we would not need a ride to the airport after all. Over the next several years, I would hear more long pauses connected to Dad, the unstated suspicions of polite people who didn't want to delve too deeply.

After Dad quit the publishing job, he became more upbeat, slightly more energized, and much more peculiar. He didn't take as many naps, but he still didn't have time to teach me to ride a bike because he was busy teaching himself to play the oboe.

Every night after dinner, Dad would take the rectangular case off the shelf, remove and assemble the black base, then hover his pinky fingers over the shiny silver buttons. He licked his lips, cleared his throat, and positioned the oboe just so before blowing some deep whale sounds. Then, he carefully disassembled the parts and put the oboe away for the night. After a few weeks, the oboe stayed on the shelf as Dad transitioned to Tai Chi. He practiced in the middle of the living room, his arms in an L, frozen as if carved by Michelangelo. Dad could hold his balance for long stretches, even after a couple martinis. I studied the strange nubby nails of his left hand that Dad said never looked the same after a gun backfired on him in the Army.

Tai Chi led straight to ESP. Dad thought he could predict things, like when the phone would ring or what number I was thinking of. He rarely got it right, but I fudged the results in his favor because being right seemed so important to him.

And then, Dad started making masks. These were no placid art projects; this was extreme crafting, Dad down in our basement in a welder's mask with a soldering gun. Using a bright blue flame, he melted metal into submission, then hammered, twisted, spray-painted, and paper-mached his vision to life and onto our living room walls.

One day, I was watching him try to meld two painted faces together, one happy, one sad, when the newspaper under the mask suddenly went up in a whoosh of flames. I yelled for Mom.

"Everybody okay down there?" she called from the top of the steps.

Dad grabbed the fire extinguisher and blasted the newspaper.

"I blame the muses!" he said, pointing to the mask and arching an eyebrow my way. "Comedy and Tragedy. The secrets to life."

Masks, literal and figurative, would become ever-present in my home.

⏪ ⏸ ⏩

On Saturday mornings, Dad started searching flea markets for precious stones and antique ring settings. He began reading library books on gold and gems, cuts and carats, and scribbling ring designs on scrap paper. He taught me that twenty-four-carat gold was purer than eighteen. Platinum was the strongest. He felt I should wear platinum. Sometimes, he'd bring home beautiful rocks, dark gray and crusty on the outside with jagged purple peaks of sparkly amethyst on the inside that looked like something only a queen could afford. He displayed the geodes on little plastic stands on our living room end tables, and I'd gaze at them from every angle.

Dad decided to open a jewelry shop. It would need a name, so he asked me to think of one. The Golden Palace? The Diamond Castle? Dad had me doodle pictures of my dream rings, gold crayon curlicues. Under each of my designs, he wrote my initials over and over in his long swirling cursive.

"A-L-C, A-L-C," he repeated, then put it together, "Alc." He smiled broadly. "That's it. That's the name. We'll call the store Alchemy."

Alchemy opened on a quaint corner in Fairhaven, a pretty town on the Navesink River, four miles from our home. The store was narrow, with two long glass cases lit with tiny light bulbs. Dad had a small worktable in the back where he sat popping on and off his black magnifying loupe, bringing diamonds close to his face.

"See those little bubbles in there?" he asked, handing me the loupe.

"Yes," I said, though I wasn't sure.

"Those are imperfections. The best diamonds are flawless."

I wandered around the store, caressing the warm glass cases, then sat on a folding chair, sliding the silver measuring circles on and off my fingers, imagining the rings of flawless diamonds Dad would make for me. When I got too bored, I'd amble next door to visit Sharon and Joan, the women who ran an antique shop packed tight with vases, dusty books, and chests. Joan was a nice lumpy old lady who stayed glued to her rocker much of the time, but Sharon was sassy. She had short dark hair and tight clothing and could emit a loud whistle using two fingers under her tongue. She had a daughter exactly my age.

"Hey, kiddo," Sharon smiled as I roamed their tables. "Is it true your father speaks seven languages?"

"Oh, yes," I said.

"Is he a spy?" Sharon shot Joan a giggly look. "Not that he said that! We were just wondering."

I could tell these ladies were fans. I was used to that. People were attracted to my father. Dad had a way about him. He knew just when to arch an eyebrow and take a drag of his Parliament, letting you know that something you'd said was percolating with him. He knew how to insert a Da Vinci reference into the appraisal of random artwork, making a crappy painting seem more valuable. He knew when to add his deep chuckle to your joke, allowing you to bubble with your own cleverness. Dad's small, strategic punctuations had the effect of making those of us around him feel smarter, funnier, and more sophisticated than we really were.

From time to time, customers actually came into Alchemy. I held my breath, waiting for Dad to approach to show off the beautiful rings he'd designed. But he stayed in the back, eye loupe on, studying the gems. It became clear that Dad preferred searching for perfect diamonds over dealing with imperfect patrons.

So I sprang up. "May I help you?"

The gentleman turned to look down at the seven-year-old salesgirl.

"This is my apprentice…Alisyn," Dad called from his back table. He always imbued my name with grandeur…as if it deserved a drum roll.

I had played out this moment in my head and imagined how proud Dad would be as he regaled Mom with the story of my sale. But it never happened.

Still, someone must have been buying Dad's jewelry because he often came home with what seemed like celebratory pieces: a pendant necklace with a red coral hand holding a solid gold dagger for Mom. For me, a gold link bracelet connected by half a dozen platinum hearts. A grown-up emerald ring in a filigree setting.

"This is an awfully ornate ring, Tony," Mom said, frowning at it. "She can't wear this."

"So, she'll grow into it."

Mom tucked my rings and bracelets into black velvet boxes in her dresser drawer, alongside all the special pieces Dad had given her: diamond rings in antique settings, a one-of-a-kind carved jade stone from the handle of a

Samurai sword. Her favorite was a necklace made of smooth amber ovals with veins the color of burnt brown sugar. The stones looked like sweet liquid honey. Sometimes I'd lick them.

A few months after Dad opened the jewelry store, I noticed the return of his multiple martinis, his faraway stares, and the *Man of La Mancha* music. *"To dream the impossible dream. To reach the unreachable star."* Even show tunes couldn't lift the heaviness of the living room air anymore. Also, the phone started ringing. A lot.

"A call will be incoming," Dad predicted from his perch on the sofa.

"From who?" I asked.

"Unclear," he said.

The back of my neck prickled when he acted as if he were plugged into a different frequency than the rest of us and could detect unseen things. I didn't openly question his powers, but I was skeptical. It didn't take a psychic to predict the phone would ring since it rang around the clock. The calls were strange. Just breathing on the other end.

"I can hear you, you know?" I'd taunt the caller, growing more emboldened as the weeks went on. "What are you, a weirdo?"

The ringing was so relentless, Mom resorted to taking the receiver off the hook for hours, a busy signal left to bleat on the side table.

It's Too Late

I was asleep but the sharp voices downstairs woke me. For a solid heart-pounding minute, I thought robbers had broken into our house.

"Do not touch me!" I heard Mom hiss. Dad's response was deep and growly, too low to make out.

Then Mom's voice, fierce like I'd never heard. "I'll have Alisyn call the police, that's what!"

I jumped out of bed and ran to the banister overlooking the staircase.

"Mom!" I screamed. "I will call the police! I will!"

A sudden silence. Dad appeared at the foot of the stairs. "It's okay, honey. Mom's okay. You can go back to sleep now."

Dear Mom and Dad, (Valentine's Day 1972—6 years old)
Never fight Becose I love you both Tell daddy to don't be anoyed about the phon call and jobs. I'm sory I din't get the phon numbar of the man. And don't ever fight. Happy Valentine and be Happy.

And remember it takes two to tango.

Love,

Alisyn

One night soon after, Mom sat behind me, braiding my hair at bedtime. Without warning, Dad kicked open my bedroom door in a loud crack. He stood in the middle of the doorframe staring silent daggers at us before turning and leaving. I started crying. I didn't know what was happening but knew that Dad kept a couple of guns in his closet and that he was starting to scare me. Another night, just before dinner, Mom, out of nowhere, heaved a whole eggplant down the length of the kitchen, narrowly missing my head before it thwacked against the wall.

I could see the unraveling even before the day they called me to the living room. Dad sat on the chair, Mom on the sofa. I stood between them.

"Mom and I have decided that I'm going to be moving to a different house," Dad said.

I had only one question. "Who am I going to live with?" I held my breath.

"You're going to stay with Mom."

I exhaled. Mom and I would be together. Everything was going to be fine.

In 1973, I did not know a single kid with divorced parents. I did know one other girl with separated parents: Sharon's daughter, from the antique store next to Dad's.

On the week Dad moved his stuff out, Sharon and her daughter came to our house, which had never happened before. Mom told me to take the girl upstairs while she and Sharon went for a walk in the backyard. The girl and I sat on my rug.

"Are you crying?" I asked her.

"No," she said.

"What's that?" I asked, pointing to a teardrop on her cheek.

"Perspiration," she said. Not sweat. Perspiration. It was possibly the most mature thing I'd ever heard. We daughters of separation had to grow up faster.

Years later, I would learn that the old Polish man who showed up twice a year with his heavy contraption to wax our kitchen floors told Mom that he'd spotted Dad at a romantic restaurant with Sharon. By then, Mom had lived with years of suspicious behavior from Dad; female students becoming overly attached acolytes; mysterious absences from work, and business trips that she discovered were not to the places he'd claimed. The Sharon Sighting was the last straw. But it turned out Sharon, too, had been deceived. On their backyard walk, Sharon told Mom that Dad had claimed his marriage to Mom was a sham, a cover for his job as a spy. Sharon thought it all added up—Dad's many foreign languages, his lack of interest in sales at his store, how he could apparently park wherever he wanted without fear of a ticket. He told her he had secret government license plates that police knew not to touch.

"Nope," Mom told Sharon during that fateful conversation, "I picked up those plates myself. I doubt spies have to wait in line for three hours at the DMV."

◀◀ ❚❚ ▶▶

The day Mom and Dad got divorced, I was late for school. I insisted on going to court to be a part of the proceedings. I imagined my invisible cameraman catching the drama as I was called to the stand as Mom's star witness. I would tell the judge about the time Dad kicked the door and how Mom and I were everything to each other. Like a scene straight out of *Columbo*, I was sure my testimony would single-handedly sway the jury and win the case.

Mom's divorce attorney rebuffed the idea of an eight-year-old being in the courtroom, but I wasn't about to be left in the hallway. So, Mom made a special appeal to the judge who allowed me to sit on a wooden bench and watch. I'd always been mature, but that morning my maturity felt hard-earned from life's hard knocks, so different from what I saw as my classmates' simple lives.

The day didn't go as I expected. Dad wasn't there, there was no jury, no one contested anything, and no one needed my show-stopper testimony. Mom raised her right hand. The judge brought down his gavel. It was over in a matter of minutes. Then Mom and I walked back across the icy parking lot to our car. When we got in, she put her head against the steering wheel and sobbed.

I sprang forward. "Mom! What's wrong?"

"Nothing, Pumpkin." She kept her forehead on the wheel.

My stomach dropped. During their separation, I'd never seen her cry. I thought she wanted to get divorced. Life seemed so much lighter without Dad's heavy silences. From the first afternoon we pulled into the driveway and Dad's car wasn't parked under the Norway maples, I'd felt the added breathing room. Plus, on the day Dad moved out, all the weird phone calls stopped.

"Why are you crying, Mom?" I leaned over the front seat, trying to get closer to her face.

"I'm just sad," she said, retrieving a handkerchief from her purse. "That my marriage didn't work."

I came to understand that Mom was not grieving the loss of Dad but rather the loss of structure and purpose and routine that even a dysfunctional marriage can provide. As independent a woman as Mom was in 1970s suburbia, she was still, at her core, the star pupil who needed instruction, rules, and a prescribed framework in which to function. Neither of us knew then that her own internal compass was broken or how badly she would lose her way once that marriage map was gone. Or how much her disorientation would derail my direction.

I hadn't told anyone where I was going that morning, but when I got to school, my teacher called me to her desk, plopped me on her lap, pulled me to her bosom, and rocked me back and forth like a baby. I stared out at my classmates' baffled faces. Even Frankie Burns, the tough kid with the dungaree jacket in the back row, looked spooked.

I knew divorce was a dirty word. I'd heard it ruined kids' lives and that I was supposed to be devastated. But I had a secret that I couldn't tell anyone but Mom. I *wasn't* devastated. I was happy. Dad had left and taken his maudlin moods and strange behavior with him. Now, Mom and I could have our nightly reading ritual without tiptoeing around his heavy quiet. Mom and I could now take as long as we wanted at ShopRite, roaming the aisles, looking for ingredients for new recipes, our pinky fingers intertwined on the shopping cart, steering it together. We could stroll to the library or idle at the bank's drive-through window where Mom diligently deposited ten dollars a week from her paycheck into my future college fund. On very hot days, we could peel off our clothes in the backyard, not even bothering to put on suits before jumping in the pool. The water soft and slippery against our bare skin.

Now I had Mom all to myself.

After Dad moved out, the music in our home changed. *Cabaret* and *Man of La Mancha* went to the back of the stack. Out came Carole King. Together, in the living room, Mom and I belted out "Natural Woman." United in our liberation, just the two of us.

Now Mom's drama students could stop by unannounced, hopping out of beat-up Mustangs in brown Birkenstocks, grabbing guitars from their backseats. Mom wore her long homemade batik skirt, and I wore my matching batik skirt. I was Mom's mini-me, helping carry out the pitcher of iced coffee, dipping my finger in her glass to taste the sweetness.

On summer afternoons, Mom would send me farther back into our yard, past my rusty swing set and the pool, to our garden to fetch the makings for our dinner. Walking barefoot over purple clover and pungent onion grass, I'd tear big zucchinis off thick stems. I picked ripe tomatoes hot off the vine, stopping to eat one whole like an apple before gathering a handful of basil and bringing the bounty back. Most evenings, the air in our kitchen was thick with the smell of pressed garlic and steam from the big silver pot boiling on the stove. Mom sautéed the vegetables, adding them to the bubbling tomato gravy, then sprinkled mozzarella on top for a zucchini stew that left long strings of melted cheese on our spoons.

After dinner, as Mom cleaned up, I went into the living room in search of a soundtrack. I'd put away my favorite Partridge Family album in lieu of her favorites. Her music became my music. Her preferences, my preferences. Her desires, my desires. I looked out the window at the fading evening light, singing a melancholy Carole King song softly to myself.

"Shall I make us some tea?" Mom asked. She spooned honey into our mugs, then we settled onto the sofa, my head resting on her shoulder. On summer nights, I was lulled by the sound of her voice, the crickets humming, and the steady beat of bullfrogs through our screened windows. I often fell asleep minutes into our reading ritual, but I didn't care as long as Mom stayed right there.

Later in bed, the creaking of our old house sometimes scared me. In the darkness, I ran my hand along the cool wallpaper in the hallway that led to Mom's quiet bedroom, listening for the gentle sound of her breath. She slept on Dad's side now. I climbed under the covers, curving my body around her warm back.

Grace

"Classy" was the word often used to describe Mom. She was different from other suburban moms. She worked outside the home, which was unusual for the era, and didn't spend time watching soap operas or playing tennis. She went to choral concerts and directed musicals. She didn't read fashion magazines; she read Dostoevsky and Tolstoy. She didn't go to see *Smokey and the Bandit*; she saw *The Bald Soprano*.

"It's just very funny and witty. And weird," she told me, as we shared a breakfast omelet at the kitchen table. "For starters, several of the characters have the same name. And it takes awhile for two of them to realize that they live in the same house and are, in fact, married. Anyway, I think you would enjoy it. It's by Ionesco, whom you like."

"I do?" I loved that Mom spoke to me as an adult and treated me as if I knew as much as she did, even though I was eight.

"Oh, yes. Remember your favorite childhood book, *Story Number Two*? That was Ionesco. It's Theater of the Absurd, which I think you enjoy."

"Why don't you like soap operas?"

"Hmmm," she said, chewing and considering. "I'm not really home at that hour in the afternoon. But I do love real opera."

"But it's so boring."

"Oh, no, it's not boring at all," Mom started, "It's quite dramatic. Take Tosca. It's thrilling. It's by Puccini, as you probably know—" Mom also routinely gave me credit for knowing things I had no clue about. "The libretto is by Illica and Giacosa, I believe. In any event, the female lead, Tosca, is a wonderful character. She sings an aria, *Vissi d'arte*, 'I lived for art. I lived for love." Mom took another bite, then went back to the *Red Bank Register* folded next to her plate.

"Keep going," I said, always wanting more.

"Well, Tosca falls in love with a guy named Cavaradossi, but he's a revolutionary, and he's in danger."

"When do we get to the good part?"

"The whole thing is good. But it doesn't end well, really, for anyone." Mom put her fork down and her hand to her heart, as though she were Tosca, "*Muoio disperato*, I die in despair." Mom let her hand drop. "And then, at some point, Tosca flings herself from the parapet. Anyway, we should see it sometime. I think you'd like it."

Mom was not only an intellectual; she was a beauty. She had olive skin and blonde hair and round brown eyes that tapered at the sides like Sophia Loren. I liked flipping through her old photo albums. She looked different in each one, as if playing different parts in different movies. In one photo, she stood against a school blackboard, a piece of chalk in her hand, sporting a mini skirt and short pixie haircut like the British model Twiggy, if Twiggy had left the Factory to become a high school teacher. In another, Mom stood under our blooming Kwanzan cherry tree, her hair set and styled for a dinner date with Dad, looking just like Ingrid Bergman in *Casablanca*. But my favorite was the black and white photo from her high school graduation, a sparkly scarf draped over bare shoulders.

"You look like a princess," I told her.

"Oh, yes," she said, matter-of-factly, stopping momentarily to study the photo. "People often said I looked like Grace Kelly, who was also from Philadelphia, and, of course, actually did become a princess. Have you ever seen her?"

I shook my head. Mom went to the bookshelf, scanned our yellowing collection of magazines, then removed one.

"She looks just like you," I marveled.

"Well," Mom shrugged slightly, "I think I also cultivated her look back then. I was sixteen when she married the prince, and I sort of dressed like her and wore my hair like her. And naturally, I liked how many people saw a similarity."

Mom mentioned things like this casually, without any wistfulness for that other time or the person she once was. She looked different now. With her stick-straight dyed blonde hair, people said she looked like Liv Ullman or Joni Mitchell. The person Mom did not look like was me. My face was oblong like Dad's, not round like hers. And my nose was bumpy with a big bridge, not a smooth ski slope like hers. Her eyes were doe-brown, mine a muddy hazel. The closest I could get to looking like her was *acting* like her, using her gestures and mannerisms. Mostly, what I heard about Mom was, "That's your *mother*? She looks so young. She looks like your *sister*." Mom would be standing right next to me, not registering the grocer's or butcher's shock, just nodding politely and moving on. She'd heard it a hundred times.

Despite being beautiful, my mother was stunningly free of vanity. She never asked if a dress was slimming or if her butt looked big in a pair of pants. I never saw her study her face in a mirror. Other than a coating of Vaseline on her lips before bed, she rarely used cosmetics. She never feared what the passing years could do to a pretty woman. I never saw her search for wrinkle cream at the pharmacy or tug the corners of her eyes upward. It was as if she were blind to her own looks—and mine, which she never mentioned. She never criticized my clothing or hairstyle choices, as so many of my friends' moms did to them. Even at the time, I recognized her judgment-free approach as a rare gift to a young girl.

◀◀ ❚❚ ▶▶

Saturdays were Dad's designated visiting days. He was always early—an hour or more—waiting in his car in the driveway, smoking and looking into the distance. It turned out he never cared about Sharon or anyone, other than me. The idea that Dad had nowhere else to be and no one else to be with felt like an undertow dragging me from our sunny kitchen toward the deep quiet of his car.

"Go tell Dad he can come in," Mom said, exhibiting the unfailing courtesy they expressed toward each other after the divorce. On some of our solo Saturdays, Dad liked to go to nice restaurants with hostesses, where I could load my plate sky-high at the salad bar. These dates in public spaces were easier to endure than the long silences of our alone time. Dad relished the ceremony of a restaurant meal: the pre-dinner cocktail, the subtle one-finger signal to the waiter for a second martini. I was eight, but I ate what he ate: broccoli rabe, lupini beans, cipollini onions.

"How about an order of clams on the half shell," Dad suggested, and when the iced plate arrived, Dad stabbed out his cigarette and rubbed his hands together in anticipation. He used the tiny fork to scoop a heap of horseradish into cocktail sauce, white shards speckling the bright red. Then Dad lifted his clam to clink against mine like champagne glasses.

"Now slurp it down." He demonstrated, and I followed. "Mmm!" His green eyes popped, as if awoken by smelling salts. "Delicioso. Let's have another."

Occasionally, to kill a couple of hours, Dad brought me to one of his girlfriend's houses if she had an art studio or something. I don't think I ever saw any girlfriend twice. People, men and women, were drawn to Dad, to his intellect and elegance, and wanted to get close to him. He didn't reciprocate. It wasn't that he disliked them. Dislike is too active and outward for my father's stillness and silence. He didn't care enough to dislike anyone. He basically tolerated people—except for me. After the divorce, Dad told Mom I was the only person he'd ever truly loved. And I felt that love every time I saw him. It felt like lead across my shoulders. Being someone's only love can be a lot to bear.

Depth Perception

Dear Mom,

I am going with Beez to Friendly's. I am using my own money. I am leaving at 15 of four. Beez's number is 741-4522. And I will get home at 5:30 or before.

Love, Alisyn

P.S.—I took my medicine and saw a bee in my room.

Being the only child of a divorced, working mother made me more self-sufficient than most eight year olds. It also made me odd.

"What's that?" kids asked, pointing to the key I wore on a chain around my neck to let myself in before Mom came home. Some kids found my key either astonishing or offensive—I couldn't tell from their frowning faces.

Almost every kid in my public school had siblings. Frankie Burns was one of six children, and he was considered the coolest kid in our grade. Older kids were always walking past our classroom, making faces at Frankie or waving to him. Frankie never waved back or giggled or did any of the things I would have done if an older kid had noticed me. I was invisible to them.

And because I was the only child of intellectual parents, I often presented as a pint-sized adult in ways that annoyed my classmates, sometimes spouting a middle-aged vocabulary sprinkled with my grandmother's 1940s lingo.

"Mr. Mac is such a taskmaster," I sighed as my third-grade class tromped in a single-file death march toward the gymnasium. "I neglected to bring my shorts. He'll probably have a conniption fit."

A scrawny boy with dandruff spun around on his heels. "Why do you always say big words? Huh?" He took a step closer as a circle of kids formed around him, staring at me. "You try to act so smart. You don't even know what those words mean. Why don't you use normal words?"

"Define normalcy," I said.

My vocabulary constabulary stood blinking, and I backed away to stand alone in the corner of the gym. It's not that I didn't have friends. I did, but I was still routinely singled out and made fun of for being different.

And nowhere was I more of an oddball than on a sports field. At recess, other kids saw a playground; I saw a minefield. For me, dodgeball meant taking a full-frontal smash to the face. The seesaw posed a grave danger of a tailbone bruise. Even a simple rope swing proved perilous, my long hair tangling in the twine until some kid had to run for a pair of scissors to cut me free.

One day during summer camp at the YMCA, a counselor insisted that I get out of the meadow of dandelions where I was daydreaming to participate in a game of softball. I dragged my sneakers slowly over to a huddle of kids, hoping some act of God would intervene before I got to the diamond. By the time I arrived, the team had decided there was only one position for which I was qualified.

"You can be the ump."

"The what?" I asked.

The umpire, they explained. This wasn't the first time it felt like other kids had taken some mandatory course on childhood that I'd missed. How did they all know the word "umpire"? How did they know how to make a bat connect with a ball?

I gnawed on my nail. "What do I have to do?"

"Nothing," they assured me. "Just yell out strikes or balls."

So, that's what I did, calling out "strike" and "ball" willy-nilly, alternating from one to the other whenever the mood struck, until I'd so enraged the other players that they threw me off the field. I glanced over at my perpetually present cameraman. *See? People really don't want me on their team.*

Mom was no athlete either. As a child, she was spared sports activities, household chores, and cooking duties so that she could study before and after dinner. This allowed her to get perfect test scores, but it prevented her from having necessary life skills. As an adult, Mom was the only person in history to forget how to ride a bike. She was terrified to even try again. She also couldn't pick up a heavy box, hang a picture, or open her car's hood without help. She routinely lost her shopping list, misplaced her purse, and locked her keys in the car *with the engine running*, which prompted multiple calls to the police, who showed up with wire hangers to snake down the window. She could eloquently expound on, say, the history of French chanson music beginning in medieval times, but could not find her way to a dinner party without missing the Parkway exit.

Mom treated her damsel-in-distress helplessness as if it were normal, part of her charm even, never demonstrating any interest in conquering it.

"You should learn how to put drops in your own eyes, Mom," I said, watching her wince as Poppy tried to administer some itchy-eye remedy.

"No, no," she said, waving her hand as if turning down dessert.

Her inability to perform simple tasks convinced me that she needed to be closely monitored, but it didn't occur to me, consciously, that her inability to take care of herself would translate to not being able to take care of me. I was more worried about her—every time she left the house. Her horrible driving didn't help. Mom had a difficult time backing out of our garage, making U-turns, and driving at night. She considered parallel parking a feat of physics akin to putting a man on the moon. She had a terrible sense of direction and poor eyesight. Basically, she possessed every quality that made someone a menace on the road. Then there was our driveway, which emptied directly onto a four-lane highway, and sat next to a vacant lot filled with wild bramble, making it impossible to see oncoming cars until our giant Oldsmobile, its front end as long as a surfboard, was sticking into the street.

"How is it on your side?" she'd ask as she edged out, inch by jerky inch.

"Um...hold on!" I craned my neck to see past our picket fence. "Not yet... wait. Wait!"

There we idled, Mom's twitchy pedal foot ready to pounce when I saw an opening between the cars roaring toward us.

"OK. Go!!" I shouted, and Mom hit the gas, often without even double-checking and with only seconds to spare before the next swarm of speeding cars.

But nothing was as scary as the accident. I was in third grade and lugging my cello, bigger than my body, along the sidewalk after school. A fourth grader walked beside me toward her car, where her mother and sister were waiting. Mom was late. Mom was often late, which always made me nervous. *Please don't let her be in a car accident.* I sighed with relief when I saw our Oldsmobile round the corner, Mom behind the wheel, sunglasses on. Then, as if in slow motion, without braking, Mom drove straight into the back of the other mother's car, the hideous sound of ripping metal echoing down the street.

"Mom!" I dropped the cello.

The girl broke into a run to her mother.

Smoke was coming from our Oldsmobile. Mom's head was slumped against the steering wheel, not moving. A man was opening the driver's side door, helping Mom out. She was bent over, blood pouring from her nose.

"Mom!" I yelled out. "Oh, God, don't let her die!"

Mom didn't look at me as the man hurried her past the crowd gathering on the sidewalk.

"Mom!" I yelled, but still she didn't respond.

"She'll be okay," the man said. "Let's get her into the nurse."

"My vision has always been bad," Mom often told people. "I don't have any depth perception. Everything looks flat, so I can't tell how far away or close things are." Years later, I came to see her lack of depth perception as a metaphor. My mother was no good at going deep; and she couldn't see things that got too close—like the back end of a parked car or her only child's desperate cry to know she'd survive.

Soon after that accident, I started driving. I asked my grandfather to let me steer the wheel of his Volkswagen while he worked the pedals. He laughed. Letting a ten-year-old drive. Ha!

"It'll be good practice for the future," I told him, and he relented, giving me the wheel on our trips from Philly to Shrewsbury. At eleven, I took my friend's mom's Buick for a spin around their apartment complex one night while she was out, my friend giggling in the passenger seat. But this was no joy ride for me. Somebody was going to have to know how to execute a K-turn on a rainy road at night when Mom got lost. I had a feeling that somebody would be me.

Will You Still Love Me Tomorrow?

Men liked Mom. Shortly after my parents' divorce, men started appearing at our door. First came Len, the divorced father of a boy in my after-school acting group. Len had black hair, a big smile, and wet kisses that he'd greet me with, which I'd wipe off with the back of my hand. I didn't like when he and Mom went on dates.

"Why can't I come?" I asked, using my body to block the door.

"Not this time, Pumpkin."

I watched them leave, then watched my babysitter sneak out to smoke cigarettes on the step with her boyfriend. I loped upstairs to stew on Mom's bed, hurt and angry but mostly scared that she'd never come back. After Len came Chuck, Mom's old college friend who lived in California. Chuck had a droopy face and didn't pay attention to me when he visited. Sometimes his phone calls cut into my reading time with Mom, so I stood next to her sighing. When that didn't work, I grabbed a pen and a piece of paper:

"Cut the crapola! This call must be costing Chuck a million bucks!"

Mom put her hand to her lips, stifling a laugh. "I'd better go," she told him.

Next was Vic, the head of the high school English department. Vic had a gravelly voice and stank of booze. His cigarettes made me particularly anxious. I watched his red-hot ashes burn long, like a smoldering Tower of Pisa, until they keeled over onto our kitchen floor. Also, he only came out at night.

One evening after dinner, Vic's dented gold Lincoln pulled into our driveway. Through the screen, I watched him open the driver's door with some difficulty, then stagger out with a brown paper bag in his hand.

I met him at the back door.

"Your mother home?"

"She's in the shower."

"Tell her I brought her something." He handed me the bag. I looked in at a small green cactus with prickly sides and a pink flower for a head.

"What is it?"

"Tell her I brought her a phallic symbol."

I dutifully climbed the stairs and walked into the steamy air of the bathroom. Mom was toweling off her naked body, her long blonde hair tucked into a pink shower cap.

"Vic's here," I reported. "And he brought you a Felix symbol."

"A what?" Mom was bent over, one leg up on the bathtub, drying droplets on her ankle.

"A falix symbol," I tried again. Mom's mouth ticked into a slight smile.

"Tell him that I'll be right down and to behave himself."

I was happy when Vic stopped pulling into the driveway.

"I don't want you to get married, Mom," I cried as she tucked me in at night.

"I'm not planning to get married," she said. "But what bothers you about it?"

"I don't want us to have different last names." That was true, but not the whole truth. Mostly, I didn't want her to love anyone more than me.

Then one night, I found her crying at the stove.

"What's wrong, Mom?" I asked, alarmed.

"Oh, oh…" she sobbed as if in pain.

"What is it?"

"I'm all alone," she cried. "I'm *so* alone."

My throat constricted. "No, you're not, Mom!" I threw my arms around her waist, knowing she'd be comforted by my presence. "You have me!"

"Oh," she said, closing her eyes. She exhaled, bringing her ring fingers up to wipe the tears. "That doesn't count."

Or at least that's what I always thought she said. And that's what I recorded in my diary. For years, I replayed those words, reliving the pain, feeling the body blow of not mattering, reminding myself that my love, as all-consuming as it was, didn't count.

Decades later, I realized "that doesn't count" doesn't sound like my mother's elevated diction. It sounds more like something my nine-year-old self would say. It's more likely my mother said, "That's not enough." Still, what I heard was that my love didn't matter in the same way a man's did. It never could. And that message stuck.

Don't Go Breaking My Heart

At the start of my fifth-grade year, Mom took a sabbatical from her teaching job to get a PhD in Creative Arts Education. Three nights a week, she drove an hour away from home to take classes at Rutgers University. So, after school on Tuesdays, I went to my friend Rachel Sherman's house. Rachel's mom, Mrs. Sherman, was usually in the kitchen and greeted me with a big smile and hug before placing a fresh sesame bagel into the toaster oven for me, soon to be slathered in butter.

Rachel's house had shiny hardwood floors and an airy family room, free of a single floating dust particle and perfect for our improvised dances to Elton John songs. Rachel and her older sister, Sydney, shared a bathroom, the contents of which were a marvel. New blue bottles of Nivea body lotion lined up under the sink like soldiers, ready to provide backup in the event the first one ran low.

I wasn't familiar with such wild abundance. I didn't know exactly how tight our money was, but I knew that Dad had stopped paying child support and that Mom was frugal in the extreme. She bought one item at a time, in whatever brand offered a coupon. When something ran out, there was no spare. I wore shoes that were sometimes too small and pants that were too short, which other kids called "floods." I wore some underwear for so many years that the elastic simply gave out.

"Most people's underwear rides up," Rachel observed. "But yours falls down."

By ten, I understood that in my life there was no backup. If I lost something, it was gone for good. So, I rationed the shampoo I liked and stopped using it before it was gone to make sure it never ran out.

Tuesday dinners at the Shermans were classic 1970s fare: meatloaf, mashed potatoes, and green beans. I ate and ate.

"Can I give you thirds, Sweetie?" Mrs. Sherman asked, before turning the focus on her own daughter. "See, Sydney, how much Alisyn is eating? Why don't you have a little more?" Sydney huffed that she was full as I stuffed another mound of meatloaf into my mouth.

On Wednesday nights, I ate a frozen TV dinner on a metal tray with the daughter of one of Mom's new classmates. This girl was what they used to call "a teenage delinquent," so some nights, she'd show up with sneaky cigarettes she'd swiped from her stepdad, and I'd take some drags to disabuse her of the notion that I was a total dork. Most nights, we just talked about her pregnancy scares.

In typical Mom fashion, she assumed I'd adapt to her evening classes and this new chapter in our lives without much need for explanation or preparation. And in typical me fashion, I coped by sitting on her bed, staring out the window, and counting the seconds until she came home. If she was late, which she often was, I called the police. I'd memorized their non-emergency number so I could check to see if there had been any car accidents between home and Rutgers. Sometimes the dispatcher sounded annoyed, but that didn't stop me from calling ten minutes later. I made a pact with myself that when the digital clock on Mom's bedside table got to 9:40, I'd start calling area hospitals.

Oh, God, it's 9:39.

I wiped my breath cloud from the chilly windowpane to see if the approaching headlights were hers. When our Oldsmobile finally appeared, turn signal blinking, I brought my palm to my pounding chest. *Thank you, God. Thank you.* Then I started sobbing.

"What's wrong?" Mom asked when I met her at the bottom of the stairs.

"You said you'd be home at nine thirty," I panted, "but it's nine fifty-five."

"Oh, I'm sorry. Our class ran long."

◄◄ ❙❙ ►►

The night before Halloween in New Jersey is known as "Mischief Night." That afternoon, Mom and I attended the bat mitzvah of a family friend. I spent much of the house party afterward upstairs with the older kids passing around a bottle of Manischewitz that someone had swiped from the makeshift bar. Occasionally, I meandered downstairs to check on Mom, whom I found standing in the exact same spot next to the buffet, laughing and talking to the rabbi.

The rabbi was tall and handsome, with twinkly blue eyes and a warm smile. It seemed like he and Mom must have met somewhere before because they were laughing like they were in on the same joke. When we got home, Mom sat on the piano bench with the coiled phone cord stretched to her ear, continuing to laugh with the rabbi. I stood next to her, tapping my fingers and gesturing toward our book.

"I'll come up and tuck you in later," she whispered. I trudged up to bed and waited, straining to hear the words through Mom's light lilt but fell asleep before she said good night.

Mom and Robert the Rabbi's love affair took off at warp speed. Robert began spending nights at our house. We spent weekends at his home. Mom started going to Temple, taking conversion classes in New York City, and spending some Saturday nights at his second place, an apartment in Greenwich Village.

On the nights Mom still cooked dinner, she abandoned our spaghetti and meatballs in favor of Robert's vegetarian dishes of potato kugel and tabouleh. The contents of our bathroom cabinet changed too. Robert's All-Natural Dr. Bronner's peppermint soap took center stage, relegating Mom's Jean Nate Bath Splash to the bottom shelf, its shiny black cap covered in dust.

Of all Mom's boyfriends, I liked Robert the Rabbi the best. I liked his friendly smile and easy laugh. The three of us developed our own private jokes. One evening we were invited to a party at the Temple that Mom and Robert feared would be dull, so we devised an exit code word. I'd just seen the movie *Bugsy Malone* and suggested "Tallulah." An hour into the party, Robert sidled over to me with wide eyes and whispered, "TAH-LUH-LAH!"

But our threesome only went so far, and on weekend mornings, I hated how Mom and Robert stayed behind his locked bedroom door long after

I was hungry for breakfast. I also hated being lumped with his two young daughters, who fought and scratched at each other while I sat and stared at Robert's bedroom door. I didn't know exactly what was happening in there, but I was resentful of Mom and Robert for shutting me out. Mom addressed my feelings of isolation by going to the library and bringing back Norma Klein's book *Mom, the Wolfman, and Me* about a single mom's sex life.

It became increasingly hard to get Mom's attention—other than when she needed help. One night, as she got ready to see a play in New York City, her voice floated down the hall, "Pumpkin, can you come in and help me pick out a shirt?"

I swung into action, becoming cheeky and irreverent, qualities that she did not possess and I knew she liked. By ten years old, I'd spent enough Saturday nights in front of the TV, glued to *The Carol Burnett Show*, to know that a good performance could hold people captive and keep them from leaving. To keep Mom in that closet, I sifted through her strange assortment of deeply discounted items for comedic material, landing on an old cardigan that could fit a fat man. "Did Archie Bunker leave this here?" I asked.

Mom laughed. "Actually, I found that at a consignment store. But I do see now it's rather misshapen."

I stumbled on a white Minnie Mouse T-shirt. "I beg your pardon?"

Mom giggled. "I admit it's not my style, but it was on the clearance rack at Marshalls. I think it was ninety-nine cents. And even then," she raised her slender first finger, "I did think twice about whether I needed it. You'll be happy to know, I wore it to the beach and did receive a couple of compliments." She smiled, and for a few fleeting moments, I felt the golden glow of being her Number One. Then, Robert's horn sounded, and she headed for the door.

I longed for our old life before Robert, our old reading ritual and togetherness. Six weeks after she met Robert, I attempted to plead my case in a note:

Dear Mom, (12/11/76)

I love you very much and I hope that you will always love me the most. Even though I love Robert, I wish that we all could do things together or just us by ourselves <u>sometimes</u>. (underlined twelve times)

Love, Alisyn

I left the note on top of her to-do list on her desk, knowing she was bound to see it when she got home from class. I hoped she would read it, rush to my room, and smother me in kisses, assuring me she would always love me the most. When that didn't happen by the next afternoon, I went back to see if my note had accidentally fallen into the wastebasket. I found it in her drawer. On the top right corner, she'd meticulously recorded the date in blue ink, then tucked it under the other cards, drawings, and love notes I had left her.

◄◄ ❚❚ ►►

Mom and Robert were in the kitchen getting ready to head to Manhattan for her Conversion class and dinner. I sat like a lump at the kitchen table.

"Can I come with you guys?"

"Not tonight, Pumpkin. It will be late, and it won't be any fun for you."

At ten, I'd been to New York City exactly twice, once with Sydney and Rachel Sherman and their grandma to see a ballet, the other with Mom's high school class to see *Godspell*.

"*Please*, can I go to dinner with you?"

Mom and Robert exchanged glances, then conferred in hushed tones at the far end of the kitchen.

"Alright," she said, her voice tight.

I jumped up and scrambled to Robert's car, sliding into the front seat, excited for the three of us to be together, Robert to my left, Mom to my right. Silence.

I clicked on the radio and sang along to Rod Stewart, but something was off. Mom's arm next to mine was rigid rather than soft. Her hands stayed folded in her lap, not holding mine, and her face stayed turned to the window, as if her neck was frozen in that position.

New York City at dusk was a swarm of energy, taxis honking, traffic everywhere. All of it scared me. I'd heard stories of grown men, like Robert, getting mugged at knifepoint.

Robert let us out at the edge of a park, people walking briskly along an asphalt path, while he went to look for a parking spot. I found an empty bench so Mom could look over her notes while we waited. I asked where we were having dinner.

Mom stared straight ahead as though she hadn't heard my question, then suddenly turned to face me. "Why did you do that?"

"Do what?"

"Why did you sit between Robert and me?" Her tone was different than I'd ever heard it, stick-sharp. I blinked at her. She lowered her voice to a snarl and pointed her index finger at me.

"You will not do this to me, Alisyn. Do you understand?"

Yes, I nodded quickly, though I didn't know what I'd done. Until that moment, it was a point of pride in my life that my parents never hit me. They never used the common 1970s punishment I witnessed at friends' houses of being bent over a parent's knee and spanked with an open hand. The times my parents disciplined me, which I could count on two fingers, they sat me down and spoke to me.

"You will not ruin this for me," Mom repeated. Her finger was already dangerously close to my face when suddenly she took her fingernail and jabbed it into my cheek. "I will not lose Robert."

My insides hollowed out. I nodded again and tried to blink away the burning. Tears spilled over and ran down my cheeks. I turned my head into the bench, away from strangers' passing faces.

The next day, Mom came into my room and sat down on my bed.

"Let's talk about what happened yesterday."

"You hit me," I said flatly, before inching away from her.

"I wouldn't characterize it as a hit," Mom said, tilting her head at me with a hopeful smile. "More like a poke, really. I'm sorry. I thought you were trying to separate Robert and me."

I didn't look at her. I didn't point out the fading crescent moon still on my cheek from her fingernail. I kept my eyes glued to a yellow spot on the wallpaper that I'd never noticed before.

"I might have time this afternoon," she said, running her hand over mine. "Maybe we can go to the library."

I wished she would leave. This kind of loss was best handled alone. I was done. Done chasing her. Done waiting for her. Done wishing she'd see me. My lifelong fear had come true. Mom had chosen who she loved the most, and it wasn't me. A wind tunnel of emptiness blew through my body.

I waited for her footsteps to fade down the hall before commencing the action I knew had to be taken. I tilted my head upward and pressed my hands together hard in prayer, the way my grandmother had taught me to do whenever I needed help. And just so there could be no taking it back, I said it out loud.

"Never again, God. *Do you hear me*? NEVER." My eyes pooled, then overflowed. "I am *done* loving Mom so much. This stops RIGHT NOW. Do you *understand*? And no matter how long I live, I will *never* let this happen again. I will *never* again love someone more than they love me."

PART TWO

/SHrap.nel/ *noun—1. fragments of a bomb, bullet, or metal that burst on impact;*
2. a term invented in 1784, by Henry Shrapnel, first lieutenant of the British artillery;
3. intoxicating New Jersey punk band that exploded onto the scene in 1978.

Secrets

As a kid, I had nightmares about being home alone when an intruder broke in and crept down the hall toward my bedroom. I tried to scream for help, but no sound came out. For as long as I can remember, I've been drawn to crime stories. The mystery, the motive, the madness. What makes criminals tick? I like trying to crack the complexity of the criminal mind, that combo of charm and cruelty. I've always innately known that in crime stories, if you dig, you can unearth the vulnerability of the villain and the mettle of the victim.

Or maybe that hunch wasn't innate. Maybe I learned it early.

◄◄ ❚❚ ►►

I walked through the back door after school one afternoon to find the screen from our kitchen window popped out and propped against the wall, breeze and bugs blowing right through the open maw. I ran next door to the neighbors to wait for Mom to come home. We called the police. The Shrewsbury police were already familiar with us from Mom's various car key mishaps and the time a raccoon was trapped in our basement. Two officers showed up and walked around, but aside from the screen being on the floor, nothing else was out of place. Maybe the wind blew it out, they said.

I was in fifth grade but knew wind couldn't prop a screen against a wall. The police left, promising to drive by to check on us from time to time.

◄◄ ❚❚ ►►

Mom was in her room, rushing to get dressed for an Alvin Ailey dance show in New York City. She was looking for her favorite necklace, the one with the smooth amber stones, the one she wore all the time. She was becoming frantic, repeating *where is it, where is it, where is it,* like she'd lost her mind. Gram and Poppy were visiting for the weekend, so the three of us fanned out into different rooms pulling up couch cushions and riffling the contents of desk drawers. My stomach was knotted. I had to find the necklace so Mom could be happy again.

"Pray to St. Anthony," Gram told me. "He'll help us find it."

I was down on all fours in Mom's closet, feeling around on the floor, when I heard her gasp. Mom was on her knees, in front of an open dresser drawer, her hands covering her mouth as if stifling a scream.

"What Mom!"

"It's gone," she said. "The jewelry is all gone."

A dozen velvet boxes sat open and empty inside her drawer, like clamshells on the beach.

"It's all been stolen," she said.

"We've got to call the police!" I told her.

She didn't get up. She stayed kneeling and staring.

"Mom! I'm going to call the police. Maybe the robber's in the house!"

She stayed put, slowly exhaling. "No. He's not. I think I know who did it."

"Who?" I shrieked.

"It was Dad."

I froze. "*No*, Mom. NO. Dad would *not* steal all our jewelry!" Of this, I was certain.

Mom's shoulders slumped. "He didn't. All of yours is still here."

◄◄ ❚❚ ►►

Mom didn't have to call the police; they called her. "We've received reports, Mrs. Camerota, about robberies regarding your ex-husband." It was even worse than we'd suspected. We learned that not only had Dad stolen Mom's jewelry, he'd also stolen a necklace from the home of the librarian at the high school where he worked, a ruby ring from the wife of his best friend, a diamond from my great aunt, and more.

Amazingly, when the police showed up at his apartment, Dad still had some of the jewelry. He provided the police elaborate descriptions of each piece's history as he surrendered them, as though they were rightfully his. But Mom's amber necklace was gone. Dad liked to give lavish gifts and had given some of the pieces to other people, like some twisted suburban Robin Hood. I was left to wonder about the provenance of my own beautiful bracelet, the one with the platinum heart links.

The police came back to our house to update Mom, who immediately shared the details with me, as she always did with important information. Apparently, when the police asked Dad why he did it, he said he needed money for his daughter to go to law school. The cops assumed I was on the cusp of a degree. Mom clarified that I was eleven.

I felt sick. I *had* mentioned wanting to be a lawyer, and Mom, Dad, Gram, and Poppy cheered me on, agreeing that lawyering would be a good outlet for my outspoken nature. But I didn't know our vague game of what-do-you-want-to-be-when-you-grow-up would carry criminal consequences. Of course, it was all bullshit. Dad wasn't liquidating the jewelry for law school tuition. He was stealing the jewelry because he felt entitled to it. Or at least that was how Mom and I explained it to ourselves for many decades.

A few days later, Mom handed me a page from the *Red Bank Register*, with one small paragraph circled in blue ink. The police blotter.

Antonio R. Camerota arrested for robbery.

"No! Why did the newspaper do that?" I flung myself onto the sofa, pulling my arms tight across my torso, a plate of armor, imagining my humiliation when my friends found out. My first lesson in how, behind every juicy headline, there's a real family's pain.

Mom didn't talk about the newspaper item. She stayed in motion, straightening her note cards on the end table as I pounded my feet into the cushions and cried. If Mom did feel any embarrassment about Dad's strange behavior, within a few weeks, she had moved on to joking about it with her friends, referring to Dad as "Tony, Man of Mystery" and "The International Jewel Thief."

I followed her lead and started joking about Dad, too, which was a helluva lot easier than imagining the moment he was fired from his job at my future high school. As usual, I resorted to song lyrics to help me process the experience. In our kitchen, I belted out Carly Simon. *"And you're where you should be all the time and when you're not, you're with some underworld spy or the wife of a close friend, wife of a close friend."* Mom laughed and laughed.

No one wanted to press charges against Dad, and shortly after his arrest, he moved eighty miles south to a beach town where he would find a different teaching job and a brief marriage. I was relieved. His absence felt better than his closeness.

◀◀ ❙❙ ▶▶

It turned out Dad *was* a man of mystery. Shortly after the jewelry heist, Mom exacted revenge on Dad by revealing one of his secrets to me.

"You have a brother," she told me.

Mom and I were in the bathroom when she delivered this news. An older brother, she told me, from Dad's first marriage, a marriage I'd never known of. I fell to the floor, taking the towel rack down with me, and sobbed tears of joy. I wasn't an only child anymore!

On Thanksgiving Day, Mom, Gram, Poppy, and I left a turkey roasting in the oven to drive to West Philadelphia to meet my brother. He was seven years older than me. Dad left when the boy was an infant and had rarely seen his son in the eighteen years since.

My brother was everything I'd hoped: tall, handsome, and cool. While the grown-ups made awkward small talk over coffee, Tony Jr. took me for a thrilling ride around Center City in his used sports car. When we parted that day, we promised to write to each other regularly. And for a couple of years, we did. Then I turned thirteen and wanted to hang out with my friends and eat ice cream sundaes at Friendly's rather than compose letters to a virtual stranger. I stopped responding and soon lost all contact with him.

Learning of a family secret at eleven, even one as wonderful as a cool older brother, does not breed trust in one's father, as if I didn't have enough reasons already to distrust Dad. It was starting to be easier not to think of him at all.

Shout It Out Loud

Even with her attachment to Robert and other distractions, Mom never missed a single one of my Back-to-School nights or parent-teacher conferences. My own approach to school, however, started to change.

"During detention," my teacher told me, "you will write fifty times on the chalkboard that you will not use inappropriate words."

"That's asinine," I told her.

"Make it *a hundred times*," she snapped.

"Asinine is not an inappropriate word!"

Halfway through fifth grade, I began challenging my teachers' asinine policies and telling my classmates to shut up. Mom thought it might be time for a different school.

Situated in an old red farmhouse twelve miles from our home, The New School was an uber-progressive elementary school that did not believe in homework, grades, or tests. The kids called the teachers by their first names. No one wore shoes. This school perfectly matched my philosophy that kids should be the masters of their own destinies.

There was just one problem. Dad hadn't paid child support for a couple of years, even before his robberies and arrest. Mom considered taking him to court to extract the two hundred bucks a month, but I didn't want her to. When I imagined him standing alone in front of a judge, it felt sad and humiliating. For both of us.

Mom told the director of The New School that we couldn't afford it. She explained that she was on sabbatical and only making half of her already meager teacher's salary. Maybe next year. But the director liked us, thought I would be a good fit, and offered me a scholarship.

The New School was tiny. Fifty kids total, divided into three classrooms. Though I was in fifth grade, I was deemed mature enough to join The Older Class, as it was called, with sixth, seventh, and eighth graders. I was delighted to discover that most of my new classmates were endearing misfits of one kind or another, too brainy or eccentric to fit into public school, and, like me, some had divorced parents.

My new best friend was an eighth grader named Cookie. She, too, was the only child of a working mom with a boyfriend, and I loved her for accepting me into her tight circle. With Cookie, I got to hear all about racy teenage stuff, like rock bands, tampons (which she called "plugs"), and sex— or, more precisely, The Bases. Cookie and I dissected and debated at what age we would ever consider going to Fourth Base.

"My mom says you have to be really careful," Cookie warned. "Because once you lose your virginity, you can *never* get it back."

I nodded, wide-eyed. "That *does* sound permanent."

Cookie and the other eighth graders were obsessed with the band KISS and played *Destroyer* on our classroom turntable at lunchtime. I needed some cool credentials, so I signed up for Columbia House Record Club and got their *Rock and Roll Over* album for a dollar.

I spent a lot of time trying to mine KISS lyrics for life guidance, but their songs about cold gin and fiery car crashes didn't come with further instructions. Even in fifth grade, I knew that KISS represented the fast lane and was, metaphorically speaking, just a Garden State Parkway exit or two away from Aerosmith, and after that came Led Zeppelin and Pink Floyd— rock-n-roll roads that led to bad acid trips. I wasn't entirely ready to jump off the Carole King covered wagon, but the KISS race car was revving its engine.

I'm not sure where most parents were in the late seventies and early eighties. Perhaps some never-ending national cocktail party or multiyear workshop on the Art of Laissez-faire Childrearing? All I know is that for long stretches during those decades, parents weren't around. Even stay-at-home-moms seemed absent a lot, maybe at the tennis club or simply in another room. We kids had to find ways to occupy ourselves. And in my neck of New Jersey, those ways often included drugs.

Drugs scared me. I was apprehensive every time I was around them—starting when I was ten. That's when a thirteen-year-old boy I met at the beach said we should get high sometime. I was so rattled that when I got home, I went straight into Mom's room, sat on her bed, and burst into tears.

"What's wrong?"

"Jimmy wants me to smoke pot with him."

"And are you interested in doing that?" Mom asked calmly.

"I don't know," I said, cradling my head in my hands. "It sounds scary."

Even though I'd vowed not to love Mom so much anymore, I just couldn't quit her. I still loved her. I loved that I could talk to her about things other kids couldn't talk to their moms about. I loved that she didn't freak out or ground me or force me to stay away from that boy.

Mom left those decisions up to me.

"I think it *can* be scary," Mom nodded, "which is why if you were ever to decide to do it, I'd like it to be here at our house, on our property, in case something were to go wrong."

"Have you ever smoked pot?" I asked her.

"Yes," she said. "Once. But it made me feel out of control. I didn't like that feeling. And I'm guessing you won't either."

I planned to follow her advice to only try it at home. But sometimes a ten-year-old's plans change. By eleven, I'd tried smoking cigarettes and sampling sips of older kids' beers. I knew the next step along the drug spectrum was pot smoking. I was frightened but came to see it the same way I saw, say, bra buying or babysitting—neither a chore nor a desire, just a mandatory rite of passage on the way to Teenageville that had to be completed sooner or later.

"I heard you can't get high the first time you smoke it," Cookie told me when we found an abandoned baggie of weed stashed in some bushes. We nervously deconstructed a KOOL cigarette, rolled up a pinch of loose leaves, then lit our homemade joint, attempting to inhale as it crumbled to the ground. We felt nothing. Second attempt, same thing.

The third time, I'd just turned twelve. Cookie and I were lying on beach chairs at her town pool, smothered in Hawaiian Tropic suntan oil and Leo Sayer on the transistor radio. The head of a boy we'd never seen before appeared over the fence—a Leif Garrett look-alike in all his wavy blond glory.

He asked if we wanted to smoke a joint with him and his friends. Tingling with possibility, we popped off our chairs and followed him down the block. Leif's bedroom had YES and Pink Floyd posters on the wall. The shades were pulled down to block the summer scorch.

We sat in a loose circle, Cookie and me on his beanbag chair. Leif lit a joint, then passed it to his buddy, who took a hit, then handed it to the next friend, who handed it to me. I took a hit and held it. Shortly after, I felt the tilt. Time shifted into a lower gear. The guys said something about Panama Red.

"We like Colombian Gold," I announced, because that was the only other pot variety I'd ever heard of. They started laughing, and I didn't know if it was at me. I also didn't know if I'd said the Colombian Gold thing out loud. Maybe I'd only thought it. Maybe I was actually whispering, and they hadn't heard me at all. Or maybe it was me who was laughing too loud. Then I was standing beside myself in the beanbag chair, watching myself try to talk with cottonmouth. *Mom was right! I did feel out of control, and I didn't like it.* But I did like being on this adventure with Cookie, and I liked the bond that came with illicit activity. That high—the high of belonging—became my drug of choice.

Stayin' Alive

I grew up with only three rules:

Rule #1—You will get a scholarship to college.

This was nonnegotiable. I knew we didn't have enough money for college. And though the divorce decree stipulated that Dad would pay for tuition, given his track record as a failed international jewel thief, it seemed unlikely. Mom had received a full scholarship to UPenn and she trusted I would follow suit.

Rule #2—You are not to get pregnant.

Mom was never shy about introducing the topic of birth control. But unlike our pot talk, she did not offer up any personal anecdote. When I tried to probe about her own experience, she literally disappeared into the dark of her closet. After that, she let Planned Parenthood pamphlets do the talking. To this day, I'm stunned by how few parents instill this rule. And how many teenagers are winging it when it comes to birth control.

Rule #3—You are not to be killed in a drunk driving accident.

Mom got a phone call. She held the receiver tight and covered her mouth. I could only make out fragments: a group of her students, coming home from a party, too fast around a curve, flew through the windshield, knocked out all their teeth, intensive care unit. I didn't know what "wrapped around a telephone pole" looked like but that's what I heard.

"Alisyn," she told me, "you are my only child. You're the only one I have. You are not to be killed in a drunk driving accident."

Yes, I nodded. I wouldn't be one of *those* teenagers.

I'll never understand all the energy other parents put into rules around food and clothing and curfews when, honestly, with Mom's Three Life Rules, so much else falls into place. I followed her three rules religiously, even after Mom was no longer around to impart them.

◀◀ ❚❚ ▶▶

Dear Mom, 5/28/78

Hi, how was the rafting trip? If you're still alive. This note is in case we're asleep when you get home. Guess what? I practiced piano for 35 minutes. Cookie and I had the last beer. We split it. I hope you don't mind. I didn't think you would. Robert took us out to breakfast. Bye. Love, Alisyn

At eleven, my risk-taking was still leavened with earnest truth-telling and note-leaving whenever Mom and I were apart, which was becoming more frequent. I had begun spending afternoons, nights, and weekends at friends' houses. Sometimes, if Mom was in the city with Robert (or on the rare rafting trip with friends), my friends' parents agreed to let us stay alone overnight at my house. We found ways to entertain ourselves, playing records, going to the mall, smoking cigarettes, splitting a beer.

I alternated between wanting Mom all to myself and wanting her to give me space. She alternated between being absent and being overly present, including coming into the bathroom without knocking. One day, she breezed into my bedroom with a glossy pamphlet. I saw the words birth control and venereal disease.

"What's this?"

"Whenever you're ready, you and I will go together to get you some birth control."

"Eww. Mom. I'm eleven."

She was completely calm. "I know. All I'm saying is *when* you're ready, years from now or whenever that is, let me know, and we'll go."

She touched my shoulder. I recoiled.

For the record, my mother says this episode happened when I was twelve. Either way, I remember it as comically early but not irrational. I already had boys on the brain and was plotting how to find one. I'd seen enough movies and magazines, as well as the message in my own home, to know that having a boyfriend upped a girl's value. Whatever superpower was bestowed through male desire, I wanted it.

But there were caveats. The boy had to have charisma; he had to be someone other people wanted, a boy who would show everybody how valuable I was. Turns out, such a candidate was headed my way.

Ethan was thirteen years old and a legend at my school. He had moved away to Cape Cod a year earlier, but his ladykiller reputation lived on. Now Ethan was back for a visit, strutting into our classroom with his faded Levi's and shiny black hair like he was John Travolta in *Saturday Night Fever*, which, rumor had it, Ethan had seen even though it was rated R. He smirked as he surveyed our homemade books bound with yarn, then swaggered out to hold court on the jungle gym. I didn't want to watch his every move, but I couldn't help it.

The day after his arrival, two kids cornered me behind the big bookcase.

"Ethan likes you," Robin, an eighth grader, whispered.

Part of me was skeptical. I hadn't really interacted with Ethan. I suspected what he mostly saw in me was fresh meat. But being new meat was better than being no meat.

Ethan's friend headed me off in the hallway. "Ethan wants you to kiss him in the loft at lunchtime."

I brought my nail to my mouth and gnawed.

"Tell him she'll be there," Robin said.

By noon I was sweating and hoping for a rain check. Then Robin dragged me to the loft and deposited me. Ethan was already up in the carpeted cubbyhole. I climbed the ladder quaking, as if it were the high dive. Up in the loft, Ethan pointed to letters he'd written on the wall.

E. J. + A. C.

Then he pressed his soft wet lips against mine. And just like that, my status changed. I wasn't outside the circle looking in: I was the bull's-eye.

As an adolescent, I started to need this type of attention. A boy's interest felt like value. It felt like sunlight. It felt like something I needed to stay alive.

Revolution

The summer I turned twelve, my old public school friend Beez called with exciting news. Her brother Dave and his band had a record coming out. A real honest-to-goodness record with a record company. It was just a 45, but still! Beez's brother was four years older than us and lived in the A-frame attic of their house that he'd decked out with dangling beads and posters of rock bands. Dave was in a garage band called Hard Attack. My main brushes with him were when I'd sleepover at Beez's and Dave would yell at us to pipe down so he could strum along to endless riffs of the Beatles' "Revolution."

When Dave wasn't home, Beez and I liked to poke around his room and stare at his posters: The Monkees, Thin Lizzy, The Beach Boys. One poster scared the hell out of me: a man with long stringy black hair and thick black makeup circling his eyes, dripping down his cheeks. A huge boa constrictor was draped around his shoulders. A shiver ran across mine.

"Who's that?" I asked.

"Oh, that's Alice Cooper," Beez shrugged in the way that kids with older siblings did. They knew things.

"Why does he have a snake?"

"He brings it on stage. I know, gross. And he bit the head off a chicken once at a concert."

"Let's go back to your room," I said.

◀◀ ❚❚ ▶▶

When Beez's brother's band came out with that record, it felt like all of Shrewsbury was excited. My next-door neighbor's cousin was the drummer. Rachel and Sydney Sherman's parents' best friends' son was the lead guitarist.

Even Mom had a connection—a fellow teacher at Monmouth Regional was the bass player's dad.

"That's Mr. Caivano's son's band, yes?" Mom asked.

"Yes!" I said, hurrying to grab five dollars from the glass jar under the oven where I kept my babysitting money.

"Is their name 'Hard' something?"

I rolled my eyes. God, she could be so out of it sometimes. The band had changed their name six months ago. "They're not Hard Attack anymore. They're Shrapnel!"

My friend Annie and I hopped off the bus in Red Bank and headed straight into Jack's Music Store. Jack's had every record imaginable, plus a glass case filled with bongs, rolling papers, and pipes. It was there in the record stacks that we first saw SHRAPNEL written in big black block letters over a photo of the five band members.

The guys all wore Army gear. One of them had on a helmet. A dog tag dangled from Beez's brother's neck. But it was the guy in the middle, in an American flag tank top, who commanded my attention. He was holding a gun with both hands. The image was captivating: his embrace of the revolver, his finger on the trigger. It looked like he was pointing that pistol straight at me.

At twelve, I was scared of a lot of things: team sports, jumping off a rope swing, going too far out in the ocean. But of all the risks in the world, this record seemed like one I might be able to handle. It was just a little 45, after all. How dangerous could it be?

Annie and I raced home to my turntable. I put the needle down, and with the first power chords, my insides ignited. *Well, I met her in the jungle, in the middle of a siege…something, something, something.* I put the needle down, again, and again, desperate to learn the lyrics and know how the lead singer got the girl. But we could only get the chorus, so we sang it at the top of our lungs.

She was my combat love, the one I'm thinking of!

Again.

She was my combat love, the one I'm thinking of!

From the photo, I had been expecting dark and loud, like Led Zeppelin with gunfire. But Shrapnel was the opposite—sunny and hot, like if the beach had a band. I loved the lead singer's voice—friendly somehow, though he was singing about bleeding on a battlefield. When he yelled, *Let's go!*, he made going to war sound fun.

I didn't know then how often I would call upon Shrapnel later in my journalism career when I needed an injection of grit in a combative interview. But from the very first time I heard "Combat Love," I knew Shrapnel was more than just music. Shrapnel was an aspiration, an identity. Shrapnel became my ticket to tribal belonging.

◄◄ ❙❙ ►►

"Who's Norman Mailer," I asked, before immediately regretting it.

"*You don't know* who *Norman Mailer is?*"

Ever since falling in love with Ethan, I expended a lot of energy anxiously awaiting his infrequent phone calls from Cape Cod, telling me of his exciting life and teenage exploits. He was fifteen now and far more worldly than thirteen-year-old me. On these calls, I tried to be my most witty, clever self but often missed the mark.

"Is he famous or something?" I asked.

"Go ask your mother if Norman Mailer is famous."

I put the phone down and ran to the top of the staircase.

"Mom!"

She appeared at the foot of the stairs, dishcloth in hand. "Yes?"

"Do you know who Norman Mailer is?"

An amused smile crossed her mouth. "Yes."

"Who is he?"

"He's a contemporary author."

"Is he famous?"

"Yes. And I'd say somewhat infamous. *The Naked and the Dead* is considered one of the great American novels. And his new book, *The Executioner's Song*, is on the *New York Times* bestseller list. I think you would like it."

I marched down to the library and lugged back *The Executioner's Song*, the size of a cinder block, then sat on the sofa, riveted. As soon as Ethan mentioned him, Norman Mailer started popping up everywhere. Turn on *Phil Donahue* after school...there was Norman Mailer. Tune in to Stanley Siegel's talk show...Norman Mailer was the special guest. Glance at the cover of the supermarket tabloid...Norman Mailer stared back at me. I quickly became something of a Norman Mailer aficionado, reading up on his multiple divorces and correspondence with convicts, ready to wow Ethan with my Mailer mastery. Then came the Norman Mailer pièce de résistance.

I was lying on my bed listening to "Combat Love" when Mom came in.

"I have something to show you." She handed me a glossy magazine called *High Times*. "Robert found it. Turn to page seventy-two."

I flipped to a long profile on Norman Mailer in which Mom had underlined paragraph after paragraph in blue ink. *(Lightly edited and condensed.)*

```
Norman really seemed to enjoy himself in the smoke-
filled, tightly packed ambiance of the tiny rock club.
It was so crowded he had to stand on a chair in order
to see the band, Shrapnel. Halfway through the concert
he elbowed his way to the front of the crowd.
```

"Oh, my God!"

"I thought you'd like that." Even at her busiest, Mom couldn't miss my dueling Shrapnel-Mailer obsessions and could still find time to do some underlining on my behalf before returning to writing her dissertation.

```
High Times: Did you like the Shrapnel show?
```

```
Norman Mailer: For me, it felt like I was an old car
and I was being taken out on a ride at 100 miles an
hour and I kind of liked it because I was getting rid
of a lot of rust. You've got to be superhuman to play
that stuff night after night and not have your senses
wiped out by it. But it has a powerful impact, I've
got to admit. I liked it more than I thought I would.
```

Seeing Shrapnel in the same sentence with someone as famous as Norman Mailer set off some explosive dominoes. This meant Shrapnel was famous. And they were from Shrewsbury. And that meant Shrewsbury was famous.

And I lived there. And Shrapnel was my favorite band. And that meant maybe I could be famous, too.

Mailer: What I felt was that the revolution that I saw starting in the late fifties is still going on. It made me feel all over again there's going to be a revolution sooner or later in this country, whether from the left or the right or up or down, I don't know. But there's something stirring…because you can't fuck with American life. You can squash it and distort it, but it just erupts.

Jeez, Mailer was really missing the point. When do we get to the part about how cute the lead singer is or an explanation of "Combat Love's" lyrics? Give me something, Norman!

Mailer: The kids have a deep sense of rebellion while they're hearing it. They're against everything else. While they're hearing it, they're with that, and nothing else counts. It's like a religion.

I read the passage over and over, memorizing it and tucking it away to show Ethan that two could play at this fame game. Apparently, I knew famous people, too. A few weeks later, *Rolling Stone* reporter Kurt Loder described a party at Norman Mailer's house. Woody Allen was there, so was Kurt Vonnegut. Special musical guests? Shrapnel.

"It figures that Norman Mailer would go for Shrapnel, a New Jersey punk band, derived from military games the band played as kids, complete with World War II paraphernalia and anti-Communist imagery, announcing the hippie movement and its music is dead."

Mailer was right. Something big was happening out in the world. And somehow, hearing *Shrapnel* on my little record player in my little bedroom felt like a portal to that big celebrity-filled world. And I was desperate for a ticket to the party.

Shrapnel

On January 19, 1980, I was a heartbroken thirteen-year-old girl, adrift and hungry for a transformative teenage experience. Ethan had stopped calling and writing. Suddenly all the value I derived from having a boyfriend, even one who existed only on the other end of occasional phone calls and postcards, evaporated. It was official—I wasn't worthy after all. Plus, my closest friends had moved on to high school, leaving me behind in eighth grade. I hated being left behind. That month I slid into a deep, inconsolable funk, the first of several losses in my life that led precipitously to a dark place.

I was achingly lonely and longed to leapfrog into the future. Instead of studying algebra or learning US history, I spent part of every school day in the loft, trying to sleep away time and fast-forward to high school, which I was sure held happiness and true love and a garden of teenage delights. Even though I had no plan for self-harm—and certainly didn't want to die—I did want my teacher and Mom to know the extent of my pain, and I couldn't think of any more extreme way to express it than to tell them I wanted to kill myself.

My teacher was concerned, but Mom wouldn't even dignify my melodrama with a response. On the many mornings when deep malaise kept me glued to my mattress, she came in and yanked the window shades up with such a snap it sent the vinyl flap spiraling around on itself. Then she ripped back my covers and told me the bus was coming. I didn't know then how different she and I were in dealing with loss. I wallowed and longed for what was. Mom stayed in motion and never looked back.

So, when Beez called on that January day to say Shrapnel was playing that night at our future high school, I hauled my carcass out of bed and started to get dressed. My closet held slim pickings. Black felt right, but I only owned one black item: a T-shirt I'd gotten on the boardwalk the previous summer at the salesclerk's suggestion. I liked it instantly, the glittery gold decal emblazoned across the chest. I ran my finger over each letter. J-A-I-L B-A-I-T.

Mom just shook her head when I wore the shirt from time to time for comedic effect. I'm sure she would have preferred I not wear it to the mall, but I liked its implication that I was a naughty risk-taker rather than my true self, a studious scaredy-cat.

I squeezed into the backseat of Beez's dad's wood-paneled station wagon between Peter Reefer, Annie, Cheryl, and Frankie. I'd known these kids since kindergarten and watched them transform into teenagers. No one embraced the role with as much gusto as Frankie. By eighth grade, Frankie Burns could pass as the stunt double for Kelly Leak, the motorcycle-riding bad boy in *The Bad News Bears*. Frankie was known around town as a natural-born hustler. He routinely showed up at my house with random items of unknown origin—a Hefty bag of weed, a half-drunk bottle of Peppermint Schnapps, a moped.

By the night of the Shrapnel show, Frankie had already provided several "firsts" in my life, including an unwanted sloppy French kiss when he and Peter Reefer appeared at my backdoor and told Annie and me it was time for us to kiss them. We were game; we knew we needed practice, so we settled onto the sofa and puckered up. But instead of a standard kiss, the boys, at the exact same moment, forced their slippery hard tongues right through our tight lips into our mouths. Annie and I leapt up, yelled obscenities at them, and threw them out of the house. Then, we marched upstairs to gargle with mouthwash and call Frankie's house to yell more obscenities at them and slam down the phone. Then Frankie called back and asked if we wanted to get stoned and hit Friendly's for ice cream sundaes. Annie and I conferred, then said, yeah, that sounded good, see them in five. That was how it worked in Shrewsbury. We were stuck with each other—and I liked it that way.

Beez's dad spun the steering wheel to the right, and there it was, filling the windshield: the promised land, my future high school, Red Bank Regional. Solid brick and windowless, the building looked about as welcoming as Rahway State Prison. A dozen lawn lights shone up at its facade, setting the school in relief against the blue ink sky, like opening night at a Broadway musical, *The Penitentiary!*

RBR, as it was called, was considered the coolest school around. It carried an air of danger from its checkered past, home to race riots in the 1970s, with student walkouts and fires set in garbage cans captured in front-page photos. Or maybe its grit came from all the garage bands born in those hallways: first and foremost, Shrapnel. Rumor had it, the Ramones had even written "Rock 'n' Roll High School" after playing a show at RBR. Part of RBR's special sauce was that kids from three different towns fed into it: Red Bank and its working-class Italian, Irish, and Black kids; Little Silver, with its Izod-wearing preppy kids; and Shrewsbury, my tiny town of middle-class white kids.

We poured out of the station wagon into the brisk January air, the parking lot a blur of headlights illuminating teenaged torsos. Frankie's dirty denim jacket was open, the word "TYRANT" scrawled in black magic marker across his T-shirt.

I pointed at it. "The warm-up band," he said.

He pointed at my Jailbait T-shirt. "Niiiice!" then laughed his woodpecker laugh. Frankie tugged open one of the heavy glass doors, and I walked through, stopping to inhale my first big whiff of RBR. I got an unmistakable hit. The wonderland of high school smelled like leftover tacos.

The tide swept us down a long corridor. Off to the left, a strange figure was leaning against a brick wall—a skinny girl with stringy red hair in a black leather jacket, hunched over, an unlit cigarette dangling from her mouth, head bobbing. I did a double take. I know her! That's Mary from my fourth-grade gifted program. Back then, she was a freckle-faced carrottop. Now I saw a harbinger of high school danger.

We sat in the linoleum-tiled lunchroom. Dozens of rows of orange plastic chairs faced a makeshift stage. The warm-up bands played and exited, leaving us in darkness for a couple of minutes. Then, one big spotlight popped on, shinning a bright circle on a huge American flag tacked to the cafeteria wall.

That's when the drumming started, fast and loud, like firecrackers. The band ran onto the dark stage, pulling guitars over their heads. Then the lead singer marched right into the spotlight, grabbed the microphone, and raised his fist.

"We're Shrapnel and we're gonna get the world!"

The guitars revved into rockets taking off. My insides ignited, and I grabbed the side of my seat in case our entire row of chairs blasted into the sonic stratosphere. Shrapnel was dressed for war. The singer's combat boots were black; his tank top was red, white, and blue. The other guys wore camouflage. Two had on helmets.

Beez's brother, Dave Vogt, had a dog tag around his neck that bounced off his chest every time he jumped in the air. His mouth was twisted in a tight snarl.

"I wanna be where the bombs are!" the lead singer yelled before picking up what looked like a WWII bomb and hoisting it over his head. The other guys turned their guitars into guns and pointed them at us. Somewhere along the way, I stopped breathing. I couldn't tell if these soldiers were trying to save us or kill us, and I didn't care as long as they kept playing. If this was high school, I was ready to enlist on the spot. A magnetic force stretched from the singer's mouth to the front of my Jailbait shirt and tugged.

"What's his name?" I yelled to Frankie.

"That's Dave Wyndorf," he yelled back. "The coolest fucking guy around."

Dave Wyndorf did something I'd never seen any singer do but had always *wanted* them to do: He acted out the lyrics. When he sang about fighting, he pumped his fist in the air; when he sang about love, he pointed his thumb at his heart. But even Shrapnel's songs about war were about love—love on the battlefield—and always begging a girl to be their baby.

Frankie nudged me with his elbow and pointed to someone just off-stage. "See him? That guy in the boots with that big belt buckle? That's Glen Buxton, lead guitar for Alice Cooper!"

I waved Frankie's finger away. "Shhh!"

The singer had his back to us. The back of his right kneecap was flexing, in and out, in and out. Waiting. Something was wrong. The lead guitar guy was adjusting some dials, shaking his head, mouthing words to someone offstage. The singer kept his arms folded across the flag on his chest, his back to us. Waiting. I teetered on the edge of my chair.

Then something amazing happened. The singer turned his head back toward the crowd, looked down at someone in the front row, and flashed a smile. A genuine, heart-melting smile. I saw it. Dave Wyndorf had just broken character—something Mom taught her drama students not to do. In that split second, it all crystallized. The lead singer was a *nice guy*. Shrapnel, I realized, was not about punk angst or violence. They were *acting*, and all at once, I was in on the act. That smile became my life preserver in a sea of danger.

Suddenly, the guitar kicked back into gear, the singer spun around, pointed out at the audience, and shouted, "I want *you* to sleep over!"

I gasped. *Me?*

Well, last night just wasn't long enough.

The cops had to wake us up off the beach.

Well, how about this one?

You can sleep over.

All the girls ain't like you.

You're the one that's so nice to me.

But I want you all to myself.

Oh, oh, Sleep over…

My tingling chest responded. *Don't worry, Dave! I WANT to sleep over!* I imagined Dave Wyndorf and me lying on my twin bed, facing each other, fully clothed, my head propped on my pillow. He would be smiling that secret smile, saying he wants me all to himself.

I couldn't blink, couldn't miss a second of this song. It felt like I'd swallowed a beehive, swarms of fluttering wings buzzing just beneath my breastbone. Pressing a hand to my chest, I opened my mouth, gulping in air. That's when the loud squeal of feedback filled the lunchroom. The principal stepped on stage.

"That's it, everyone! It's eleven p.m. Curfew time. The show is over."

"No!" I screamed.

"SHRAP-NEL! SHRAP-NEL! SHRAP-NEL!" The crowd started chanting and stomping their feet.

All of a sudden, the guy off to the side with the boots and big belt buckle jumped up on the stage, grabbed a guitar, and hit a chord that shook the cafeteria. Shrapnel fired up their guitars again. The drummer's arms flew into a frenzy.

Vogt jumped straight up into a high split, like his pants were rocket-propelled.

Wyndorf pointed at us. "You know this one!"

I ain't got no class,

I ain't got no principles!

Wyndorf was singing, but the principal wasn't leaving. Everyone sang-screamed. *School's. Out. For. Ever!*

The principal barked into the microphone, pointing to someone in the back to call the police. I looked around for an exit, but all I could see were kids climbing onto chairs, fists in the air, singing their lungs out. Suddenly, the roar of guitars wilted. Shrapnel was playing just as furiously, but we couldn't hear them anymore. On stage, the principal stood with a limp black electrical cord in his hands. But Shrapnel didn't stop playing, and the crowd didn't stop screaming. The back row started chanting, then the next row, then the next. *"FUCK! YOU! FUCK! YOU!"* Frankie grabbed my arm, pulling me up on a chair, then I, too, was shouting and stomping. Screaming profanity at a school principal was not my usual style, but here I was, saying *Fuck You!* to the authorities, to eighth grade, to Ethan, and all of life's unfairness.

The bright greenish cast of cafeteria lights clicked on. The music stopped.

"RBR!" Wyndorf shouted. Then, Shrapnel was gone.

I lowered myself from the chair, my head spinning like I'd fallen off the Tilt-A-Whirl. The echo of guitars still hung in the hum of the fluorescent lights.

As I staggered out of Red Bank Regional that night, I felt as if a door had been blown open, blasting me into a different dimension. I knew everything that had come before was a past life. And fuck Ethan anyway. He was a child. Shrapnel were soldiers. But something else happened in the rapture of that night, something communal and transcendent.

Decades later, the kids in that room would still talk in Technicolor terms about how that Shrapnel show blew our minds. Even the hardcore metal music lover who would travel the world to see Motörhead and The Damned a hundred times remembered that night as a lightning strike. So did the high school football player who would become a San Francisco 49er and win two Super Bowls, and the future Manhattan bond trader who would leave it all behind for Fiji. Even Frankie, who would later marry a famous heiress and become an overnight multimillionaire, then lose it all to heroin. And yes, even the lonely girl who would later land her dream job as a national news anchor and go on to interview presidents and celebrities, would still recall that Shrapnel show as a peak experience that not much else in life could match.

Even Glen Buxton, Alice Cooper's guitarist, would later marvel in an MTV interview about the intensity he experienced that night at RBR, and how Shrapnel set off a chemical reaction that blew the doors off the cafeteria.

That night we learned the power live music had to change our lives and the intoxication of telling the authorities to fuck off. This was our time, our show! We knew we were witnessing the start of something big, that revolution Norman Mailer had described, with Shrapnel leading the charge. Shrapnel was going to get the world.

At the exit, I saw a folding table with rolled-up posters and when I got home, I stood on my floral bedspread, dug my nails under the tacks that held KISS to my wall, and threw their poster to the floor. I gingerly unrolled Shrapnel and tacked them into their rightful position, right next to my bed. I lay down and stared at that poster for a long time.

And I want you all to myself. Oh, oh, sleep over. I had to hear the song again, had to memorize more lyrics. But the only way to do that was to *see* them again. Mom poked her head through the doorway.

"How was the concert?"

"Amazing," I said, not taking my eyes off the poster.

"What part of it was amazing?"

"Just…everything." There was so much I wanted in that moment. I wanted to be like Shrapnel, on that stage, all eyes on me. I wanted effortless charisma. I wanted to play the guitar. I wanted to be a lead singer. I wanted to be friends with Shrapnel. I wanted to go to their shows every night. I wanted to be their girlfriend. Mostly, I wanted Shrapnel to love me as much as I loved them.

"I just have to see them again," I told her. "Somehow."

Mom nodded, then turned to head down the hall. "I have faith you'll find a way."

PART THREE

at·tach·ment/əˈtaCHmənt/ *noun—1. affection, fondness, or sympathy for someone or something; an affectionate relationship between two people; 2. the act of attaching to something; 3. the process of clinging to a person or place for survival.*

Dreaming

The summer before high school, I went for my annual visit to see my South Philly cousins, Julie and Jianna, at their beach house in Wildwood, New Jersey, a hundred miles south of Shrewsbury. I loved Wildwood with its glorious white sand beach under the lively boardwalk where we would dance to disco blaring from amusement rides. I looked forward to this trip all year—another chance to copy my cousins' city-slicker ways. Julie and Jianna, meanwhile, considered me a hopeless hick from the hinterlands.

"Is that what youzz wear in the sticks?" Jianna asked, eyeing my ratty "Let's Party" T-shirt and homemade cut-off shorts. My cousins dragged me into their Pepto Bismol-colored bathroom to commence an urgent makeover. With their prompting, I spent the entire visit spraying Sun-In into my mousy brown hair and rubbing coconut oil over my sallow skin, trying to oven-roast it into a savage tan. In the space of two weeks, they transformed me from a country bumpkin in a ratty T-shirt into a blonder, tanner bumpkin in a fuchsia tube top.

I became an apprentice in my cousins' lifeguard appreciation program. This meant spending hours every day traversing miles of hot sand up and down the shoreline, stopping at each stand to flirt with the buff lifeguards. My cousins worshiped lifeguards the way other girls worshiped Donny Osmond or Shaun Cassidy, studying their hobbies and horoscope signs. Under their tutelage, I, too, became fluent in the universal language of lifeguard. That summer, I felt the power of my burgeoning teenage body and saw how boys started lingering around my beach towel. That summer, I was also determined to make my dreams come true, regardless of long odds or obstacles, and my dream took the shape of a lifeguard.

In my family, the beach held magical and medicinal properties. There were very few ailments a day at the beach couldn't fix. Allergies acting up? The ocean air will clear your sinuses. Poison ivy? Let the saltwater shrink the blisters. Tired? The sun's rays will revive you. I came up with my own prescription. Need more self-worth? Find a lifeguard.

When I got back home to Shrewsbury, I zeroed in on the one I wanted. He had a creamy coffee tan and worked at Trade Winds, the beach club in Sea Bright that I'd been sneaking into all summer. With his red swim trunks on and that silver whistle around his neck, he exuded an air of ease with his station in life. I was feeling confident, too. I'd returned from Wildwood not only tanner and blonder but with one of Julie's hand-me-down bathing suits that she'd given up when it started to bag in the butt. It was a pelican pink number, cut low enough to reveal cleavage and high enough to expose hip bones. I stole a glance at the lifeguard up on his stand. I liked that he looked strong. I liked that he was trained to save me if I went too far out in the ocean. Maybe I was looking for safety before venturing into the wild world of high school—a literal *life guard*.

Still, I needed a way to get him to notice me. So, I marched down to the water's edge, right past his stand and straight to the jetty. I set one foot on the first rock, then stepped to the next. The piercing sound of a whistle. He stood atop his stand, shaking his head no. I tilted my head and opened my arms, like, "What?" He used his first finger to call me over.

I strolled over as casually as possible, my hand acting as a visor against the low slant of afternoon sun. "What's the problem?"

He told me I had to stay off the rocks, which I knew. He asked why he'd never seen me before, which he had, a half dozen times. I found out his name was Robbie, and he was from Rumson, the wealthy town two over from Shrewsbury, filled with gorgeous mansions that lined the road to the beach. I debated daily which one I should live in when I grew up. There were too many to choose from! I asked if he was going to the beach party that night. He was. He told me to stay off the rocks. I agreed, then walked back to my towel, heart pounding through the pelican pink.

The sun went down. The ocean breeze picked up. The sand under my bare feet cooled to room temperature. Two kegs got tapped. Our Shrewsbury posse cranked up The Ramones, while the Rumson side of the beach had Bruce Springsteen on a never-ending loop.

"There you are," a voice next to me said.

His whistle and lifeguard jacket had been replaced by an Izod shirt. He said it looked like I could use another beer. I followed Robbie the Lifeguard over to the swath of sand where "Born to Run" was blasting. By that point, I would have followed him off a short pier into the dark ocean. I was still in my bathing suit when we kissed in one of the deserted underground cabanas, his warm arms wrapped against the hot pink strings across my shoulder blades.

◄◄ ❚❚ ►►

I couldn't wait for Mom and Robert to meet Robbie. I wanted them to like him and knew they would. Robbie turned out to be a steady, funny, and devoted boyfriend. Plus, he had the same name as Robert! Something about that symmetry was deeply satisfying to me—mine and Mom's love lives on parallel tracks, both finding the right guys after our long searches. But apparently, devoted and steady were not qualities Mom put at the top of her list.

"I'm afraid he's a little…straight," Mom said, after meeting Robbie for the first time.

I should have seen it coming. I knew that she preferred offbeat, unconventional types. I knew that she favored her quirky drama students over the straitlaced ones. I already knew she didn't bond with preppy people and that she never liked "that whole Irish-Catholic drinking culture," as she characterized some of our neighbors. But until then, our preferences were so aligned that I had never noticed her capacity for judgment, nor did I know that when my desires deviated from hers, she was incapable of seeing what might be best for me.

"He smokes pot, Mom. OK?" I snapped. "Does that make you feel better?"

"That's not what I mean by straight," she said in her measured way. "I mean, conventional."

"He's a fantastic boyfriend!" I said, crossing my arms at her.

"I agree," she nodded. "That's why I'm concerned. I'm afraid you'll get bored before long. You might end up hurting him."

My eyes started burning. "You know what?" I shouted. "Not everyone has to be a VEGETARIAN! Some people can just be WASPS! I like WASPS!"

Then I stomped my feet on every single stair up to my bedroom and power slammed my door. My mother didn't know me. I would never outgrow Robbie.

Rock 'n' Roll High School

On day one of high school, I decided that the penal institution known as RBR was the perfect place for me. After the boundless freedom of my middle school and home life, I liked the rigid structure of RBR. I liked the assigned seating, standardized tests, and obnoxious buzzers that signaled five short minutes to scramble to the next class. I particularly liked how the older kids, the seasoned veterans, waged open war with the militant hall monitors whose mission was to catch us in the slightest infraction and issue a demerit until we'd chalked up enough for a Saturday detention or in-school suspension.

By the time I arrived, only the bass player of Shrapnel was still there; the rest had graduated. But there were other garage bands—Steel, The Worst, Tyrant, Blitz—and every morning in the parking lot before the bell, music cranked from car stereos—Alice Cooper and The Ramones, Sabbath and The Stones. RBR was Rock 'n' Roll High School! The cool kids smoked and joked and bitched about how lame school was and debated daily whether they'd be busted if they cut class, which lent the entire parking lot a prison yard vibe filled with potential escapees trying to dodge the warden. I listened to the grousing, knowing I could never join their rebellious ranks. Mom's *Life Rule #1* could not be broken: I had to get that scholarship to college.

No place captured the high school ecosystem better than my biology class, which was filled with every classic eighties archetype, including the perky cheerleader, the creepy loner, and the super-stoned pothead. But there were also some unique-to-RBR characters: the long-haired guitarist of Steel, who spent most of the class poking the jean jacket of the lead singer, who sat behind his beautiful blonde girlfriend and crooned some of his answers to her. On the far side of the room sat a senior—a Joan Jett-look-alike named Judy—

who wore head-to-toe black leather regardless of weather fluctuations and was so tough, rumor had it, she'd stabbed her boyfriend with a switchblade, landing him in the hospital. In my memory, she wore her black motorcycle jacket over her gym uniform during PE class, but can that be right?

As for stock characters, no one played his part better than Mr. Horton, our curmudgeonly teacher. Mr. Horton had been at RBR for decades and, according to his past students, was grumpy and cantankerous even back then. I couldn't tell if he'd simply run out of gas on his way to sign the retirement papers or if he kept teaching out of sheer masochism. Either way, his disdain for us was deep and unvarnished, and he seemed genuinely pissed that we continued to show up for seventh period every day. Each afternoon, well after the bell signaled the start of class, Mr. Horton stayed behind the door of his "laboratory" in the back of the classroom, which we soon discovered was his hiding place for smoking cigarettes. When he finally emerged, he did so with a visible cloud of smoke trailing behind him, as if his body were smoldering underneath his white lab coat.

Even the cool Steel guys and knife-wielding Judy had to respect Mr. Horton's lack of giving a fuck. I personally found his naked contempt for us completely endearing. I loved the way he returned our graded tests with the same resigned wrist flick as a jaded blackjack dealer in Atlantic City, tossing losing cards across our desks. Mr. Horton did not suffer fools, which meant he had zero patience for our questions. One afternoon, the class stoner, Shawn, who had spent every day of the past eight weeks face down asleep on his desk, suddenly stirred. Mr. Horton was at the board in the middle of a lesson on hereditary traits, droning on about how different breeds of dogs could reproduce so long as they were similar in size. "Meaning," he said, "a Chihuahua cannot breed with a Great Dane." At that, Shawn snapped out of his stupor, lifted his head, and announced with salacious delight, "Ohhhhh, I get it."

The rest of us sat nonplussed as Mr. Horton put down his chalk, trained his bloodshot eyes on the boy, and said, "Go back to sleep, Shawn." And that was that. We never heard another word from Shawn. RBR was everything I'd hoped for.

Little Pink Barrette

On Friday and Saturday nights, Robbie and I went to parties in Rumson. These gatherings were straight out of the Preppy Handbook in the homes of people with last names like Peterson, Chamberlin, and Smith. So different from the Red Bank houses of families named Scoppetuolo and Mastrianni. And Camerota.

The guys at these parties were tall and sandy-haired, clad in wide-wale cords and Docksiders. They chatted in Rumson code about court times and nine irons, words that made no sense to me. Here's something else that didn't make sense to me: the Fair Isle Sweater. Girls in Rumson wore these things *out at night*. These sweaters were made of thick wool, often in lime green or bright pink, and had necklines so high, they could neuter even the shapeliest girls. Fair Isle Sweaters were the polar opposite of tube tops. They screamed, "Nothing to see here, folks! You can't even tell if I *have* boobs!"

I loved the routine and reliability of having a boyfriend and enjoyed going to these clean and comfortable houses with Robbie, though I wouldn't have minded switching up the Springsteen soundtrack for some Shrapnel, which no one in Rumson had even heard of. Robbie's friends were always quick to twist off a beer cap or light a cigarette, and after the night I won the who-can-name-the-next-Clapton-song contest, they warmly welcomed me into their posse.

Still, I never felt completely at home, never knew what to say about whether Stowe was less icy than Sugarloaf. To me, Robbie's classmates seemed to bask in their easy lives, knowing that college would be paid for from their fathers' flush bank accounts. Their toughest decisions seemed to be Princeton or Yale, Villanova or Notre Dame—and I secretly resented their parental help, which I didn't register as envy, but rather as smug superiority, knowing I'd have to con my own way into colleges and clubs and thinking that made me better.

◄◄ ❚❚ ►►

You can only make out in someone's car for so many weeks before the subject of sex comes up. By early November, I was already equipped with an A+ in my first-semester sex ed class and an epic, though untested, commitment to birth control. So, after two months of making out in Robbie's car, he and I proclaimed our mutual love and started discussing whether we should lose our mutual virginities.

But I was nervous and quickly became consumed with how I'd know when the time was right. I asked God for a sign, and he immediately sent one in the form of Tracey Goodman's barrette. Every day that baby pink barrette glared at me in Algebra class, blinking like a pink plastic beacon, warning of caution ahead. It stared at me sideways from Tracey's hair and begged some nagging questions: *Had she voluntarily clipped that thing on her own head? Or was that the handiwork of her overbearing mother? And how could I lose my virginity when my classmate still wore pink plastic barrettes?*

The barrette forced me to think back to a time when I was a barrette-wearing child—before Dad's heavy silences, his arrest, and job losses. Before the revelation of his secret son and a more recent marriage after my mom (that he'd also hidden from me), that resulted in a quickie divorce from a wealthy widow who figured out he was more interested in her inheritance than in her. I tried to think of a time before Mom met Robert and started studying for her doctorate, before I had to fend for myself during her absences. But even back when I wore barrettes, I never felt like a child. If I lost my virginity now, it would be another point of separation from the team I was supposed to be on, another cleaving from the pack. My old oddball status was never far behind, and I wasn't eager to stand alone in the corner again.

I also had another overwhelming worry, one that gnawed at me daily; I had a strong suspicion that immediately upon shedding my virginity, I would look different. I couldn't put my finger on it, but I was pretty sure something about my physical appearance would change, and the other kids would see it. I'd wear some kind of adult aura that wouldn't wash off.

"Here comes the non-virgin," they'd whisper, and after that, I'd be relegated to lonely no-man's-land.

That's it, I decided in the middle of Algebra. Case closed. Though I loved Robbie, I could not spend the next year on Sexually Active Deserted Island. The barrette won.

The Cool Table

I was in the lunchroom, trying not to stare but staring anyway. I'd seen them before, but on this November day, I studied their table with particular interest. Through crisscrossing red lunch trays, I watched them laughing and lounging, coming and going in ways that suggested little regard for class schedules. I recognized two of the Steel band members from my biology class, but I was more focused on the girls. Three of them were standing, telling a story, or a joke perhaps, before heading outside to the smoking patio. In their faded Levis, Converse high-tops, and leather jackets, these girls exuded self-assuredness. There was not a barrette in the bunch. I felt certain that if I could somehow make it over to their table, my tortured virginity issues would vanish. Those kids would understand.

But I didn't stand a chance. I was doomed to the forgettable freshman table where the girl next to Beez had chewed up potato chips decorating her braces. Sometimes I could come up with a ruse to try to infiltrate a club I wasn't a part of. But this one was impenetrable. I didn't have a leather jacket or red high-tops, and I certainly didn't have the guts or glory to navigate a cool table.

At RBR, being cool required comfort with living on the edge: the edge of expulsion or arrest, addiction or self-destruction. It required the ability to tell a good story, often about some brush with "the authorities." Coolness required taking risks—with drugs, alcohol, or sex. Coolness earned you a nickname. It was what allowed Frankie to reportedly have sex with a junior and earn the nickname Frankie Panky, and then to pass out from a Quaalude and wake up as Frankie Stanky. It's what allowed guys like Peter to smoke a shitload of weed and forevermore be known as Peter Reefer. I could fake some of it, occasionally coughing up a saucy wisecrack, but nothing nickname worthy.

Being cool meant not giving two shits whether teachers or parents liked you, not caring if you failed a test or got sloppy drunk at a party. Mostly, coolness required detachment. That was the hardest part. My longing for belonging was too intense.

I turned back to The Cool Table. *What were they laughing at over there?* That's when I saw her stand up. Sydney Sherman—older sister of Rachel, my friend since nursery school. Sydney Sherman—of the well-stocked bathroom with the never-ending Nivea! Rachel and I were still friends, but I couldn't very well ask her sister to help me catapult to The Cool Table. That was the definition of uncool. No, this had to be done stealthily.

My pulse kicked into a higher gear. Why was Sydney standing? Was she leaving? Maybe this was my only chance! I sprang up and grabbed my books. I had to hit the timing just right. My eyes on the target, I quickened my step, squeezing between plastic chairs, hoping no one was charting my peculiar course.

Sydney turned her head in my direction. Her eyes flickered. "Alisyn!"

"Oh, my God!" I exclaimed. "What are the chances? Is this your lunch period?"

"If lunch is what you call this gruel, then yes. Where do you sit?"

I waved my hand in a vague direction. "Over there. You know, with some...freshmen."

"Oh, you should totally sit here with us."

I could have kissed her.

The next day, I marched directly to The Cool Table and put my books down before anyone could stop me. Sydney quietly and conspiratorially filled me in on "the vitals," as she called them. *So, that's the guitarist in Steel, and the beautiful girl with freckles on his lap is Michelle. She's whispering in his ear now, but by the end of lunch, one of them will usually have stormed off. Over there is Winkie, the gorgeous tomboy in leather. And you have to meet Viv! Whenever she's sprung from detention. You've probably seen Sally Wyndorf. You know, Dave Wyndorf's little sister? And over there is Dawn, the flaxen-haired, doe-eyed beauty...*" Sydney sometimes spoke as if she'd just given an oral report on

Edith Wharton in Honors English, and it was still on her tongue. Meanwhile, my brain had short-circuited somewhere around Wyndorf. Not only was this The Cool Table, it was also a luge chute straight to Shrapnel. I pulled out a chair, sat down, and never left.

The kids at The Cool Table talked about music. They talked about the bands they'd seen and plotted their next shows. They talked about Lou Reed and Iggy Pop—who they called Lou and Iggy. They talked about Johnny Thunders, the New York Dolls, and David Johansen, who they called DavidJo. They talked about the Ramones and the Dead Boys and clubs called CBGB and Max's Kansas City, where Shrapnel played.

I had nothing to add to these conversations and I feared my silence would soon become conspicuous. No one likes a barnacle that only feeds off the juice of other people's stories. Looking back at that time, what I'm most struck by is Sydney's generosity. From the day we reconnected, she let me bum her cigarettes, borrow her clothes, and—in the every-girl-for-herself jungle known as a school lunchroom—Sydney gave me the ticket I so coveted. She shared her seat at The Cool Table.

No one at The Cool Table openly discussed sex. They were too cool for that. But somehow just breathing their sexy air put my ambivalence to rest. A few weeks later, back in Algebra class, gazing at my classmates, I was surprised when a feeling of equanimity swept over me. An inner voice said: *You are different than your classmates and that's okay.* Suddenly, as I looked at their virginal freshman faces, I couldn't remember why I'd been worried about not fitting in. How silly to think I would look different afterward. Now it all seemed so obvious—my classmates would not reject me. They'd never even know.

Born to Run

If I'd known New Year's Eve would be The Night, I might not have worn Mom's long-sleeved Danskin leotard and matching wrap skirt. I might have opted for something with, let's say, easier access.

Thanks to Mom's *Life Rule #2*, I never considered having sex without birth control. So, once I believed I was mentally and emotionally ready, Robbie and I drove to the unmarked brick building in Red Bank to pick up the goods. Pulling into the parking lot felt illicit and grown-up. He waited in the car in case we saw someone we knew.

I spent some time perusing the literature in the waiting room, reading about the effectiveness of diaphragms versus condoms. Once in the exam room, I sat in a crinkly paper robe, my legs swinging off the table. A white-haired doctor kindly but determinedly tried to steer me toward birth control pills, telling me he thought they'd be easiest for me. I told him I wasn't comfortable taking hormones every day. He told me they were low-dose and safe. I told him we barely kept aspirin in my house.

"We'll give you a six-month supply for free."

I perked up. "Well, okay. I mean, if that would mollify your anxiety."

The doctor swapped a glance with the nurse. "Yes, that would mollify our anxiety."

And just like that, I waltzed out to the parking lot with a brown paper bag stuffed with free pills and freedom. And get this: The doctor told me that to be extra safe I should take the pills for an entire month before ever having sex, *and I did that.*

After that visit, I became something of an unofficial birth control clinic ambassador—regularly trumpeting their services and, later, driving friends in need there. Robbie did, too. A few weeks after our visit, Robbie's history teacher asked his class which charity they'd like to donate bake sale proceeds to. Robbie raised his hand and suggested Planned Parenthood. His class cracked up. He wasn't joking.

Being a contraception champion was never political to me. It was practical. I share my story now because I don't hear many people talk about their "awesome first time." Maybe everyone is keeping it their little secret. Maybe nobody wants to brag. All I know is that a loving relationship + birth control makes it possible, and I'm living proof.

◄◄ ❚❚ ►►

That night the party was in a big Rumson house with all the usual trappings: tons of kids, a couple of kegs, absent parents, and Bruce Springsteen on repeat. Because it was New Year's Eve, the guys were in suit jackets and ties.

Just before midnight, Robbie and I stole away from the crackling fire in the crowded living room and went upstairs to what appeared to be a dark guest room. We knew we didn't have long before our absence would be discovered and had to make it quick. In the light of the digital clock on the nightstand, I began trying to wrest my arms free from the black bodysuit, as skintight as a surfer's wetsuit, then unwind the wrap skirt. A straitjacket and chastity belt would have been easier. Robbie tugged different flaps of fabric, laughing as he tried to help.

We were both nervous. Then, as if the Universal DJ in the Sky was in charge of the turntable, the stereo downstairs cranked up, and the first beats of "Born to Run" began. There in the dark room on a twin bed, it was just Robbie and me. And Bruce.

Springsteen and the E Street Band started narrating the action. The song begins with steady vibrating guitar chords, matched by a throbbing drumbeat as Bruce belts out how he's sweating it out on the streets at night. Then the drumming starts driving faster and faster, and Bruce describes being fuel-injected and boys trying to look so hard. Next, Bruce begs Wendy to let him in and to wrap her legs 'round his velvet rims and strap her hands across his engines. I'd heard "Born to Run" a hundred times, but I thought it was about riding a motorcycle out of town. *Wait, is it actually about sex?*

As with any well-timed song, I felt the invisible hand of God at work and knew this song was specifically selected for me in that moment. As the climax of the song approaches, Clarence Clemons starts wailing on his sax. The momentum builds and Bruce rasps out how he wants to die in an everlasting kiss. Then the guitar, drums, and sax combine into an explosion of musical fireworks. That's really how the song goes.

I rested my head on Robbie's shoulder for a moment, then jumped up and hurried to pull on the Danskin contraption before anyone knew we were missing. A round cherry wood mirror hung on the wall, and I stopped. Robbie had opened the door a crack, and in the long triangle of hallway light, I stared at my own reflection, turning my head side to side, looking for any visible sign of virginity loss but saw only my same self looking back. I smiled at my reflection. *How ridiculous to think I would look different.* We tiptoed down the stairs and sat back down on the stone fireplace, blending back into the crackling festivity of kids raising their cups in toasts, moments away from midnight.

Robbie's freckled friend Mike bounced up. "Hey, where have you guys been?"

"We were outside at the keg for a while," Robbie answered.

Mike cocked his head at me. "You sure?"

I nodded. "Yeah. Why?"

"I don't know," he said, narrowing his eyes on my face. "There's just something different about you than before. You look different."

Walk on the Wild Side

I've always been a charisma hound. It seems to me that with charisma, you can get whatever you want, even make someone love you forever. I saw it with Mom and Dad. But mostly, I learned it from Vivienne.

Viv was wild and fearless. She was an honorary member of The Cool Table, though she rarely showed up. She couldn't be bothered to sit still and eat a meal, though once I saw her swipe the sandwich of some self-important douche in the lunchroom and eat it in his face without uttering a word.

I met Vivienne in drama class on the first day of second semester. I waltzed into the classroom, confident that my new teacher somehow knew I was the daughter of a fellow drama teacher and that I would therefore be her favorite. The seats in front of the classroom were taken, leaving only one open desk in the back, and when I saw it, my boots froze on the linoleum. The area next to that seat was darker than the rest of the room, as if the light had burned out just above that spot.

In the black hole underneath was a girl with black hair pulled back in a ponytail. Her dark eyes were ringed in black liner. She had on a stretched-out red sweater and old jeans with writing scrawled up and down the legs. I also noted that all the boys' desks were turned a tick in her direction.

I took my seat and attempted a smile, but she didn't look over. Up close, I could read the riot on her jeans: JIMI HENDRIX carved in dark blue ink into the denim on her left leg. THE RAMONES scrawled in black marker along her right thigh. SEX PISTOLS painted in red nail polish along her right calf like a not-so-concealed weapon. She was rooting around in her purse, actively ignoring two handsome, sharply dressed Black guys in front of her.

One, in a pressed shirt and skinny tie, was turned all the way around in his chair to talk to her.

"Why you gotta be so cold?" he asked.

"Why you gotta be breathing?" she answered, not bothering to look up from her purse. She pulled a small pot of lip gloss from her bag. "Black honey, my favorite," she purred, licking her lips. "Oh, sorry! I don't mean you." She burst into a throaty laugh, which set off a belly laugh in the smitten guy.

The smell of cigarette smoke radiated off her, but there was another element that made me think she might ignite: a kinetic energy, an agitation. I tried to settle into my seat but got the distinct feeling she might slit my throat.

"Alright, class," Mrs. Maxwell began. "Welcome to Intro to Drama. We will be covering the history of theater. And, of course, we will be performing."

I clicked my four-color Bic into the ready position and sat up straight. The storm system next to me sank deeper in her seat.

"Who can tell me which musical is based on the myth of Pygmalion?" Mrs. Maxwell asked.

An over-zealous sophomore in the front row named Joanne Grasso, who was perpetually running for student council, shot a meaty hand in the air and waved, "*No, No, Nanette!*"

"No." Mrs. Maxwell said.

A loud snort sounded from the darkness next to me. "PIG-malion?" the girl said to Joanne's round backside. "You should have gotten that one."

"That's enough, Vivienne," Mrs. Maxwell said.

"*My Fair Lady*," I offered.

"Thank you, Alisyn," Mrs. Maxwell said.

She told us to think of other examples of modern plays with Greek roots. I had been scribbling for several minutes when a pang of nausea suddenly twanged the back of my throat. I swallowed hard, before a flush of heat whooshed up my face and my mouth started watering in that way that happens right before vomiting. *Oh, no! I should not have taken my Pill on an empty stomach.* I put my hot face down on the cool surface of the desk and took deep breaths. I closed my eyes.

"Miss Camerota and Miss O'Leary!" My eyes snapped open. "I will not tolerate sleeping in my class. You may both gather your books and see yourselves to the principal's office."

"But...I'm not feeling well," I stammered.

"Vivienne, what's your excuse?" Mrs. Maxwell demanded.

Vivienne reached for her book on the floor. "I was just bored shitless."

Mrs. Maxwell clapped her notebook shut. "I suggest you both come to class with more energy tomorrow."

I rose slowly, my body burning with mortification. But the expulsion infused Vivienne with energy, adding a spring to her step. I followed her out the door to the empty hallway, then stood disoriented.

She spun toward me. "What's your prob?"

"What?" Being this close to this girl's force field made me suddenly conscious of my hair. Why on earth had I used a curling iron that morning?

"I'm thinking you don't get sent to the office much," she said. "Wild guess."

I knew I had a choice to make. I never shared personal information with classmates, and I could have lied, but part of me wanted to let Leather Tuscadero here know I wasn't the innocent freshman she was mistaking me for.

"It's my pills," I said.

"Pills?" Vivienne's dark brown eyes flashed and connected with mine for the first time.

"Yeah, they make me feel sick sometimes."

Her face lit up. "And tired, right?"

"Yes," I nodded. This was encouraging. Maybe this captivating creature and I could have a connection. But I was antsy. We couldn't stand in the corridor long without arousing the attention of a hall monitor, so I started moving.

"What pills do you have?" Vivienne looked truly interested in me now, nodding with anticipation. "Percocet? Demerol? Tuinals?"

"There's more than two in all," I said, not knowing the words she was using and straining to remember the name on the dispenser. "There's probably twenty-eight. I think they're called Ortho Novum."

Vivienne slowed down. "What kind of pills are those?"

"Birth control pills."

She stopped cold. "You're on birth control pills?"

"Yes," I said, savoring the shock. *See, you she-devil? I'm not the prude you took me for, even if I don't have Sex Pistols scribbled on my leg.*

"Wait. How *old* are you?"

"Fourteen."

"REAL-lee?" Vivienne folded her arms and looked right at me, then pulled open the door to the principal's office.

I was spellbound. Like everyone, I found Viv equal parts intimidating and hilarious. One lunch period, the girls at The Cool Table were discussing an upcoming Shrapnel show at the famed punk club CBGB, which sounded thrilling and far away and like someplace I'd never be able to convince Robbie to go. The girl talk turned to the Shrapnel band members.

"I love Dave Vogt's puppy dog eyes," Dawn sighed.

"I like Phil, the dark brooding type," Sydney said.

Viv was known to have cool boyfriends but never spoke of her love life.

"What about you, Viv?" Michelle asked.

Viv flashed us a sultry smile. "I wouldn't mind a piece of Shrapnel in me."

Soda came out Sydney's nose.

◀◀ ❚❚ ▶▶

Mrs. Maxwell assigned Viv and me to direct each other in scenes. I chose Blythe Spirit, thinking Viv would enjoy playing a mischievous ghost who could torment that eager beaver Joanne. But the few times I tried to get Viv to work on it, she blew out of class before I could corner her. Finally, I chased her into the crowded corridor. "Hey, I think we need to rehearse."

"What?" she asked, looking annoyed.

"The scene...we have."

"Riiiight," she said, squinting into the far distance. "I'm thinking that's optional."

"No, no." My pulse quickened. "No, that's for our grade."

She sighed. "What do I have to do again?"

"I'm directing you in—"

She cut me off. "Can you come into the bathroom? Away from the maddening throngs."

I glanced at the black-and-white clock on the wall; four minutes until the bell and one demerit until a Saturday detention for my chronic lateness.

"I have to get to biology," I said.

"Hey, sugar," she said, spinning away from me, "take a walk on the wild side." Viv shifted soundtracks and started belting out a Janis Joplin song to the shuffling hallway crowd.

"Sing it, Viv!" A girl yelled.

I broke into a jog behind Viv's long strides. From twenty feet back, I watched Viv spin right into the wooden bathroom door. I was afraid she'd hurt herself until I realized that was how she entered rooms.

"It's cool," Viv said before being subsumed in smoke.

"It's cool," I repeated, several beats behind her.

"It's cool" was the secret code for the bathroom that signaled to everyone inside that it was cool to keep smoking. When the door opened without "It's cool," everyone immediately flushed her cigarette down the toilet or doused it in the sink, in case it was the dreaded Miss Wilson, the hundred-year-old, fear-inducing hall monitor. Sometimes the door would open without the secret code, and everyone would flush away freshly lit cigarettes only to find someone like Tracey Goodman or Joanne Grasso swinging in. Then everyone would go apeshit, berating them for their uncoolness. I found the bathroom biosphere fascinating. On the day I chased Viv inside, roughly six girls were in there, smoking, reapplying lip gloss, peeing, or melting their black eyeliner with a match for smoother application.

Viv squinted at herself in the mirror. "My hair's not following instructions today."

Viv's looks were so irrelevant to her allure, I had to ask. "What do you want it to do?"

"Stand on my head and spit wooden nickels," she said, then hoisted herself onto the white porcelain sink and lit a Marlboro Red. She took a huge drag, exhaling a long slow smokestack as if she'd been holding it in her lungs for hours.

"The performance is eleven days away," I said.

Viv let her head fall back against the tile. "Good. Then we have another ten days before we need to think about it."

"I think you're going to like this scene. It's about a dead wife who comes back and haunts her husband and his new wife. You can haunt Joanne!"

"Can I punch her in the face?" Viv asked.

Just then, the door opened. "It's cool!"

Something was off. The voice was high and croaky. Eyes darted. Suddenly, Miss Wilson teetered around the corner.

"I *got* you!" she screeched. "Now, who in here was smoking?" By then, no one was holding any evidence, and the girls closest to the door ran out. "Was it *you*, Vivienne?"

Viv affected a wide-eyed expression and shrugged her shoulders as Miss Wilson walked up to her. Then Viv blew a chimney's worth of smoke right in her face.

"To the office!" Miss Wilson croaked. The bell rang.

"Shit!" I said.

Miss Wilson swept her bony arm at me. "You, too!"

Viv and I were headed to the principal again—and some little part of me was happy, even excited, for that walk on the wild side.

◄◄ ❚❚ ►►

I could hardly wait to see the coven Vivienne called home, what graffiti was sprayed on the walls, what drugs were spilled on her nightstand. But her khaki-colored ranch house was standard-issue suburbia: four modest bedrooms, a sunporch, and a formal living room with a piano that looked untouched. Viv's mother also seemed utterly normal, with shiny dark hair and warm caramel eyes. She greeted me with what appeared to be vast relief.

"Oh, you're here to practice a scene? Isn't that nice, Vivee? Oh, that's terrific."

I sat on the edge of one of Viv's twin beds, waiting for some cue that she was ready to get to work, but instead, she kept picking up the needle and putting it down on her albums: the B-52's, the Ramones, Generation X,

Patsy Cline. When she tired of the music medley, Viv led me down to her dark basement with a TV, beat-up black pleather couch, oval table, and huge ashtray.

Watching Viv smoke, which she did a lot, was a voyeuristic experience, like watching someone take a bubble bath or meditate. Like maybe she and the Marlboro wanted to be alone. She'd light the cigarette, stare at its burning tip for a beat before wrapping her lips around the filter, drawing on it deeply. Then, she'd lean back and open her mouth to let the plume billow out over her face. I chewed my cuticles, waiting to start our assignment.

At around 5:00 p.m., a loud garage door went up, and Viv stiffened. A tall man in a winter dress coat and briefcase walked through the basement door.

He stopped to stare at us. "Up to your usual level of productivity, I see."

"Ignore him," Viv told me.

"What do we have here?" he asked. "A Mensa meeting, I assume." He spoke in a booming Brahmin accent, as though he were a Shakespearean actor in an amphitheater.

"We're doing homework," she snapped. "Get out of here."

"You're getting my daughter to do actual schoolwork?" he asked me. "Clearly, you have the patience of Job."

"God!" Viv yelled. "Leave us alone!"

"Very well. You can get back to saving the world." He marched out and up the stairs.

"Sorry," Viv said, grabbing another cigarette. "He's such a fucking asshole."

Dance This Mess Around

Viv's energy drew people in like moths to a blowtorch. Guys—from basketball players to Dead Heads—could smell the danger and wanted to possess and protect her.

When I look at photographs of Viv from that time, she appears as a flash of light, an over-exposure of energy, a lightning bolt too fast for the camera to catch. "It's like we're seeing the trails of her acid-trip," Sydney once noted, trying to explain yet another photo where Viv's image was replaced by a white-hot streak.

I wanted to be close to Viv and to *be* her—to be so desired yet care so little. Sydney was also mesmerized. Teachers were less enamored. They saw Viv as a flight risk, and the school's layout didn't help. RBR was originally conceived as a late seventies model of collaborative classrooms without walls. That experiment was short lived once the administration realized a thousand rowdy, mutinous kids had to be reined in. But some parts of the school still operated with the failed open-floor plan, meaning six classes would be in session simultaneously, separated by a few non-sound-proof dividers. On many days, above the din, a teacher could be heard ordering Vivienne to the office. I'd turn to see her spinning out of class, arms wide open, like a skydiver whose chute failed to open.

◀◀ ‖ ▶▶

Parties in Red Bank were always loud with music, thick with smoke, and cloaked in darkness so neighbors wouldn't catch on. Some Friday nights, I began swapping out preppy Rumson parties with Robbie for grungier Red Bank parties with Sydney. By then Sydney and I looked almost identical:

same brown roots growing under the same brassy Sun-In highlights, same petite body type. Many mornings we'd board the school bus only to discover we were wearing the exact same Levis and puffed shoulder shirt from Pants Place Plus. Classmates began to mistake us for each other, and I loved having her as my twin.

When Sydney and I arrived at one Red Bank party, the B-52's were blasting from the stereo, setting the scene in a minor chord. We moved fast through the dirty kitchen toward the living room, looking for her boyfriend, Conor, last seen sitting next to the notorious slut Tammy.

Just as we passed the staircase, I saw a blur of motion. Viv was at the top of the steps teetering around, clutching a half-empty bottle of vodka as two figures fluttered near her like handmaidens from a fairytale. Seconds later, I heard cascading thuds and looked back to see Viv crumpled at the foot of the stairs, her handmaidens frantically descending to kneel beside her, trying to stand her up. Viv let out a loud cackle. But her descent wasn't funny to me.

Then someone yelled, "Police!" and kids started scattering. The cops were coming through the back door with flashlights like laser beams. I followed four other kids out a window onto the lawn, where I saw a girl on all fours combing the blades and crying. "I dropped my black beauties," she sobbed. I couldn't stop to look for her drugs. I had to find a ride home. The togetherness was over.

◄◄ ❚❚ ►►

I don't want to claim that Monmouth County was a den of drug use. I'm sure there were many people there who never touched drugs. But starting when I was a teenager, an ever-expanding panoply of illicit drugs became a regular part of the stories my friends and I heard (and told). So much so, that later in life, when I met someone who didn't know what purple microdot was, I assumed they'd been raised in a nunnery.

I've tried to tally up the number of friends I watched fight the demons of drug abuse, but I lose count after a dozen and I'm very skittish about even referencing the ugly episodes I witnessed. Those aren't my stories to tell. Somehow I was spared the agony of drug addiction and alcoholism.

Even famously addictive nicotine couldn't get its claws into me. I used cigarettes as a personal punctuation mark, an exclamation point on an exciting night, rather than something as common as a comma. But let's not pretend I was able to dodge the addiction bullet because I had more willpower or stronger character than the others. After decades of examining this, I believe the only difference between some of my dearest friends and me is that no substance ever lit up my neurotransmitters the way it did theirs. Every additional beer or cigarette made me feel worse and made them feel better. Simple as that.

But I can speak with authority about the excruciating pain of watching friends spiral down. I've loved addicts and can testify to the silent scream of not being able to do a single fucking thing as they steadily and dramatically kill themselves. For a long time, I made the mistake of thinking their addiction would stop if only they tried harder. If only I found the right words. If only they needed me more than they needed the drug.

◀◀ ❚❚ ▶▶

Robbie's senior class was going to Ft. Lauderdale for spring break, and I didn't want him to go. I was afraid he would forget about me, or cheat on me, or have too much fun without me.

As I was worrying about my boyfriend, Mrs. Maxwell was holding auditions for RBR's spring musical, *The Boy Friend*. The beautiful tomboy Winkie and I got parts as dancers in the chorus. After some play rehearsals, Winkie took me to her friend Mark's house in Red Bank. Through a dark smoky living room, we walked single-file upstairs to Mark's tiny bedroom where he and his cute best friend Matt would be drinking beer, smoking butts, and playing killer tunes—Squeeze, Joe Jackson, Johnny Thunders, Adam Ant, The Vibrators, and Shrapnel. Mark and Matt told great stories about going to Shrapnel shows. I desperately wanted to go with them but knew that spending Saturday nights in New York City with two senior guys would be a tough sell to Robbie. Not much happened in Mark's room but somehow that soundtrack percolated with possibilities, and I wanted more.

It was during those music-filled afternoons that I came to believe the chasm between Springsteen and Shrapnel, Rumson and Red Bank was becoming too big to straddle. I feared I would have to choose a side. I started picking fights with Robbie, setting up impossible choices, forcing him to decide between going on his class trip or staying with me, when what I really wanted was to go see Shrapnel.

At home, something was going wrong with Mom and Robert. She didn't say anything, but I could see he wasn't around and Mom wasn't going to his place. This worried me. After our parallel successes, I feared instability in Mom's love life spelled instability in mine.

Dad had moved again—to a different South Jersey town where he'd found a job teaching German and Spanish at another high school. In our weekly phone call, he'd mentioned that he might try to see me in the school play, but since he'd missed my eighth-grade graduation and fourteenth birthday, I didn't count on it. By then, Dad's world had shrunk. He'd gone from international traveler to a man who didn't often venture outside his tiny town, or even his own living room. Our visits were down to Christmas and a summer weekend. I didn't care. I had boyfriend issues to worry about.

On opening night of *The Boy Friend*, I was giddy from the cast bonding and audience applause. When the curtain went down after our final bow, I made my way, light-headed and breathless, out to the audience to find Mom and Robbie, Gram and Poppy. I stood pressed against the seats as families shuffled by. Poppy helped Gram into her sweater, Mom searched her purse for the car keys. Suddenly, Beez's brother, Dave Vogt, was in front of me. It was a disorienting jolt to see a piece of Shrapnel standing before me in regular clothes, rather than hanging on my wall in camouflage.

"You were great up there," he said, then leaned forward and kissed me on the cheek, as if we were cousins at a family reunion. I had to resist the urge to bring my hand to the spot on my face where his lips had just been.

"What have you been up to?" he asked.

"Oh, you know, play rehearsal." We stood nodding at each other until his father tapped him on the shoulder.

"Guess I gotta go." He gave me a quick nod.

Flushed, I watched him walk away.

"Good job!" Robbie said. "You pulled off that cartwheel. Wanna go grab a slice?"

I did want some pizza. But I also wanted to go to the bar where some of the cast was going. And I wanted to know where Dave Vogt was going.

Robbie pulled into the parking lot of Danny's Pizza. He turned off the engine, and just as we were about to get out, I saw Dave Vogt and Phil Caivano, Shrapnel's bass player, crossing the parking lot toward the entrance. They were laughing. Vogt swung open the door. Without thinking, I sank into the bucket seat below the dashboard.

"What are you doing?" Robbie asked. "What's happening?"

I blubbered some sentences about Mark and Matt and Winkie and the music in Mark's room and how I really wanted to go see Shrapnel. Robbie's face registered only sad confusion.

◀◀ ❚❚ ▶▶

The day after Dave Vogt kissed my cheek, Robbie left for his class trip. That week Shrapnel played a Battle of the Bands concert in Red Bank at the Carlton Theater, once a majestic jewel of a building, now worn and faded. I hadn't seen Shrapnel since the RBR show more than a year earlier and I was eager to confirm that the earth-shaking event hadn't just been in my head. Steel was playing the Battle of the Bands, too; plus Blitz, Frankie's band; and the Blushing Brides, a Stones tribute band.

I ran up the thick red carpet of the grand staircase and stood on the second floor, taking it all in. To my right, down the long mezzanine, the door to the women's lounge flew open and Viv spun out, a cigarette balanced between her lips to ask Sally Wyndorf for a light. To my left, Frankie and Peter Reefer hung over the balcony railing. Frankie said something and Reefer's face lit up red. I knew they were baked. I knew them so well.

Looking down into the orchestra, I saw Dawn and Michelle on the edge of their red velvet seats, waiting to cheer on their Steel boyfriends. Two rows behind them was Shawn, the stoner from biology, looking stoned, and against the wall was Judy, intertwined with her boyfriend. I guess they'd patched things up after the stabbing. Any direction I turned, I knew someone, knew their story, and loved them. Then my throat got thick, and liquid pooled in my eyes.

"Hey!" Sydney said. "What's wrong?"

"Nothing. Nothing's wrong. It's just that everyone's here, you know?" My voice caught. "And we're all together. And everyone's connected and..." Tears spilled down my cheeks.

"I know!" Sydney said. "I just saw Conor next to Tammy. *And I don't even care.*"

I laughed and somehow that made me cry more. I knew just what she meant. Some nights were bigger than our petty jealousies. Some nights were so big, they connected us to the cosmos.

"It's like if a lightning bolt struck me dead right now, it would be okay," I said, my voice quivering. "Like I know what it is to be completely content."

"Oh, great," Sydney said, "now you're making me cry." She coughed, then laughed and whisked at her tears before digging into her bag and bringing out a tissue. She blew her nose loudly. "God! I'm a mess!" She looked around. "Is Rob coming?"

"Rob," I repeated, unable to immediately place the name. For a second, I thought she meant Mom's boyfriend, Robert.

"Rob," she repeated to my blank face. "Your boyfriend."

Robbie.

The lights flickered. We ran to our seats. Arms flew in the air as Shrapnel marched on stage. Caivano hit a guitar chord. Vogt took his angry wide-legged stance and scowled out at us. Wyndorf grabbed the microphone and yelled, "Have no fear! Underdog is here!"

Shrapnel cranked into a supersonic version of the Underdog theme song, and we screamed, "Speed of lightning! Power of thunder!"

By the time the opening riff of "Sleepover" started, I was dizzy. I hadn't heard the song in more than a year, and now it was going by too fast.

Well, last night wasn't long enough.

The cops had to wake us up on the beach.

Well, how about this one?

You can sleepover...

I needed to hear it again and again and again. Then I started sobbing the way only a fourteen-year-old girl can when, on one perfect night, her life is complete.

Robbie came back three days later, but I was long gone.

That was the last relatively stable month of my teenage years.

Price of Admission

Shrapnel was playing at CBGB, the iconic punk club located in New York's bombed-out Bowery neighborhood, where Blondie and the Ramones and the Talking Heads and any other cool eighties band you've ever heard of got their start.

"Oh, my God," I said when I saw the name on the fake ID Mark had scored for me. "Monica Buonincontro?" I was in the front seat between Mark and his older brother, Pat. A cold beer bottle had turned room temperature between my squeezed knees as I used the green glow of the dashboard to study the paper license.

"I couldn't find one that said Ali-skin," Mark laughed. He'd recently taken to calling me Aliskin as a nickname, or Skin for short. I think he simply liked the rhyme. But I loved the nickname's risqué connotation of exposed flesh combined with the reference to punk rock skinheads. I acted like I took the name in stride. Truthfully, it was a high honor. I'd arrived.

Before we left, Mark's brother had chopped a gram of cocaine into lines on Mark's bedroom mirror. I had no interest in coke, though I'd heard it spoken of in reverent terms: something expensive and reserved for special occasions. So, how does someone with no interest in cocaine end up snorting cocaine?

Imagine you live in a land where everyone eats white bread. You've seen the reports that white bread isn't good for you, but there it is, at block parties and backyard barbecues. You don't like the white bread, but you can't help noticing that everyone seems more excited when white bread is around. White bread makes every event feel more festive and celebratory. Songs get written about it. People are so excited by white bread, they're even excited to share it with you. They want you to experience its thrill. And in that way, white bread comes to feel like one of those "motivators" who work the dance floor at weddings and bar mitzvahs, cultivating active excitement. And you like exciting dance floors—even if you aren't crazy about consuming all that white bread.

The downside to white bread is that it kills some people, but only after it destroys their lives. Throughout high school, some of my friends developed such a strong taste for cocaine they burned through their paychecks, then their savings. One friend died in a mysterious single-car crash in the middle of the night, supposedly after being three weeks late to pay his dealer; another hid in a closet for twenty-four hours with crippling psychosis, certain that burglars and rats had invaded his apartment. Three years after my first exposure to coke, I would scramble to soak a cold dishcloth for a friend who had spelled out his own nickname in chunky caterpillar lines, then snorted the whole thing, sending his heart into overdrive, and making his face a sweaty raspberry. Again, those are their stories to tell. My story is that I never liked the heart-racing, cheek-chewing, chain-smoking, money-wasting of it all.

Mark's brother parked on some grim Lower East Side street, and we took our places at the end of a line of leather outside CBGB. I was so close to Shrapnel, I couldn't get carded and have it fall apart now.

"The last time we were here, we saw somebody get shot," Winkie suddenly remembered. "We heard a gunshot, then this guy got tossed out of a car right in front of us, bleeding from his head."

"Really?" I gulped.

"ID," the bouncer demanded and I handed it over. "Name?"

"Monica Bone-in-quantro," I said with an Italian flair, hoping it bore some resemblance to the real thing.

"Date of birth?"

"8-17-1962." I said it quickly to show how second nature my own fake birthday was to me. The bouncer didn't budge.

"Oh. Wait. I mean, 7-18-1962!"

"Bingo," he said, flat as a board.

I stopped breathing. "Sorry. Numbers confuse me. Plus, I'm extremely drunk."

"Trust me," Mark piped in, sticking his big head over my shoulder. "She's ALL fucked up." The bouncer sighed. I knitted my hands together and pressed them to my lower lip. "*Please*," I whispered. "*I love Shrapnel.* I have to see them."

A stream of air came out the bouncer's nose. He pushed open the door.

"Gawd!" Mark said, slapping my shoulder as we headed for the bar. "You almost gave me a heart attack. That's the last time I take a fourteen-year-old to CBs."

CBGB smelled like stale beer, leather, cigarettes, and dog shit. It was darker than I liked and crowded with burly biker types and tattooed skinheads. Being at CBs was like being in a madhouse of graffiti: Every door, wall, surface, square inch was covered in letters and symbols. Graffiti on top of graffiti, layers and layers, marking time like rings of a tree. The bathroom stalls and sink were coated in colors, decorating the cramped, dirty space used for drug-doing and drama. The toilet was covered in graffiti. There was even graffiti *in the toilet bowl.* I tried to check the mirror on the way out, graffiti covered my reflection.

Out front, the lights went black and we pressed toward the foot of the stage. I positioned myself behind a short girl in a plaid Catholic school kilt, combat boots, and a mohawk. The skinhead next to me had a safety pin through his cheek. *Well, last night just wasn't long enough.* I sang to myself like a psalm.

A guy with a bushy beard and dark sunglasses ambled onto the stage.

"All right, all you animals," he shouted in a thick New York accent. "Get ready to rattle yuh chains for yuh masters!" Everyone cheered. "But first, listen up! I got some instructions for yuh. The next time yuh mutha asks you what's the difference between punk rock and New Wave, I want yuh to spit on her!"

A guttural roar from the crowd.

"And tell her, 'That's punk rock!' And then, I want yuh to *apologize* for doing it. And tell her, 'That's New Wave!'" The room erupted. "Now, without further ado, here are the commandos of punk rock themselves! It's Shrapnel!"

I cupped my hands to my mouth and screamed.

Chop Up Your Mother

Being born on June 21, I considered summer my personal birthday gift. From the second I opened my eyes on summer mornings, I could feel that crackle of yellow energy, that atmospheric glow just outside my window. On those mornings, the pull was ever-present: The air humming with crickets and a trilling sparrow's song, stirring my insides and reaching around my rib cage to tug me eastward to that magical place. The beach.

Without Robbie, I was free to go to the beach every day and free to sit in Mark's sweltering bedroom every night, listening to music. When the heat got unbearable, we climbed over wooden fences and went pool-hopping in our underwear or grabbed a couple six packs and drove around, to a party or back to the beach.

One night, we drove under a train overpass that Rumsonites were known to spray paint with messages like "Springsteen 4ever" or "Class of '81!" My eyes blithely grazed the latest message: "Goodbye Alison. Thanx for the memories. Punk rock is life."

A sharp prick shot up my spine. The name was spelled differently but the message was unmistakable. Had I decided punk rock was life? No, and I was hardly masquerading as a punk rocker. My hair was still Laura-on-General-Hospital-long, not spiked in a Mohawk. I didn't wear safety pins in my face. Occasionally I tried them as earrings, but no one noticed. I didn't own a leather jacket or red Converse high-tops. My one attempt at an edgy aesthetic was my Boardwalk-bought leopard-print shirt. But on me, leopard looked as tame as a house cat. I bought hot pink lipstick, but on my mouth, it was more Debbie Reynolds than Debbie Harry.

Still, those steamy nights of music were sticky with the vague promise of future Shrapnel shows. That's the thing about becoming a groupie; it takes on an addictive quality, my personal form of dependence. And like a junkie jonesing for a hit, I was desperate to score tickets and rides, searching for the perfect high. If Shrapnel swapped out "Underdog" for "Special Forces" in their set, I had to immediately find another show. If they played "Siegfried Line" but not "Girl in Trouble," back to another show I had to go. Most urgently, I had yet to learn all the lyrics to "Sleepover," so I couldn't even sing it to self-soothe during the long lapses between live shows. I knew only snippets, which I sang over and over, much to Viv and Sydney's amusement as they traded there-she-goes-again looks.

"Don't you love Shrapnel?" I beseeched Sydney.

"Yeah, I do," she said. "But no one has it quite as bad as you."

She was right. I had it the worst. Maybe if Shrapnel had put out an album, that could have placated me. Perhaps if I could have heard more of their songs on my record player, I could have kicked the cravings for the next show. But with groupies, it's always about more than the music. It was the band's charisma and energy and secret smiles that were impossible to turn away from.

◀◀ ❚❚ ▶▶

Mom never told me that she and Robert broke up or where she met Gary, but there he was at our kitchen table. Gary had a fancy new car and what I guessed was a high-paying job as a psychotherapist, though Mom didn't seem very interested in him. I assumed he would soon be gone, and I braced for the next round of suitors to show up.

"Gary and I are going to the opera at Lincoln Center," Mom informed me as she chopped cucumbers for a salad and I stirred the seashell macaroni in boiling water. I was still in my bathing suit from the beach when Mom asked me to help with dinner while Gary sat idly at the table, which pissed me off.

"You ever go to the opera?" Gary asked me.

"Nope."

"You should," he said.

"I don't have time," I told him. "I'm going to CBGB tonight to see the Dead Boys and the Sic F*cks. And maybe the Vibrators." I knew the Vibrators weren't playing; I just threw them in for shock value. Had I known that I'd be surrounded by skinheads with baseball bats later that night, I might not have been such a brat. But that summer, my mouth was set on smart-ass mode.

"I know you're trying to be provocative," Mom said without looking at me. Her voice had a world-weariness lately, with none of the zest she'd had around Robert.

"Nope," I lied. "Those are just the names of the bands."

◀◀ II ▶▶

Being at CB's was better than being at the opera with Mom and Gary, but I wasn't happy about the blood. In the middle of the Dead Boys set, Stiv Bators, the lead singer, slashed his own stomach with the mic stand, causing blood to squirt everywhere. This was my dirty little secret about punk rock that I couldn't share with Mark or Matt or Winkie (I'm afraid to admit it even *now*)—I hated the blood-squirting, head-banging, body-slamming nihilistic elements of punk rock. But that stuff was part and parcel of punk. It's like saying you like opera but hate the singing. If I wanted to keep scoring rides to see Shrapnel, I had to suffer through the hardcore bands they played with.

I made deals with myself. Maybe if I did a Kamikaze shot and hit the bathroom in the middle of "Hey Little Girl," the Dead Boys first set wouldn't seem so long. Maybe if I could endure the screeching feedback of "Sonic Reducer," I might discover a hidden ditty in the Dead Boys's playlist that allowed me to stick it out through a second set. If only I could get past the self-destruction of Stiv Bators, "Combat Love" would be around the corner. At another show, Stiv drank a bottle of Jergen's body lotion and puked on the equipment. This guy was no charmer, no Dave Wyndorf.

Some nights I was so desperate for Shrapnel I went to CBs even when I knew they weren't playing, hoping for, I don't know what? A glimpse of their poster behind the cash register? A surprise appearance? To fall in love with another band as an antidote to my addiction? On this night, I was willing to give the opening band, the Sic F*cks, a chance. Their song "Chop Up Your

Mother" was kinda catchy on the bootleg tape Mark had. Then the lead singer took the stage all sloppy and lumpy.

"Hey, man, who let us the fuck back in?" he asked.

The skinhead to my left growled and raised his fist.

"Good to see all the skins here tonight," the singer continued, spitting into the microphone. "Come on! Get fucked up and murder someone!"

Feedback squealed from the speakers into my eardrums. The two guys in front started throwing their bodies into each other, and I was about to get an elbow in the face. Then I felt it in my gut, that old hollow feeling. The Sic F*cks were no Shrapnel. I could never love them. There was no cure for my brand of addiction.

I tapped Mark's shoulder, cupping my hand to his ear. "I'm tired."

"Dead Boys have another set after the F*cks!" he yelled. "Don't you want to see if Stiv falls off the stage again?"

"Tempting. But no thanks."

"Well, suit yourself!" Mark said like a goofy game show host, like who would ever turn down that parting gift?

I knew the unwritten penance for bailing early. I turned and swam upstream through the crowd of clenched faces and fists. Punk rockers looked angry, even when they loved the band. I made my way to the door and stepped out onto the dark street. I walked in the direction I was pretty sure we'd parked, noting the street sign, East Second and Bowery, in case I couldn't find the car and had to make my way back to CBs. I moved fast past the metal gates pulled down over storefronts and buildings spray-painted with sinister shapes, like swastikas and elongated triangles. *Our neighbors suck* was scrawled in red paint on the outside of what looked like a flop house. Above it in black: *Stun + gun = cops*. Hustling past parked cars along the curb, I looked behind me, then turned the corner. I couldn't erase that story about the guy getting shot in the head, so my skin was prickly as I walked toward a pile of dirty clothes against a chain link fence. All was still, until I got right up to the pile. Suddenly it jerked.

"Ahhh!" I jumped over a wino's leg splayed across the cement, a wet circle on the crotch of his pants. "Oh, God!" I blurted, backing away. A car honked and zoomed by, then I bolted half a block to Mark's Mustang, grateful to find it unlocked. I got in, slammed down the lock, and sat still for a few minutes, trying to catch my breath as I watched a brown paper bag from an overflowing garbage can waft around the curb. I turned and climbed over the front seat.

Being in the backseat alone reminded me of a time—I must have been four or five years old—in the back of our Oldsmobile. Mom and I were at the train station, waiting for Dad to come home. The night sky was pitch black. Rain was coming down in sheets, hammering the windshield. Trains had come and gone, but no Dad.

"Stay here," Mom said over her shoulder. "I'm going to look for him."

"No!" I shrieked.

"Just stay in the car," Mom said, grabbing the umbrella.

I stayed in the backseat, straining to see through the torrents, crying and yelling, "Mommy!" I screamed for what felt like forever. I have no memory of Mom returning to the car that night, or if she ever found Dad, though, of course, she must have. I only remember her leaving.

My eyes popped open at the sound of something horrible. In those first foggy moments, I wasn't sure if the fleeting echo was real or the remnant of a nightmare. I didn't know if I had been asleep for hours or mere minutes but my left cheek was resting in a slippery pool of my own saliva. Right outside the car window I heard voices, staccato shouts. For a second, I thought maybe Mark, Matt, and Winkie had come back, but the voices were strange and too close, almost in the car. I lifted my heavy head and dragged the back of my hand across my wet mouth. Just as I pushed upright, I caught a blur of movement, a swinging baseball bat, a cluster of skinheads, followed by that awful sound again, a violent shattering of glass as the bat crashed through the passenger window of the car right in front of Mark's. My throat closed.

Falling back down, I rolled into the foot well and onto the floor mat, curling my body into a tight ball, my heart pounding through my eardrums. In that split second on the floor, I knew Mark's windows would be smashed next. I didn't know how long it would take the skinheads to get what they wanted or if I could hide with shards of glass raining down on me. I also knew I was a witness to a crime and that the skinheads wouldn't like that. I pressed my palms over my ears to stop the sound of shattering glass and started praying.

Please, God, let me make it home alive.

Girl in Trouble

Something scared the skinheads off. They bolted before finding me. But that wasn't the end of my brushes with danger that summer. Three weeks later, I was at a party, having a grand time in Mark's humid backyard filled with fireflies and laughter, with our summer soundtrack of Squeeze playing. It was almost two in the morning, most of our stated curfew times. Bert, one of the motorcycle-jacket-wearing Shrewsbury guys, borrowed the car of his best friend Kuts, to drive five of us home. We'd all been drinking beer, but to my fifteen-year-old brain, no one seemed too drunk to drive. It started drizzling, and at the intersection of Branch and Maple, as we turned left, an oncoming car skidded into us. For a few seconds, we sat stunned from the crash, then Annie threw open the passenger door, and everyone scattered into a row of dark trees. Other kids knew not to wait around for the cops to find bags of pot on them.

By the time I got out, everyone was gone. I took cover behind a dripping tree and watched Bert storm around, his arms flying like he was about to punch the other driver. A police car's lights painted cherry red streaks on the wet asphalt. Bert started waving his hands and yelling at the cop, too, which I thought was unwise, but then the cop drove away. I popped out of the trees.

"What'd the cop say?" I asked.

"Oh, man, that was Melvin. I play hoops with that kid. He told me I stink of booze and to get out of here."

Bert said he had to go tell Kuts about his car and asked if I wanted to come. I said no thanks, though I didn't have another plan. He drove away, holding the dented door closed. I looked around. The accident felt minor compared to being abandoned by the gang on a rainy road a couple miles from home. A different police cruiser drove by.

"Hey!" I yelled. "Police! Help!!"

The police car's brake lights flashed, then backed up. I rode in the front seat, not the back like a criminal. When we pulled into my driveway, the house was dark. I thought about waking Mom to tell her about my night but then thought better of it. This came too close to violating Life Rule #3, not to get killed in a drunk driving accident. Also, it felt like a long time since Mom and I had shared important moments of our lives with each other and during that time, I'd started to write some new life rules:

Alisyn Adage #1—Never Get in a Car with a Drunk Driver…Unless You Need a Ride Home.

Two weeks later, Matt was behind the wheel of his dad's car. Six of us loaded in, heading home after a party. One of our friends, Waldo, was driving a separate car. Halfway down Pinckney Avenue, Waldo crossed the double yellow line and roared past us on the left, flipping us off. He swung back into our lane, almost taking Matt's front end off.

"Oh, no fucking way!" Matt laughed, then swung out across the double-yellow and gunned it, trying to pass Waldo.

"Slow down!" I yelled. Everyone laughed.

Just as we caught up alongside his car, Waldo sped up, preventing Matt from getting back on the right side of the road. I saw the T intersection ahead. I felt Matt accelerating. I saw the stop sign. I screamed as we flew through it. Matt cranked the wheel to the left, his tires squealing and skidding across Broad Street. The car jumped the curb and mowed down a sapling in front of Pathmark.

Everyone cheered. I was still screaming.

"Let me out!" I screamed. No one moved. I began clawing at their laps, the door handle, the window.

Matt looked over the seat at me. "Calm down. I'll drive you home."

"Let me *out!*" I clawed and clambered across Mark, then spilled onto the sidewalk, gasping for air. I watched their taillights drive off and hated them for leaving me stranded again, hated them for not caring about my life, and for not being afraid for their own. And I hated myself for needing them so much.

But nothing screamed "vehicular danger" louder than Kuts's notorious green Dodge Dart. Shrapnel was playing in New York City, and I wanted to go even though Mark, Matt, and Winkie couldn't. I resorted to hitching a ride with the aforementioned Kuts and Bert, the two most intimidating, leather-jacket wearing, hard-drug-doing characters in the Shrapnel orbit. Having to make conversation with Kuts and Bert for an hour-long car ride, much less an entire night, was inconceivable, so I roped a girl I barely knew from Rumson named Heather into going with me. Heather had no idea what to expect, and I didn't fill in the blanks. I didn't warn her that Kuts drove a dented 1970 Dodge Dart—still broken from our recent accident and his other brushes with death—or that he'd have Motörhead cranked at a deafening volume. I also didn't explain that Shrapnel was playing with the Dead Boys and that the last time I'd seen the Dead Boys, I'd narrowly escaped skinheads with baseball bats.

"Who needs a beer?" Bert asked, peeling a can of Miller from its six-pack noose and holding it up.

From the second Kuts sped onto the onramp of the Parkway and floored it into the fast lane, I had a feeling this trip was a mistake. Until that moment, I was not fully aware that Kuts was the shittiest driver in the world. I was also not aware that he would drink beer after beer and repeatedly struggle to find a light for his cigarettes, at times taking his eyes completely off the road to reach for his lighter that had fallen in the footwell. During the ride, my throat swelled up so thick with anxiety, all I could do was watch the red needle vibrate at eighty mph and Kuts's car careen close to the cement divider. Red brake lights flashed in front of us, and my own foot reflexively slammed the floor mat. When an eighteen-wheeler appeared out Heather's window, a solid wall of metal boxing us in, Kuts sped up, racing the truck. Trying to subliminally suggest we slow down, I asked what time the show started, knowing it was hours away. Kuts said 7:14, which didn't make sense but made Bert laugh. I didn't know it meant a Quaalude.

I'd never heard of Zappas, the place Shrapnel was playing, but I practically pushed Heather through its front door, grateful to be out of the Dodge

Dart death trap. And when Shrapnel marched on stage and played "Girl in Trouble," the hell ride seemed worth it.

If she's a girl in trouble, I'm in trouble,
Cause I'm in love with her...

Zappas wasn't as crowded as CBs or the Fast Lane, so I got right up front. About two songs in, Dave Vogt stepped to the front of the stage and saw me. His eyebrows went up with a quick, surprised nod. And as soon as they finished the first set, Vogt came out from backstage and headed straight for me.

"Hey!" He leaned over and kissed me on the cheek. Our new greeting, apparently.

"Hey!" I said, my insides lighting up from being singled out in the crowd.

"What are you doing here? Who are you here with?"

"My friend Heather," I said. "And Kuts and Bert."

The friendliness left Vogt's face. "Where are they?"

"Well, I last saw Kuts at the bar. Actually, ON the bar. Sleeping."

"Sleeping, huh?"

"Yeah. He must be very *tired*." I smiled, thinking Vogt would laugh, but he didn't. He scowled like he was disgusted with Kuts. Or me. Then he marched his combat boots over to the bar without saying goodbye.

After Shrapnel's last set, I wanted to go home, but I knew Kuts and Bert wouldn't hear of bailing before the Dead Boys. So, I stood bored watching Stiv Bators hop around on an imaginary pogo stick. He wore a jean jacket with the arms ripped off and a thin black necktie but no shirt. He had a piece of bologna safety pinned to his chest. Three songs in, he hung himself with the microphone cord. *Check, please.*

The minute the Dead Boys were done, I dragged Heather up to Kuts's motionless body. He was face down on the side of the stage. I poked him. Nothing. It was possible he was dead. I was relieved. Now Bert could drive us home.

"Everybody out! Show's over," the bouncer yelled.

Out on the sidewalk, I looked around but didn't see Bert. I went back to the side door and banged, but no one came, and there was no handle to open it. I banged again. We walked around the front. The sidewalk was empty.

"Do you remember where we parked?" I asked Heather.

She said not really and that we shouldn't be walking around there anyway.

If we couldn't find Bert, I said, we could always take a taxi to Penn Station. I didn't tell her that I didn't have a single cent on me. Nor did I tell her we were about to miss the 1:43 a.m. The last train home.

"You know we're not in Manhattan, right?" she said. "We're in Queens."

I did not know that. I had a nervous habit of picking my cuticles, and now one was bleeding. Heather started crying. She said her parents were going to kill her.

"They would never let me come here! I have a tennis tournament at eight!"

Directly across from us was a rundown automotive shop, its lot littered with garbage and a wrecked car on cinder blocks. On the opposite corner was a grimy storefront with thick metal prison bars over its windows and a big cracked "Check Cashing" sign with long shards of glass missing, like stalagmites. The street looked deserted, but it didn't feel that way. A streetlight kept pulsing its electrical current. A Shrapnel mantra looped in my head.

If she's a girl in trouble, I'm in trouble

Cause I'm in love with her…

How did the rest of the song go? How does the girl get out of trouble? That's when I saw it—an old maroon van creeping down the block. It's headlights shone into our eyes, lighting us up on that corner. The feeling of prickly pins spread across my neck. We stood frozen as the van rolled to a stop right in front of us

"What are you DOING?" Vogt asked out the passenger window.

"Dave! Oh, thank God! We can't find Bert! And Kuts passed out!"

Vogt turned his head to Wyndorf at the wheel and said, "KUTSY!" Lots of laughter. "You can't be standing out here!" Vogt said. "Get in the van."

Climbing into the back of that van, I felt I'd hit the lottery. This was Shrapnel off-stage. Shrapnel sans helmets. The Shrapnel I longed to know. Heather and I sat on canvas sandbags on the metal floor. I tried to absorb every word the guys were saying so I could record it later in my diary, but the motor and Jo Marshall on the stereo made it hard to hear anything but snippets; their manager, a guy named Legs McNeil, apparently quite the schmoozer, was the person who came up with the name "Shrapnel" after Gene Simmons from KISS told the guys they had to have a one-word name. The guys said that Dee Dee Ramone told them some crazy record producer named Phil Spector had held him at gunpoint, but he'd escaped. The best tidbit was that the cartoonist who drew the Spiderman comic strip loved Shrapnel and was turning the guys into superheroes in a comic book. I lay back, my eyelids dropping. Shrapnel had rescued me. Shrapnel were *my* superheroes.

Hunger

Earlier that summer, Mom received her doctorate in Creative Arts Education, the culmination of four years of coursework and night classes, writing and presenting a dissertation. I assumed the only thing that would change was that now her students would call her Dr. Camerota. I didn't know that at forty-one years old, after almost two decades of teaching, she was bored and hungry for a new challenge. Nor was I aware that Monmouth Regional was scaling back her drama classes amid budget cuts.

Mom's feelings were undetectable. It was summer, and I was at the beach all day and at parties most nights. Mom stayed busy with her psychodrama workshops, never betraying her growing discontent. She also never gave an inkling of how crushed she was by her breakup with Robert. I had no idea she was starting to consider Shrewsbury, the center of my universe, her prison cell. I also didn't know just how tight money had gotten. While working on her dissertation, Mom taught three classes, not five, which meant she was making only three-fifths of her meager salary. Mom was up-front with me— on this point at least—we had slipped into the lowest rung of the middle class.

Mom's current boyfriend, Gary, had a good job. He had that new car. Our house was starting to need repairs. One morning, our glass shower door came off its hinges into my hands, and Mom and I didn't know how to fix it, leaving water to soak the bathroom floor. Wouldn't it be nice to have a man's help and not have to worry, Mom sometimes mused. But we both knew Gary was dull. I didn't know how she could settle for him, though I was starting to suspect she could never be without a man. And I was starting to suspect neither could I.

Mom traveled to Seattle for a week-long psychodrama conference. She planned to stay with her old friend Walter, a former teacher from Monmouth Regional, who had moved to Washington State years earlier with his girlfriend. I stayed at home, figuring I could spend my nights bouncing between sleepovers at Sydney's and Viv's. But it didn't work out that way. Sydney had to go see her grandmother, and Viv was grounded. Some nights, I couldn't reach Mark or Matt or Winkie, and I knew it was uncool to call too many times. So, I sat on my bed alone, my stomach sick with the knowledge that no one ever needed me as much as I needed them.

One night I stood in front of the open fridge door staring in at its scant contents—a Tupperware of half-eaten tabbouleh, a jar of Dijon mustard, and some old relish. I turned to our cupboard. Two cans of forgotten mandarin orange slices, three boxes of linguini, a couple cans of chopped clams, and a bottle of olive oil. I was too hungry to cook any of that.

I turned on our old black-and-white TV, adjusting the metal hanger antennae until the screen stopped flipping round like a slot machine. Oh, good, my old friends Gopher, Issac, and Julie could join me for dinner along the Promenade Deck. I sat down across from my *Love Boat* companions and funneled forkful after forkful of the tabbouleh into my mouth until the bowl was empty. But I was still hungry. I grabbed a sticky half-gallon of chocolate ice cream from the freezer, swallowing spoonful after spoonful until the carton was done. I liked keeping my mouth full, so I would feel no emptiness.

I was a bottomless pit—the child famous for asking for thirds and fourths during sleepovers at friends' houses. I was the insatiable teenager who ordered the nachos and the bacon cheeseburger and the ice cream sundae and ate it all and whatever else was on the table, if someone else was picking up the tab. Yet, I could never get full. Even now, I save food well past its expiration date, because you never know if there will be another meal. But in retracing these stories, I'm forced to examine whether my hunger was real. I *felt* like I was starving. But was it true that I didn't have enough food? Or was the insatiability about something else entirely?

I went to the cabinet below the oven to find my glass jar of dollar bills from babysitting, then waited to see the headlights of the delivery guy in our dark driveway. He arrived in time for me to finish an entire pepperoni pizza with Mr. Rourke and Tattoo keeping me company. Some nights I didn't turn off the TV until well after the test pattern came on. Some nights I watched the color bars pixelate into a single bright beam before fading to black.

I knew of a party that night in Red Bank, but the host, Rex Gareth, always creeped me out. He had jet black hair, a black mustache, and wore a spiked metal dog collar around his neck like a medieval ogre. He was older than us, long out of high school, and apparently aimless. Sometimes I saw him skulking down Broad Street talking to himself. Even cool kid Frankie was wary. "Rex Gareth is a sick fuck," he told me. "He's hardcore."

"Rex Gareth is a volatile douchebag with a short fuse," Viv said. "I wouldn't go to his party even if I wasn't grounded. I'd rather be grounded."

I heard a rustle right outside the dark screen window—the same screen Dad had knocked out to steal Mom's jewelry. Was the delivery guy still there? Had I locked the door after he left? I went to the phone and dialed a number I knew by heart, then grabbed five singles and waited for the taxi to show up.

Throughout high school, there were plenty of fun parties with nothing but keg beer and laughter in humid backyards. But there were a few nights when things happened that forced my brain to process nonsensical events and ominous images, like the night that two of the handsome jocks in our crowd showed up at a mellow backyard party but struggled to hoist themselves onto the waist-high deck where the rest of us were standing, repeatedly trying as their arms collapsed under them. Or the night that Frankie's lips were stretched over his teeth like an old man whose dentures had fallen out as he insisted, "I osstt all my teett. Do you shee my teett?"

On nights like that I'd hear low rumblings. Something about a trip, to somewhere like Tompkins Square Park, a notorious drug den. Or a ride on something called *the Dust Bowl Express*, which I came to understand meant Angel Dust, the powerful anaesthetic known for physical disassociation and super-natural violence. The murmurs felt dark and mysterious and made my neck itch.

Rex Gareth's apartment was up a flight of stairs caked with dirt. From outside, I could hear the Dictators screaming "Search and Destroy." Inside was a smoke pit. I was relieved when the very first person I saw was Dave Vogt, over by the keg in the kitchen, but he didn't return my smile.

"What are you doing here?" he asked.

"Looking for a beer," I said, hoping that sounded cooler than saying I was lonely and scared at home. I found the only unused plastic cup on the counter and pressed the black lever on the keg to fill it. Vogt went back to talking with Bert, and I turned my attention to Wyndorf, who was talking to Shrapnel's guitar player Daniel, and wearing a black leather vest over, of all things, a tight yellow Shaun Cassidy T-shirt.

"Hey, there," he said, when I got so awkwardly close he was forced to acknowledge me. I was pretty sure he had no idea who I was, despite having recently saved my life.

"I like your T-shirt!" I yelled over the music.

"Oh," he laughed, glancing down. "I think it's my sister's. I found it on the floor. But then I decided to wear it. Irony. Ya know?"

No. I didn't. I was too busy staring at his lips.

He turned back to Daniel, and when my silent presence grew too weird, I inched away back to the kitchen.

That's when a roar came from the living room, a monster breaking free of his chains and turning on the crowd. A vortex of black. Rex Gareth was spinning. Something shiny was in his hand.

"He's got a knife!"

"*Knife! Knife!*" The word ricocheted around the room. A tornado of bodies swirled with fists flying. I screamed and looked for Vogt, but he was gone. A windowpane shattered as something or someone went through it. I ran for an exit door, but it was the bathroom. I bolted inside, leaning all my weight against it, trying to latch its small silver eye hook, my hands trembling. My legs turned to jelly and I fell to the floor, then crawled into the tight space between the toilet and the tub, curling my body into a ball.

A fist pounded on the bathroom door.

Dear God. Dear God. Dear God.

I knew I should let other people hide in the bathroom, but I was too scared to open the door. And then, in a violent bang, the door flew open. There was Dave Vogt. In the threshold, his face contorted.

"Come on! *You gotta get out of here!*" He sprang across the tile and lifted me off the floor, standing me up and tucking my arm under his, interlocking his fingers with mine. I pressed my face against his back as he pulled me through the maelstrom, using his left forearm as a shield. When we got to the door at the top of the steps, he yanked it open, and we ran down the stairs and straight to his father's station wagon.

"*Get in!*" He jumped in the driver's seat and peeled out of the driveway. I sat with my hands over my mouth, trying not to hyperventilate. We rode down Maple Avenue in silence. I was still shaking.

Vogt turned to face me. "You shouldn't be around that stuff."

"I didn't know it was going to be like that."

He leaned his arms over the steering wheel to look both ways at the stop sign, and I studied the side of his face, his tousled brown hair falling against his cheekbones. In that moment, I loved him—for fighting his way through the danger for me, for kicking in the door, for rescuing me again. For being my superhero. His pretty girlfriend flitted across my mind, so self-possessed in her RBR baton twirler uniform. I'd heard she was headed to UVM in September. I guess guys in Shrapnel came gift-wrapped to confident girls like that.

"You can't keep coming to places like that. OK?" Vogt pressed.

I stared out the window at the dark shadows of houses with their shades pulled down and nodded but knew I was lying. I had just become part of the gang. I wasn't about to give it up. The gang was all I had.

The Unreachable Star

I remembered Walter from my childhood, when he used to sit in our backyard, laughing with Mom and drinking iced coffee. I always suspected he had a crush on her but thought she wasn't interested. In my memory, he was the color gray: common, slightly drab. Mom mentioned, in passing, that Walter was coming out to visit from Seattle. *Sure, whatever,* I thought. I knew he had three daughters who lived in New Jersey. What about his girlfriend? I asked. They broke up, she said.

When I got back from my annual trip to Wildwood, Mom mentioned that Walter had said Seattle is a nice place to live, or, as she began referring to it, "The Pacific Northwest."

"Right on Puget Sound," she said. "It's very beautiful."

She might as well have said Bali is lovely, all those palm trees and turquoise water. It meant nothing to me in real life. It bore no relation to our white poured-concrete house surrounded by pink azaleas. It had no relevance to my days on the sand in Sea Bright with Sydney or my nights at Shrapnel shows. Her musings, like Walter himself, were easy to ignore. But when he left our house that month, Walter left behind a small newspaper clipping for me from *The Seattle Times*:

Tonight and tomorrow night, The Heats rock Astor Park…The Lenny Kaye Connection (featuring the guitarist with The Patti Smith Group) comes to WREX…Juice Newton plays Parker's at 9:00 p.m.

I frowned. "Who cares?"

"See?" Mom said, "There are interesting bands in Seattle, too. Walter thinks you might like The Heats."

I didn't give a shit what Walter thought. My sensible mother had stopped making sense.

◀◀ ❚❚ ▶▶

Another hot, humid August night in Shrewsbury meant another keg party. Every backyard party was dark, making it hard to see faces, but I knew everyone's outlines so well that I spotted Vogt's wiry, tight build right away. When I got up close, his mouth jumped to a sideways smile. The party was mellow, without the attendant danger that usually exploded near us. He was happy to see me this time, not pissed I was there. We hung out near the keg, talking and laughing, mostly about what a shitty driver Kuts was and how one time Kuts actually fell out of a friend's car while it was moving and *got run over*. Everyone thought he was dead until he popped up and said, "I fucking ripped my Ramones shirt!"

Vogt asked if I wanted to go to another party, and I said yes. He took my hand, and we wound our way through dark woods, the moon making the sky a milky white. It was back in the thick of the trees that we started kissing. In the eighties, people used to say that kissing a smoker was like licking an ashtray, but that wasn't true. Vogt's mouth tasted smoky sweet, and tangy with beer. With my lips against his warm neck, I realized that all boys' summer skin had the same sweet scent of salt and soap and fresh-cut grass.

Vogt pulled off his shirt and laid it on the ground. I wrapped my arms around his muscular back and looked up at the stars. I knew right then that whatever happened next, at the next party, or next week, or next month, or with Mom and Walter, or years from now, none of it mattered. The only thing that mattered was this moment. Because what I wanted, what we *all* wanted, was about to be mine. I was about to stamp Shrapnel permanently into my diary. This is what ambition looked like for me at fifteen because that night I would have been hard pressed to name a more impressive accomplishment. I imagine this is how Academy-Award winners feel, knowing that regardless of where life takes them, no one can ever take away that coveted prize.

Back at home, I slid under the cool sheet and tucked it tight against my bare skin, feeling snug against the vastness of the universe.

And I want you all to myself,
Oh, oh, sleepover...

◄◄ ❚❚ ►►

The next afternoon, our house phone rang. Once, twice, three times. After the third ring, I figured Mom was busy downstairs, so I darted into her bedroom and picked up the receiver to hear a conversation starting.

"...Mrs. Camerota. It's Dave Vogt."

"Oh, hello, Dave. Do you want to call her on the phone in her room?"

I cupped my hand over the receiver and screamed, "I've got it!"

"Alright. Nice talking to you, Dave." Mom hung up. By then, I was shaking.

"Hey," he said. I'd never heard his voice on the phone, but it was familiar in an unexpected way, like I'd known it my whole life, which I guess I had.

"Sorry, I didn't know this was your mom's number. I found it in the phone book."

"Oh, that's okay."

"So, hi."

"Hi."

He laughed. "I had fun last night."

"Me, too."

"I was wondering if I could see you again."

I gulped. "Yeah, definitely."

"I was hoping maybe you wanted to come to the show tonight?"

I said yes then put the phone back gently in its cradle but stayed seated, my heart thrumming at double speed and my hands in prayer position covering my mouth. Sex was one thing. *But a phone call? In the middle of the day?* I had a feeling that might mean Vogt actually liked me and that I might be in deeper than I'd bargained for. I took a huge breath and stood up to walk out of Mom's room. And when I did, there she was, leaning against the bannister, arms across her chest.

"That was Dave Vogt?"

"Mm, hmm." I tried to sound casual, as if he called all the time and she'd somehow missed it. Mom didn't step aside, forcing me to squeeze past her to get to my bedroom. As I did, I caught a shot of her face and saw an expression I recognized, the same one she wore whenever I got an A on a test or a part in a play. She could never have known about my night. She likely thought this was the beginning of a courtship, rather than the consummation of the life-and-death link that Vogt and I already shared, but I could see she was happy for me. Happy that I'd gotten what I wanted.

◄◄ ❚❚ ►►

I liked the way Vogt's eyes lit up when he saw me at shows, how his mouth jumped into a crooked smile. I liked how his attention shone on me like a spotlight for everyone to see. Then he came closer, and I stiffened under a bridle of guilt. He liked me *too* much. I didn't have to win him over. His affection was too available. And though I could not have articulated it at the time, available affection made me squirmy.

Dave Vogt, it turned out, was sort of shy. He wasn't the caricature of angry soldier charisma I was drawn to at shows. Also, I still preferred what I considered the clean stability of Waspy homes over the gritty graffiti of CBGB. The truth was, I didn't want to be a punk rock girlfriend after all. I'd already gotten the brass ring: a perma-piece of Shrapnel carved into my belt of belonging. After that, I didn't need more. I liked Vogt, and I really liked that he liked me, but I liked him up on stage, from afar. It turned out that the part I liked best was trying to reach the unreachable star.

Nothing Left to Lose

At the start of sophomore year, after my reckless summer, I was relieved to get back to RBR's strict rules and rigid structure. But all was not well there either. Over the summer, Viv's downward spiral had worsened. One night, she was drunk behind the wheel of a friend's car and drove off Tower Hill, the highest point in town, flipping the vehicle. She was rushed to the hospital and survived, though a lightning bolt scar sliced through her right eyebrow as a forever reminder to the rest of us that she was literally going off a cliff.

I tried to talk to Viv about her drinking. One night at a party, I saw her stagger through a hole in the bramble. She was disheveled, her hair mussed. One of the handsome, cocky jocks was right behind her, wearing cut-off shorts and a smug smile. Everything about it set me off. I was sick of seeing her wasted and not giving a shit about anyone or herself. She sat down on the curb next to me and lit a butt.

"What are you doing?" I said.

Her eyes struggled to find purchase on my face. Her black liner was smeared.

I leaned in. "You need to *stop this.*"

"What?" She blew out a channel of gray smoke.

"Don't you see?" I said. "*Everyone* loves you. You can do whatever you want with your life."

"What are you talking about?"

I knew I was violating cool code but I couldn't stop myself. "You *drink* too much."

Viv took a long drag. "You've got it all figured out, huh, Skin?" Then she pushed herself up and walked away.

I couldn't have known that night that Viv was rabidly self-medicating, trying to numb her complex PTSD after an overdose and sexual assault at thirteen years old. And though all of us lined up, hoping for a chance to glimpse the inner mainspring that made Viv tick, she never let anyone see inside. There was no way of knowing her, really. But I only learned this much later.

◀◀ ❙❙ ▶▶

One afternoon, Vivienne's mother was looking for her, calling down the hallway. "Viv-vee? Viv-vee?" She went into Viv's room, opened the closet door, and screamed in horror.

"And that's when I took my dad's tie off my neck and came out," Viv told us in the lunchroom.

Sydney and I exchanged some frightened side-eye, waiting for the punchline.

"What did your mom say?" Sydney asked.

"Nothing," said Viv. "She was just crying. I told her, 'Next time it will be you.'"

◀◀ ❙❙ ▶▶

At home, Mom's talk of moving was picking up steam. Wouldn't moving to the Pacific Northwest be an interesting life experience, she wondered aloud. But she didn't have a job there and didn't appear to be looking for one. She also didn't appear to be crazy about Walter, who, it turned out, lived in Olympia, not Seattle. None of it made sense, and I prayed that logic would prevail and prevent Mom from driving us off a cliff, too.

Then she called a realtor to appraise our house. I watched them walk the grounds, Mom pointing out the particulars.

"Think of it as an adventure," Mom told me. "Think of all the stories you'll have for Sydney and Viv. Think of the new people you'll meet."

"I don't want to meet any new people," I said. "I want my friends."

She continued spouting nonsense.

"Change is good. You can find your people anywhere."

By fifteen, I already knew that wasn't true. I knew I would never find another Sydney and Viv. I knew there was no other Red Bank Regional. And I knew there was no substitute for Shrapnel.

I was grasping for ballast. At the end of August, I'd reconnected with my first love, Ethan, who was now seventeen and eager to have an honest-to-goodness relationship with me. But I was more interested in protecting myself. So, I took up with Ethan as well as one of his closest friends, a Jim Morrison-lookalike, who I'd sneak up to see in New York City. Duplicity was becoming the device I used to avoid hurting someone's feelings—primarily my own. Even then, I already expected people to leave, so I didn't consider duplicity a con, I considered it an insurance policy. I liked having a boyfriend and another waiting in the wings, for when either one abandoned me. Later, I was stunned to learn how badly I'd hurt people. I didn't think I mattered enough to cause any pain.

In October, Mom went through with it. She took a leave of absence from her job and rented out our house. She announced we would be moving the following month. I went into full meltdown mode, beseeching her to snap out of it or for anyone to stop this madness. After her edict, my mother assumed the role of remote queen, retreating behind a solid wall of silence and pulling up a drawbridge against my pain and panic. Gram, Poppy, and Mom's closest friends appeared shell-shocked into submission, which only made me more hysterical. Dad met the news with taciturn acceptance. He lived sixty miles away and had long since given up having any say in our lives.

"If that's what Mom wants," he told me, "you need to try it."

I couldn't breathe. I desperately needed someone, anyone, to take my side.

◄◄ ❙❙ ►►

That month, Viv went missing. First from her homeroom some mornings, then the lunch table, then one day she disappeared completely. Rumors flew.

I grabbed her brother's arm in the hallway, "Where is she?"

"She's gone, Alisyn. That's all I can tell you."

I ran to the payphone on the wall, digging in my purse for a dime.

"Please, Mrs. O'Leary. My mom says we're moving. Can I please know where Viv is or get her number to say goodbye? *Please!*"

Her mother was sympathetic but resolute. "I'm sorry, dear. I can't. We just don't know if Vivienne is ever coming back."

◀◀ ❚❚ ▶▶

Mom's closest friend, Muriel, threw a small dinner party before we left. Just a few people, including a woman we'd never met, a part-time palm reader named Verna. Mom didn't believe in mystical messages, but I did, and I was desperate for answers from anywhere, even Mom's palm. At the end of dinner, Mom capitulated and unfolded her hand. Verna took one look and blanched. She stammered something about how we should probably wrap up; it was getting late; this was all just for fun anyway.

"*What is it?*" I screamed. "What do you see?"

Verna, dedicated to her craft, dove back in. She petted Mom's palm gently, as if trying to wipe away whatever evil harbinger it held. She took a deep breath.

"I see a break. A disruption in the lifeline. Not a death. But a loss of something."

"Like *what?*" I cried.

"Something big. Something permanent."

I became inconsolable.

"Can't you all *see?*! We should *not* be moving! It's going to be bad. We're going to *lose* something."

The adults fell silent. The more hysterical I got, the more Mom's face flattened. Muriel cleared the table of plates. Mom searched for her purse, said we should go. But her palm was screaming loudly that we should stay, and no one was listening.

◀◀ ❚❚ ▶▶

I refused to pack. I lay on the floor, wailing in agony. In pinched silence, Gram and Poppy moved around my fetal self, folding my belongings gingerly into boxes and suitcases. Sydney threw me a going-away party filled with the kids I'd once admired from afar at RBR, now my closest friends, whose stories intertwined with mine. They hung a big poster on the wall filled with goodbye messages. They swore they'd write. But I knew their lives would go on without me. I knew there would be more parties and more inside jokes. More break-ups and hook-ups. More Shrapnel shows. Someday we'd find out where Viv was.

And I would miss all of it.

The next day, I wandered the halls of RBR hugging people in despair. I slobbered on Mrs. Maxwell, then blubbered to Mr. Horton about how much I loved him, hugging him and leaving tear stains on his smoky lab coat, making his bloodshot eyes even redder. And my classmates. How stupid of me to have taken them for granted. On the day I was leaving, I loved them all and felt their superiority. They got to stay.

When the bell rang and the time was truly up, I walked out of school in a surreal stupor. *Where was I even going?* I turned and reached my arm out, pointing up at the school's brick face and in my most melodramatic Scarlett O'Hara way, said:

"I will be back, Red Bank Regional. Mark my words. I will be back."

◄◄ II ►►

On Thanksgiving morning, our drawers were empty, the car trunk stuffed with our dishes, my photo albums, and Ramones records. Mom decided our furniture would stay behind for the renters, leaving the living room eerily still, like the scene of a sudden abduction.

Pulling out of the driveway, I had to avert my burning eyes from our house and the windows begging us not to leave. Mom's face was dry, her jaw set—a robot lacking human receptors. A million years earlier, I'd longed for just the two of us to go somewhere together—and now here we were, just the two of us, but I was all alone. Desperate for comfort, I reached for my trusty companion, the radio, searching for lyrics from someone who could feel loss.

But that morning, Janis Joplin spoke only to Mom:

"Freedom's just another word for nothing left to lose."

"That's right," Mom said, nodding at the radio, gripping the wheel. "That's why we're moving."

One mile away, at the outer edge of Shrewsbury, Mom pulled the Chevette up to the bank's drive-through window, where, for as long as I could remember, she had dutifully deposited ten dollars a week into my future college fund. Without a word, she withdrew every cent.

PART FOUR

nos·tal·gia /näˈstaljə,nəˈstaljə/ *noun. 1. a wistful desire to return in thought or in fact to a former time in one's life, to one's home or homeland, or to one's family and friends;*
2. a sentimental yearning for the happiness of a former place or time.

Take It On the Run

Some people are forward-facing; some are present-centered. I'm backward-looking. I recall past events as though they were yesterday. I remember conversations verbatim. I know what song was playing on the stereo and who told which joke. Sometimes I can even still feel the tingling sensation of that other time. Nostalgia has been with me almost as long as my imaginary cameraman.

How fitting that the word nostalgia comes from the Greek *nostos* (homecoming) and *algos* (pain or ache). It's hard to imagine a more acute ache to return home than I experienced after leaving. I once read a psychiatric description of nostalgia as "a vehicle for traveling beyond the suffocating confines of time and space." Those suffocating confines were all I had now.

I've never found a word for my condition. Extra-sensory memory, maybe. Perhaps the part of my brain that controls memory, the temporal lobe, isn't the standard size of a prune. Maybe mine is a pomegranate. Maybe my hippocampus, where episodic memories are formed and indexed, is enlarged and heavy on the hippo. It's dangerous, this thing. Needing to be in another place and time.

◄◄ ❚❚ ►►

I landed in Olympia as if I'd fallen from a distant galaxy, stupefied by this new atmosphere, dense with fog and the alien scents of damp cedar chips and burning pine from wood stoves.

Walter had rented us a nondescript two-bedroom house, furnished in beige, in a generic development. For the first few days, Mom and Walter stayed behind their closed bedroom door. When the silence inside became suffocating, I left to wander the silent streets shrouded in gray mist. There were no people, just street after street of profound quiet and evergreens draped in fog. And yet, out there alone, I still believed the magic of companionship might find me, though I knew it would take more than my imaginary cameraman. This was a job for a studio audience of angels who I hoped were watching over me. I still believed that I was a survivor and that maybe my soulmate was waiting around the corner to rescue me from the house of beige. I still believed that, against all odds, something miraculous might happen on Monday at my new high school.

On Monday, Mom dropped me off at the front of the school, and I walked into a damp mass of mullets, flannel shirts, and bell bottoms. It was clear that Mom and Walter had lied—there were no cool kids here who listened to punk rock. REO Speedwagon seeped from their Walkman headphones.

Two particularly perky class reps were assigned to usher me around, pointing out wood plaques commemorating state championships. They invited me to their after-school club called Young Life, which in the middle of the first meeting, I discovered was a Christianity club involving virginity vows. On the drive home, I proselytized to my student shepherds, telling them of the big world out there filled with sex, drugs, and punk rock.

"You don't have to live this way," I told them.

Three weeks after we arrived, Walter broke up with Mom and went back to his ex-girlfriend. Only the swiftness surprised me. He would need Mom and me to move out right away. Mom sat on the edge of my bed.

"What are we going to do now?" I asked.

"I don't know," she said. Mom didn't cry. She immediately left for a prepaid weekend psychodrama conference in Port Townsend. I stayed behind with Walter and over taco salads at a Mexican restaurant, listened to him tell me he "wished it had worked out differently." It just wasn't meant to be, he said, as if he could wrap up his shit sandwich in a dirty little bow. He hoped I'd accept his apology. I stared through him, seething, then pointed my fork at his face.

"You made me leave everything I had and everyone I love—all for *nothing*."

"But now," he said, "you and your mom can go back to New Jersey."

Dad, International Man of Mystery

Mom, high school graduation

Me at two. Mom's caption: "Our family"

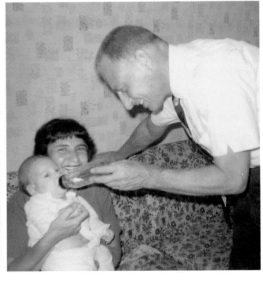

Gram and Poppy loved feeding me

Mom and me, deeply connected

*My adolescence:
a ShopRite teddy bear,
KISS poster, and Ethan*

*In Wildwood with my puka shell
necklace, pink tube top, and favorite
lifeguard*

*Illustrations of RBR
by Sydney*

My first day at RBR

SHRAPNEL

COMBAT LOVE

COMBAT LOVE
HEY

LEAD VOCALS: WYNDORF, LEAD GUITAR; DANIEL
RABINOWITZ. RHYTHM; DAVE VOGT. BASS; PHILIP
CAIVANO. DRUMS; D. CLAYTON.
PRODUCED BY JONATHAN PALEY AND LEGS McNEIL.
MIXED BY ED STASIUM SPECIAL THANKS TO ARTURO
VEGA JOEY RAMONE THE RAMONES JONATHAN
PALEY TOM HEARN JEFF SHEILDS.
Copyright 1978 by SALUTE RECORDS, Inc.
15 West 1700 St. (Apt. 104) N.Y.C. 10022

SHRAPNEL
SAT.
SEPT 11
FAST
LANE

FRANK MASSO IN CONJUNCTION WITH Legs McNeil
presents
WORLD WAR III - (bring your battle gear)
N.Y.C. SHRAPNEL
with
BACK BY ARMY
DEMAND!

they
SCARED ME
...AWAY
WARHOL

the true
COMMANDOS
of rock-n-
roll

SHRAPNEL

Go Cruisin

SHRAPNEL
SHRAPNEL

MARCH 4, FAST LANE

4th Ave One Block From Ocean, Asbury Pk.

Tom Hearn

Me at fifteen, still trying to meld with Mom

*RBR posse
(Sydney and I as twins)*

A sunny day in Bellingham, Chad, Hera, Jake, and I

I routinely put less than five dollars in my gas tank

Me and Tommy at a Fourth of July back-yard party

Not sure how my co-workers could tell I wasn't happy

Some self-reflection during my Seoul searching

My popcorn tin, stuffed with memories

"My mother left her job," I reminded him. "I transferred schools. We rented our house. We have nowhere to live."

At fifteen years old, I still believed that the celestial courtroom in the sky would mete out justice, squarely and rapidly. So, I was scornful, but calm. I told Walter he had ruined my life, and he would pay for it. It was not up to me anymore, I explained. It was in the hands of the universe now.

He sort of laughed. "Bad karma, huh?"

I told him I felt sorry for him. I said I hoped the universe's revenge didn't involve his three daughters, but I suspected it would. Only then did his face go slack.

I knew Mom must be feeling blindsided and embarrassed. She'd set out from Shrewsbury for a new life and instantly struck out. I knew that returning would be complicated by renter's rights and that it was unlikely we'd find another house in Shrewsbury. Still, I believed Mom's rational self would resurface to figure out the details, and proper order would be restored.

Two days before Christmas, I flew alone back to Philadelphia on a ticket I'd begged Gram and Poppy to buy me before we left. I spent the next week on planes, trains, taxis, and buses, going from friend to friend, making sure no one had forgotten me in the month I was gone: Christmas Day in Philly, Christmas night in South Jersey with Dad, the next day on a train to Sydney's house in Shrewsbury, the following night a party in Red Bank, then on a bus to meet Ethan in New York City. Friends greeted me with fierce embraces.

Alisyn Adage #2: Leave People and They Love You More.

I saw it everywhere. I told everyone that we were coming home, and most of the adults were too polite or confused to pry into what had gone wrong. They were just relieved we were returning. On New Year's Day, I was in Sydney's room when Mom called, sounding strangely upbeat. I expected to hear the plan, flight details perhaps. She told me she had met a man. His name was Mac. Walter's best friend. We would be living with Mac now, one hundred and fifty miles north of Olympia in the town of Bellingham.

"It's a college town," she said. "Right on the water. I think you'll like it much better than Olympia." I collapsed on the chair and sobbed on Sydney's desk.

◄◄ ‖ ►►

Mom and Mac met me at Sea-Tac Airport. I got in the back of Mac's van, numb and uninterested in hearing about his life story. Here's what little I learned: He had the rugged good looks of Nick Nolte in *North Dallas Forty*. Like Mom, he was originally from Philadelphia, and, like my cousins, had a thick Philly accent, which felt comforting in some small way. He was the director of a drug rehab center and a former heroin addict. He smiled into the rearview mirror, told me he knew I'd been through a lot, but thought I would like Bellingham. I didn't tell him that I already liked him better than Walter. Or that I was sure he, too, would soon be gone.

Bellingham was another strange land laden with fog. Mac lived in a tiny fishing cabin on the bank of a lake with his Labrador retriever. I was allergic to dogs. There was no bedroom for me. I slept on his scratchy sofa covered in dog hair.

Our first forty-eight hours were spent going between unremarkable cedar-shingled homes, looking for a rental big enough for the three of us. It was dark by the time the realtor showed us one that wasn't ugly. By then, I just wanted the upheaval to end. We started hauling in boxes before the paperwork was even signed. I needed to unpack. I would be starting another new school on Monday.

Mom didn't explain how exactly she'd met Mac, and I didn't want to hear it anyway. There was nothing she could say that would make dragging me here to live with a stranger feel right. I watched her open a cardboard box marked Kitchen Stuff and wipe down utensils, gamely shuffling our belongings from Shrewsbury to Walter's rental to Mac's van to this random house.

"Think of it as an adventure," Mom said.

I thought of it as a descent, watching this woman who had once been my heroine shape-shift into an unrecognizable lover of mountains and streams, fishing boats and big dogs. But in this strange land, a body snatcher called Mom was all I had.

We started to unwrap our porcelain dinner plates from layers of newspaper, trying to find places for our fragile pieces in someone else's kitchen. That's when the realtor blew back through the door. There'd been a mistake. The owners did not accept our terms. They wanted us out. We had to leave *now*. The police were on their way.

Mac didn't bother stabbing out his cigarette before grabbing a stack of plates and tossing them into the cardboard box without any cushion. I could hear cracking as he hustled the boxes to the back of his van. Mom and I scrambled to turn off the lights, then ran to Mac's van and peeled out. A patrol car rounded the corner. Mom looked over the seat at me.

"All part of the adventure," she smiled.

In the darkness and rain, we followed the realtor's taillights to the carport of another house. It was a split-level, the nicest we'd seen, with wall-to-wall oatmeal carpeting and a built-in dry bar. I sat on the floor of the empty family room while Mom and Mac conferred in the corner.

"This is out of our price range," Mom told the realtor.

"We'll take it," I said.

Mom and Mac traded uneasy looks.

"I'm not going to another house," I told everyone.

The realtor—a khaki-clad man in his forties, who looked like a dad, crouched next to me. "I think Alisyn is right. This is the one. A family named the Hennesseys live next door. If I can make a prediction, I think when you meet the Hennesseys, everything will be alright."

Heartbreaker

Bellingham was the darkest place on earth. I stared out the window into the pitch-black night and wondered if I would ever know where I was. The day after we moved in, Mac baked a loaf of brown bread that Mom and I carried in a dishcloth to the Hennessey's front door. We rang and a beautiful woman in form-fitting dark jeans and moon boots opened the door.

"Oh, you beat us to the punch!" she said. "Kimberly and I were just about to bring some lemon squares over."

Down the hall bounded a girl with golden hair and green-gold eyes. A Nordic princess in loose loungewear. They didn't make mother-and-daughter duos like this in New Jersey. The girl beamed at me, as if us arriving was the best thing to happen here in a long time.

Mom and I sat in the Hennessey's living room, lightly chatting about our arrival, sparing them the real story. But I couldn't stop staring at a photograph. It was innocently sitting in a 4x6 gold frame on their coffee table. The person in the photo didn't look real: his hair was too blond, his blue eyes too twinkly. Perhaps someone had stuck a young Robert Redford in a frame.

"Who's that?" I finally asked, pointing to it.

"Oh, that's my brother, Jake."

"Where does he live?" I felt my heart sinking. I knew the answer would be somewhere far away, somewhere out of reach.

"He lives here. Downstairs. You'll meet him."

I forced myself to look away.

◄◄ ❚❚ ►►

Everyone in Bellingham knew Jake. He was a world-class skier, a scratch golfer, a killer windsurfer and mountain biker. His physical prowess was legendary and natural, without lessons or endless practice, just a God-given grace that allowed him to turn 720 helicopters off hair-raising ski jumps and spray rainbow waterfalls on a slalom waterski after a dry start from the dock. Jake had graduated from high school seven months earlier and was at loose ends, building homes with his father while he figured out his future. Most summers, Jake worked on a commercial fishing boat in Alaska, one of the most dangerous jobs on earth, one from which some guys in Bellingham never returned. I would come to learn that Jake himself was considered a prime catch, an elusive white whale that scores of girls had tried to snare without success.

But that first day, when he walked through his front door, I didn't know any of that. I only knew that in my fifteen years, I'd never seen anyone so at ease in his own skin. He pulled off his gloves and motioned to our house.

"We thought we saw movement over there. Welcome." He gave a rakish smile. "You have any boxes that need unloading?"

In our brief interaction, I saw it all so clearly. Jake was too charismatic, too charming, and too beautiful for lonely old me. Maybe once upon a time, on a sunny beach far, far away, I could have bikini-schemed my way into his heart. Maybe if I still had cool friends or somewhere to wear my leopard-print shirt, I could have wisecracked a way for him to notice me. But I had no identity anymore. And for the first time in my life, I knew someone was so far out of my league that it wasn't worth trying. I already knew that yearning for Jake would only end in heartache. For my own survival, I decided, I would ignore him entirely.

◄◄ ❚❚ ►►

In the mornings, I walked to the bus stop in blackness. In the afternoons, I walked back in perma-dusk. The drizzle never let up. I told Mom I wanted to go home. I told anyone who would listen that I would soon be returning to New Jersey, though I had no way of doing so. Mom believed it was only a matter of time before I adapted to my new surroundings.

"It's good to experience different cultures. Think of how much more of the world you've seen than Viv and Sydney."

That was the problem. Seeing new things without my friends as witnesses made the vision useless. Even a sight as breathtaking as the Pacific Northwest felt pointless with no way to share it.

"Besides," Mom repeated, "you can find your people anywhere."

Anyone who thinks like-minded people are just lying around waiting to be discovered never moved from Red Bank Regional to Sehome High School. Kids in Bellingham didn't listen to the Ramones or Squeeze or Shrapnel. They listened to REO Speedwagon, Sammy Hagar, and the Scorpions. They didn't wear leather or Levi's. They put pineapple on their pizza. I longed for someone to bond with, but I couldn't spot any potential friends in a sea of damp fleece.

One afternoon, Jake passed by the sliding glass doors of our empty family room. I looked away. I didn't like to see how his blond hair started to wave just past his ears, how his lithe body looked in jeans, or how he seemed to glide instead of walk. He waved at me. I reluctantly lifted my hand to wave back. He walked over; he knocked. I didn't bother getting up from my beanbag chair or turning down the Ramones. He slid open my door.

"You looking at some pics?" He pointed to the photo album open next to me, which I'd been flipping through, morosely staring at my old life. "That from back East? Can I take a look?"

I didn't like being this close to him, didn't like him thinking of me as some charity case he had to be nice to. Jake leaned in.

"Who's that?" He pointed at the photo of Robbie and me in front of the fireplace just after midnight on New Year's Eve. I looked down at my past self.

"Oh, that's my old boyfriend."

"How old is he?"

I said eighteen, and Jake seemed surprised and intrigued about the wild ways back East. *Yeah, that's right! I had a life once. You'd never know it, but I used to be more than your little sister's classmate sucking her thumb in here!*

"Where's that?" Jake asked, pointing to a picture of me in my leopard shirt and Sydney's black leather jacket.

"Oh, that was one night in New York. I think we were going to CBs or the Peppermint Lounge or somewhere."

"What's CBs?"

"CBGB," I sighed. "It's a punk rock club. It's where the Ramones and Blondie play…and Shrapnel…" I heard my voice trail off.

"Like, 'This ain't no Mudd Club? Or CBGB. I ain't got time for that now'?" Jake sang.

Yes! Now we were getting somewhere! Jake knew the Talking Heads song.

"Whelp," he said, straightening back up and giving me his grin. "We don't have CBGB here. But we do have a Little Caesars Pizza. Kimmy and I can take you there some night and show you how Bellingham tears it up, too." I offered a snort. It was sweet of Jake to be polite to the lonely new neighbor. But I was ready for him to go now.

◄◄ ❚❚ ►►

A month after we moved in, half the road washed away. The unrelenting rain combined with frozen ground created mudslides that swept giant chunks of asphalt and some free-standing garages down an embankment into the lake. The next night, Kimberly invited me to a party at her boyfriend's dorm. Mom, who never expressed concern about my safety, was so struck by the biblical flooding that she actually asked Kim, as we stood in the kitchen, if she was sure we should be driving at night along a cliff that was crumbling into the lake.

"Oh, don't worry," Kimberly said. "My brother Jake is an excellent driver." For some reason I felt safer than I had a second earlier.

I climbed into the back seat of Kimberly's Rabbit. Jake turned to check on me. "You all buckled in?" The rain was heavy, and the road was dark, but Jake orchestrated the stick shift, radio station, and lighter for his Marlboro with ease. Halfway to town, at a bend in the road, sat a lonely gas station with a flickering neon sign, the last gasp of civilization for another five miles. Jake pulled into the lot, and the car fishtailed.

"Watch this," he said, "The owner hates when I do this." Jake yanked the emergency brake and cranked the wheel to the left. The car went skidding sideways, pinning me to the seat like the Scrambler at a carnival, and sliding straight toward the plate glass window of the convenience store. Inside, the owner's eyes went wide. Then the car stopped short, smack up against a snowbank. Jake looked back at me. "Sorry 'bout that. Sometimes I gotta liven things up or Bob gets bored. Anybody need anything?"

I watched Jake amble into the fluorescent light, and the owner wag a finger at him. The owner followed Jake to the refrigerator, then back to the cash register, running his mouth while Jake laughed. It was obvious the owner loved Jake. I was afraid I did, too.

The dorm party was a disaster, packed and loud, and the guy at the door told us we couldn't come in. Rumor was some kids had a bunch of coke and didn't want outsiders there. Kim's boyfriend got agitated and pushed the guy before Jake tugged them apart. Right as we gave up, I yelled at the door guy that he was being a total douche, and he could take his keg and shove it up his ass. Jake grabbed my arm.

"Alisyn! Is that how they do it back East?"

"It is in New Jersey," I said.

The next Saturday night, I was alone. *Nothing to do. Nowhere to go-oh,* the Ramones taunted me. I called next door. Jake answered. He said Kimberly was night skiing at the mountain. I liked his deep voice and wanted to keep hearing it. I asked if he knew of anything happening...anywhere? He said he was going to the neighbor's to play pool, I could come along if I wanted.

"But you'd be stuck with me," he said.

I said that might be okay.

First, Jake wanted to swing by the ice rink for an impromptu hockey game. A girl I recognized from the school bus was there, so she and I drank a couple of beers and shared a cigarette while the guys played. Jake glided around, shooting the puck through the goal again and again, skating backward as the other guys chased him, hooting and laughing. I had to look away.

"Are you with Jake Hennessey?" the girl asked, eyes glued to him.

"No. He's just my neighbor."

Jake killed it on the pool table, too, banking shots, shooting with the cue behind his back and his eyes closed, cracking up the neighbor boys. I looked out the window into the pitch black. After midnight, Jake and I headed out across the neighbor's yard. Days of freezing rain had formed an icy crust over packed snow. I walked skittishly, slipping and sinking. Jake held out his hand,

and as I reached for it, he swept me up in his arms, carrying me like a bride across the threshold.

"We're going to have to get you some better boots," he said. I wrapped my arms tight around his shoulders and tilted my head up to the sky. The fog had cleared, and in the vast blackness, a blanket of a million stars shone.

Back at Jake's house, he asked if I wanted to watch some TV. On the couch, he leaned over to kiss me, and I melted into his body. We kissed for hours, and when I finally stood to leave, Jake stood too and wrapped his arms around me. I knew better than to ask when I would see him again, but I cracked.

"Maybe we could do this again some weekend…" I could have kicked myself.

He looked into my eyes. "Do I have to wait that long?"

◄◄ ❙❙ ►►

Amid the mullets and bell-bottoms at school, I met two cool senior girls.

"So, you live next door to Jake Hennessey?" one of them asked. "Be careful. He's a heartbreaker. He never goes out with anyone."

I nodded like I was taking that under advisement, but by then, my make-out session with Jake had revived some of my Jersey girl moxie, and I thought, *Ladies, ladies. I'm not like other girls. I don't get attached to guys that way. I'll never let Jake know how much I like him. I've got this. See, I'm the girl from New Jersey who got a piece of Shrapnel.*

I was in a bathroom stall at a movie theater when I heard a group of girls enter, speaking in breathless whispers. The Bunnies were a clique utterly unique to Sehome High School: A group of extremely pretty, sports-car-driving, rich girls known for flagrant gossip and high drama. On a normal day, the Bunnies had no use for a new girl from New Jersey but this was apparently no normal day.

"Oh, hi!" the Bunny with a little nose and the longest lacquered lashes said with a big fake grin.

"Oh, hi!!" Two others mewed in unison.

This threw me. In New Jersey, we didn't feign friendship. If Viv didn't like you, she called you an asshole and sauntered away.

"What are you doing here?" The long-lashed Bunny's nose twitched. "Who are you here with?"

"My neighbor."

"Jake Hennessey?" demanded the turquoise-eyed one.

"Yeah. Do you guys know him?" I kept a straight face.

For a second, the cat had the Bunnies' tongues.

"There you are," Jake said as I approached. By then, the Bunnies had him surrounded. "You gals must know Alisyn. She's new to town. You've probably seen her around school."

The Bunnies didn't take their eyes off Jake. Long Lashes spoke up.

"Oh, Jake, I'm having a party next weekend. My parents are out of town. You should definitely come."

"Sounds like trouble," Jake said. He threw his arm around my shoulder. "Maybe we'll swing by. Al, you ready to head out?" I nodded. "We'll catch you gals next time." Jake smiled at them, then steered me out the door. In the parking lot, he bent down and whispered in my ear. "*Stay away from the Bunnies.*"

"Why's that?" I assumed their prettiness would allow guys like Jake to overlook any annoying personality traits. I'd heard they dated older guys and had parties with cocaine. I'd also heard that Jake had slept with a couple of them.

"You know why they're called the Bunnies?" Jake asked.

"Because they drive convertible Rabbits?"

He laughed. "Because they hop from guy to guy. They're bad news. *Baaad* cinema."

At the time, I thought Jake was sharing gossip about the Bunnies. It never occurred to me Jake might be afraid of his own heart getting broken.

Hold Me Now

A couple weeks after the brush with the Bunnies, Jake took me to a club in Vancouver, Canada. The music was different from back home: Haircut 100, Thompson Twins, A Flock of Seagulls. But the euphoria of a dance floor is the same everywhere, and this was the closest thing to New York City I'd felt since moving away. Mom and Mac were gone for the night. So, I was surprised when, back at my house, Jake stopped seconds short of sleeping together for the first time.

"Is this okay, Al?"

In the moonlight through the window, our eyes connected. I knew what he was asking. *Are you sure this is okay? Are you sure you won't get pregnant or that I won't somehow hurt you, even accidentally?*

I didn't tell him that, for me, sex was the simple part. I didn't tell him that in a lifetime of being afraid of so many things: catching a ball, climbing a tree, going off the high dive—the one thing that didn't scare me was sex. I was a natural, completely at ease in the connection, the whispers, the closeness. I didn't have any weird hang-ups. I didn't need to be drunk or the lights to be out or the sheets pulled up. Not to say I was more technically proficient than the next girl. I was just as perplexed as anyone by the cover of Cosmo promising the secret to a perfect blowjob. What was that secret? I was still appalled by slutty girls who slept with lots of guys who never cared about them. *Have some self-respect, woman!* And I didn't understand girls who had sex just because a guy wanted it. Why? I also didn't understand sitcom jokes about "faking it." Why would anyone ever do that? Why would you have to?

I had sex on my terms, only when I wanted, and only with guys I really liked. And when I wasn't attracted to someone, I was violently unattracted;

the mere thought of their touch repelled me. Even when I was attracted, I often turned the guy down. I saw that the more I said no, the more he came back. I knew the secret to sex was what happened next, and I knew how to play that part, too. I required no promises of undying devotion.

Alisyn Adage #3—Do Not Demand Commitment.

I didn't call the guy afterward or beg for his attention. I was satisfied with the tacit bond that sex creates between two people, the secret smile across a room for the rest of our lives. And that night, I was naïve enough to think that would be enough with Jake.

◀◀ ❚❚ ▶▶

Jake's favorite challenge was feeding me. Burgers at Red Robin. Nachos at Dos Padres. I devoured it all.

"One lumberjack breakfast coming right up." Jake was standing at the stove making me breakfast. "Two pancakes, two sausage patties, and two eggs over medium, as requested. You want any toast with that?"

Jake's parents knew of our budding romance and were generally okay with it, as long as we were back in separate beds by morning.

"Oh, Jake, honestly," his mother clucked, coming in to grab a banana before her aerobics class. "Alisyn can't eat all that."

"Mom, have you ever seen Al eat? She knows she's full when food starts falling *out* of her mouth."

Occasionally I tried to reciprocate. One morning I called out our kitchen window to Jake drinking coffee on his deck. "Want to come over for breakfast?"

He squinted to see through the screen. "Whatcha making?"

I hadn't thought the offer through that far. I looked down at the counter. "Grapes?"

"Grapes?" Jake said. "I'll be right over!"

Jake admitted once that he sometimes felt he played the role of father figure in my life and wondered if I felt that, too. "Uh, no," I replied. "That's creepy."

It took me a while to realize he wasn't wrong, but I didn't see him as paternal—he was *parental*. He paid for everything, drove everywhere, and protected me from the cold. He clothed me in long johns, mittens, ski pants, and goggles before taking me up to the mountain to try to teach me to ski. In those early months in Bellingham, I had no idea that I was in the process of transferring every ounce of dependency I'd ever had on Mom to Jake and then some. Being with Jake meant I was the anointed one. I was the Chosen One. Of all the girls in Bellingham, Jake had picked me. And there was nothing in the world more special than being loved *the most*.

Back then, I didn't emotionally register my father's absence because his presence had felt like absence for so long. It was easier for me not to be around Dad than to try to fill the silent distance sitting next to him. When I moved to Bellingham, Dad called me at an appointed time every Sunday. For someone with great episodic recall, I don't remember these calls. I'm guessing they were full of meaningless small talk, which was easier than hearing about his job losses or drinking. Even asking him to send missing child support checks made me feel sorry for *him*. I imagine I told him about the weather or some test grade I got, but I knew better than to ask anything that would trigger his evasiveness. You can't get blood from a stone. And you can't bond with a secretive man, no matter how much he loves you.

◀◀ ❚❚ ▶▶

I'd told my New Jersey friends that I'd return for the summer. It was a less than half-baked plan—I didn't have any job prospects or place to live. And now I didn't want to leave Jake. Still, the night I hung up after breaking the news that I wouldn't return, I wrapped my arms around my knees, rocking and sobbing.

Without thinking, I was at Jake's sliding glass door, the glow of Johnny Carson on TV bathing him in blue light. He was stretched out in his recliner, hands behind his head. I tapped on the glass.

"What's going on, Al?" he asked when he saw my tear-streaked face.

"Nothing, really." I blew out a breath. I shouldn't have come in this state. But I was looking for something, some reassurance that I'd survive if my old friends forgot about me, some vow that even though I already loved Jake too much, he wouldn't leave me.

"Come here," Jake said, sitting up and patting his thigh. "Come tell Uncle Jake what's wrong."

I let out an unexpected laugh and sat on his lap. He brushed the wetness from my face. "What's going on with you," he asked softly.

"I decided not to go home this summer." I stopped talking, but the tears kept falling. Jake wrapped his arms across my back and under my knees, pulling me to him. "And I guess I just wanted to come over..." I paused to keep myself from revealing too much, "to make sure I made the right decision."

"You did, Al," he whispered, rocking me back and forth, back and forth.

Satellite of Love

I couldn't take my eyes off Jake, the way he moved, the way his eyes twinkled when he told a joke. I saw how other guys stole his funny lines, and girls stood too close. Jake told me he loved me, but I didn't know why. Why didn't he choose that cool girl from the ski team who won the national championships, I wondered, as I watched their easy banter, speaking their shared ski language. In Bellingham, people put huge value on the ability to ski black diamonds at Mt. Baker and catch air windsurfing on Lake Whatcom—Jake's specialties. Few people in town seemed to care if I aced an English test, what college I might go to, or how I was able to convince the bouncer at CBs to let me in to see Shrapnel. I started to think the only thing making me visible was the glow reflecting off Jake.

And I hated feeling invisible.

One afternoon, Mom came into my bathroom carrying an armload of fresh towels and caught me staring into the mirror.

"What's up?" she said.

"I don't think I'm pretty enough for Jake."

"Why do you say that?"

"I just don't. There are so many other prettier girls."

Mom met my reflection. "I think if Jake was just looking for pretty, he would have made a different choice. You're more interesting."

"Everybody loves him," I told her.

"Everybody loves you, too."

"Not like that."

She looked at me. "I think it can be hard to have two stars in a relationship. Sometimes someone has to be the satellite. And I don't know if you're good at being the satellite."

Alisyn Adage #4—Act Like You Don't Care.

By then, I'd learned that Jake liked to pull me close, then withdraw. I knew that after an intimacy burst, Jake's attention could stray back to smoking and joking with his buddies around the keg or planning the next ski trip that didn't include me. His retreats left me silently spinning, frantic to win back his attention by resorting to my old trick of performing—laughing at another guy's joke or bandying a double entendre as one filled my beer. Only then would Jake reappear, back to whisper our connection in my ear. Jake's was the kind of intimacy I knew best, the kind that came and went. Only fools believed in unconditional love. Realists like me knew that one wrong move and people withdraw their love from your savings account without a word. You have to keep performing to keep 'em coming back for more.

Some nights, Jake disappeared. He said he was going out with his friends. And there'd be sightings of the three of them, Jake, Chad, and Brent. Look! Over there! Pulling away from the party or the pizza joint. Somehow I kept missing them. "Did you see Hennessey? He was just here."

It drove me crazy. What were they doing? Were any girls with them? Those nights felt like horror flicks where the danger stays shrouded in shadow. At one small house party, Jake, Brent, and Chad went into a bedroom and locked the door, leaving me outside.

"What the fuck is that?" I said to Tina, the Bunny who drove the Rabbit.

Tina shrugged. She'd gone out with Brent for years. She was used to his disappearing act, to being his satellite. "You know they do blow in there, right?"

Back in New Jersey, drugs were so commonplace most didn't require closed doors. But in Bellingham, risky behavior seemed to be the sole domain of the male species. Jake didn't want me around such stuff. I saw it as the height of chauvinism.

"We should go get our own blow," I said. "And let's pick up a case of beer, too." The Bunnies were happy to play along with some East Coast rabble-rouser. I hoped that partying with new friends could fill my emptiness.

But on the nights Jake chose something or someone over me, I felt the withdrawal acutely.

One late night at Brent's house, Jake and Chad said they had to leave for a little while. I didn't want Jake riding Chad's motorcycle. I didn't want Jake to leave. He said he'd be back soon. Hours passed. My heart raced. I pressed my face to the window, waiting for that single headlight, begging God to let Jake come back in one piece. It was the same old sick feeling I remembered all too well. I demanded Brent let me call the local hospital to see if there'd been a fatal motorcycle accident.

"They'll be back," he said, like he was dealing with a child. And in the most aching way, he was.

My stated curfew, 2:00 a.m., came and went, and I swung between terror and fury. Sometime after 2:30, we heard the low gurgle of an engine. Jake and Chad walked through the door.

I fell to the floor.

"Where were you?" I screamed. "You *left* me! I had to be home at two. You fucking *left* me!" I was screaming and crying. Jake stood frozen in the middle of the room. Chad and Brent were wide-eyed, spooked by the banshee. But I couldn't turn off my rage. All that pent-up anger from years of worrying and waiting.

Jake drove me home in silence. The next day I watched him through the kitchen window as he bounded down the outdoor steps to get firewood or bring in groceries, without so much as a glance in my direction. I recognized something in his face, something I'd seen in the faces of Mom and Dad. The look of disengagement; the look of someone who could compartmentalize sadness, someone who would go on living, even if it was without me. I couldn't do that, couldn't stash my sadness out of sight. I knew no one could ever take Jake's place. I would die without him.

◄◄ ❚❚ ►►

I doubt there's ever been a stronger credo in my life than Alisyn Adage #5: Leave Before You Get Left.

Why would anyone allow themselves to stand by helplessly, their face wet and contorted with despair, as someone they loved left them in the rearview mirror? I had spent much of my sixteen years desperately trying to avoid that scenario but there I was, standing in Jake's driveway, bawling. The day he left for college, I stood with Jake's mom and sister watching him load the last bag into Brent's back seat. Jake came and wrapped me in a bear hug. But I couldn't be consoled.

"Oh, for heaven's sake, Al," his mom said, wrapping an arm around me. "He's only going over the mountains."

"Over the mountains!" I wailed.

"He'll be back to visit," Kimberly assured me.

Jake called that night. He said he missed me and he'd call again soon. But he didn't call the next night. He called four days later, but I missed it. I called him back, but he wasn't home.

Chad went to visit Jake. There was a girl. Long blonde hair, killer skier. But Jake didn't like her. Her cheeks had a layer of hair, like sideburns. But, man, she loved Jake. It was so fucking funny how much she loved Jake. Chad and Brent laughed their heads off. I was losing my mind.

◀◀ ❚❚ ▶▶

About a month after my junior year started and Jake left, I walked in gray mist home from the bus stop and through my front door. Mom and Mac were on the living room floor, a map spread out before them.

"Come join us," Mom said.

I took a seat cross-legged on the carpet. Mom was kneeling back on her heels. "Mac's been offered a job."

"OK," I said.

"It's a very good job," she said. "It's a bigger rehabilitation facility, and it's more money."

"I'd be the director," Mac said.

"Great," I said.

"The job is in Pittsburgh," Mom said.

"Ooookaay," I said slowly.

"Which is obviously much closer to New Jersey," Mac said. "And it would be terrific for your mom, too. There'd be more work for her there."

"There's a hospital called Western Psychiatric," Mom added, "where they have a psychodrama program."

Mac's eyes slid over to Mom. I could sense breath holding, waiting for me to wig out.

"Soooo," he went on, "they want me to start as soon as possible. They need me there in two weeks."

I nodded.

"We were just looking at the route here." His finger traced an eastward line across the Rockies. "It'll take about five days to drive if we push it." He stopped. They looked at me.

"Sounds great. Congratulations."

"So, do you think you can start packing this weekend?" Mom asked.

"Me?" I raised my eyebrows. "Oh. I'm not going."

"What do you mean?" Mom asked.

"I mean, it sounds like a good opportunity. For you guys. But I'm not going. I'm not moving again."

Heavy fog cloaked the foothills beyond the picture window, but my mind was as clear as a beach day. I was done with their adventure. I was done being the only one with crystal clear vision who could see the stop sign up ahead as the car careened across an intersection. Being the only sane person in an asylum is not vindication; it's a crazy-making-scream-inducing horror show. I was done screaming. Mom was leaving, and I was ready to let her go.

"What will you do?" she asked, which, years later, I realized was a particularly emotion-free response from a mother whose sixteen-year-old daughter had just declared their life together was over. But at the time, I saw it as standard Mom and me. She was pressing forward. I was left to figure something out on my own.

"I'm not sure," I said, standing up, my legs stiff from sitting. "Give me a couple hours. Can I have the car keys?"

◄◄ ❚❚ ►►

Hal and Cynthia Eriksen were the parents of Brent, Jake's best friend. They owned a real estate firm, the signs for which dotted sidewalks of office buildings around town. The Eriksens had a beautiful lake house, two luxury cars, a ski boat, and a private plane. They had two sons. What they did not have was something Cynthia had always wanted: a daughter.

That afternoon I sat at the Eriksen's dining table, wiping away tears as my desperation sank in. I needed someone to save me from more upheaval. I didn't want to move again, I told them. I didn't want to start over at another new school. I had close friends now. I couldn't bear to leave. Mostly I couldn't bear to be that far from Jake. But I didn't tell them that part. The Eriksens knew everyone in town. Maybe somebody had a room to rent?

That evening just after dinner, the phone on our kitchen wall rang. I ran for it as if waiting for test results.

"Hal and I talked it over," Cynthia said. "We'd like you to live with us. We'll figure out the details tomorrow, but I wanted to let you know as soon as possible."

Mom drew in a breath and nodded when I told her. "That's what you wanted, isn't it?" I said yes, and she said she was happy for me. I didn't have to convince the former high school teacher that moving in the middle of junior year would be bad for my grades and bad for that future college scholarship. I knew Mom desperately needed a paycheck. She'd never found a job in Bellingham, and though she busied herself with cooking nightly dinners and daily grocery runs, I knew it was unsustainable. Above all, I knew she had lost the authority to make me go.

Years later, she would say, "I wanted you to have the freedom to do what you wanted with your life and become the person you were supposed to be. Having parents who didn't give me that freedom, I knew that didn't work out too well."

On the day Mom and Mac were leaving, I wrote a goodbye letter.

10/24/82

Dear Mom and Mac,

Good luck with everything. I hope everything works out for all of us. But if it doesn't, we'll make adjustments. If there's one thing I've learned, it's that nothing is permanent. So who knows where we'll be in a year? We've all made the choices we think are best and now we're doing them!!! This will certainly be a learning experience. But after this one, let's stop learning for awhile, O.K.? Well, you're both yelling at me right now to help you pack, so I gotta go. I love you!

Finding that letter decades later, I see so much in its breezy blank spaces. I see a teenager keeping it light and airy to avoid the painful and humiliating reality of being left behind. I see a girl who knew that this was the moment that Verna-the-Palm-Reader had foretold a year earlier of something permanent being lost, but also a girl who was done screaming out warning signs for her mother. And there was something else glaring in that letter that took me years to see. The author of that note was a girl who had learned to project a sunny surface in response to her mother's chilly distance, a bubbly cheerleader's answer to the remote professor. I didn't know then that Mom's remoteness was a cover for her own secrets. All I knew was that it had been a long time since I'd felt her warmth. I relied on Jake for that now, though he, too, had left.

On the day Mom left, when all our dishes and clothes were once again packed up and the house was empty, I stood again in the Hennesseys' driveway next to Kimberly and her mom, the mist between us thick as gauze. Mac loaded the last box in the U-Haul, hitched to his car, and Mom sat in the passenger seat, looking small. Mom later told me she was afraid to look at me, afraid she would break down and make me feel worse. All I saw was the side of her face. An emotionless mask. I envied her ability to do what was impossible for me—swap out one place for another, one guy for another. Mom rolled down her window and reached out to stroke the top of my hand with her thumb.

"We'll call you as soon as we arrive."

I heard Kimberly's breath quiver. She put her arm around me. I was crying, which was a common state for me, not because Mom was leaving, but because I knew I could never get anyone to stay. How strange that this was where our journey ended. Mom leaving the place she chose and me staying somewhere I never wanted to be.

"Wish us luck!" Mac called out, shifting into gear, starting to roll away.

"Drive carefully!" I yelled. But Mom had rolled up the window. The car came to the end of the block. The brake lights flashed, then turned left and disappeared.

I felt a knot loosen and a rope fly free from its hitch—an unexpected feeling, unmoored but free. Freedom from worrying about Mom, freedom from her lack of depth perception, her helplessness, her love life, her any-port-in-a-storm decision-making.

For so long I was a passenger on her misguided ride.

And now, it was over.

Freedom's just another word for nothing left to lose.

Now, I got it.

Skidmarks on My Heart

I moved into the downstairs family room of the Eriksens' lake house. We agreed I would extract $200 a month from Dad and hand most of it over to the Eriksens for food and rent. The space they gave me wasn't an official bedroom; it had no door, but there was a closet and half a wall that gave me some measure of privacy from their often-used pool table.

The Eriksens were happy to have me, but they were stricter and more orderly than Mom. They objected to my clothing strewn on the floor and my dresser drawers flung open. I was grateful they'd taken me in, but I was lonely. I often felt so desperate for a familiar face that once when I saw a New Jersey license plate on the highway, I trailed it for miles in the Chevette that Mom had left behind, praying it might be someone I knew. I wished that Jake would call more often. I wished he'd come back.

◄◄ ❚❚ ►►

In October, Jake came home from college for the weekend. I wanted all of his attention and a candlelight dinner. But I didn't tell him that, and Jake was bent on partying with his buddies, which is how I ended up standing hurt and resentful in Kurt's wood-paneled attic, waiting for Jake while he and Brent measured out a mound of psilocybin mushrooms that had been drying on newspaper under Kurt's futon for a week.

That's when Chad arrived with a girl I recognized from school. She had the locker next to mine and smiled at me as we swapped out books between classes. She had pale blonde hair, sea-green eyes, and an ephemeral air that allowed her to levitate down the hallway above the drudgery.

"This is Hera," Chad said.

"Oh! Hi," I responded, grateful to have a companion. "We know each other."

Hera wore the blank expression of a Botticelli angel. "No, we don't."

I paused. "Yes, we do."

"I don't think so."

This was weird. I thought everyone knew me as the Jersey girl in straight-legged jeans. Plus, she'd been smiling at me for a month, though now her mermaid eyes stared through me.

"Well," Chad said, breaking the awkwardness, "you two can get to know each other." Then he disappeared with Jake behind a closed door to weigh the shrooms.

Hera, it turned out, wasn't being rude. She was *so* ethereal that she didn't register earthly events like an East Coaster in Levi's landing one locker over. Hera, I would learn, wasn't concerned with social status, or diets, or clothing, or cliques, or any other garden-variety high school issue. She read books: Anaïs Nin and science fiction. She liked knitting. Like me, she was the daughter of a divorced, unconventional mother who didn't fit any suburban mold. Like mine, Hera's father lived in a different state and was defined mostly by his absence. Most remarkably, at fourteen, she too had fallen in love with a punk rock band, Psycho Pop, and had also ventured to a big city, in her case Seattle, to follow them around. She, too, had slept with the guitar player, Nikki. Her own Dave Vogt. Hera and I also shared the singularly intoxicating and maddening experience of being the girlfriends of Jake and Chad, two in-demand and often unavailable guys. Within a few months, Hera and I would become inseparable.

Jake returned to school after that weekend, and one of the older popular guys in town started paying attention to me. I liked the status of being seen in his sports car. I liked his company. I liked that he liked me. Mostly, I liked the idea that if somebody else fell in love with me, Jake would see my value and remember to love me the most. With the new guy, I felt less lonely. Less invisible. Then I slept with him. Then he told Jake.

◄◄ ❙❙ ►►

On Thanksgiving weekend, exactly one year after Mom and I pulled out of our driveway in Shrewsbury, Brent Eriksen threw a blowout party while Hal and Cynthia were out of town. It was my first Thanksgiving spent away from my family. I heard Jake was back in town, but he hadn't contacted me, and his silence made my body ache. I was standing right by the pool table when he showed up.

I was desperate to tell him my side. But he wouldn't look at me. Then he was leaving, and I was sobbing. He went out the sliding glass door but doubled back and came to me. He wrapped my body in his, lifting me off the floor. Then he whispered goodbye and let go.

Jake cut off all communications. I cried through portions of every day, suffering one crying jag in Spanish class so extreme that Señora Diaz didn't know what to do but have Kimberly escort me to the nurse. Hera sat in my Chevette for long soulful, heart-to-hearts, raindrops streaming down the windshield. Even the Bunnies tried to help by plying me with beer and late-night greasy burgers at drive-thrus. And for a few seconds in their sports cars, singing to the Go-Gos, I could pretend I would survive without Jake; then the night was over, and the music stopped, and I was alone.

On Your Radio

I flew back to New Jersey to embark on an exhausting circuit of mandatory family holiday visits: Christmas Eve in South Jersey with Dad and his new girlfriend; Christmas in Philly with my grandparents, aunts, and uncles. At some point on Christmas Day, Mom appeared at Gram and Poppy's door, struggling with her suitcase and purse, unable to ascend the icy but salted steps, needing my uncle's arm and my aunt's hand to relieve her of the pie she was precariously carrying.

Mac didn't know where to park, so Poppy grabbed an overcoat and went out to direct him. Once inside, Mom said yes to Gram's polite offer of some hot tea, though it was clear Gram was busy with the Christmas meal. To me, Mom's needs seemed to eclipse everything, and I felt the walls of the narrow row house closing in.

There was something else I detected in those walls beyond the smell of musty mothballs. I sometimes got a strange feeling at Gram and Poppy's—a dread that seeped into my stomach, creating a sinkhole from my throat down to my pelvis. The feeling was peculiar because Gram and Poppy demonstrated hourly how much they loved me, cooking my favorite meals, hanging on my stories, endlessly tickling my back. Still, that secret sinkhole seized me unexpectedly, from a source I'd never been able to identify.

That Christmas I was especially out of my mind, desperate to get to Sydney's because Shrapnel was playing a midnight show at Big Man's West in Red Bank. I treated that show like a life-saving drug, my last chance to revive all that had been lost. My transition to needing friends over family was complete, and only Shrapnel could deliver salvation.

So, the second the pizzelles, dried figs, and Sambuca were cleared from the dinner table, I made such a stink about needing to see Shrapnel that Gram and Poppy agreed to get in their cold car and drive me two hours north to Shrewsbury. At 8:00 p.m., I was in Sydney's bedroom, sweeping purple eyeshadow onto my lids.

"I can't believe my mother is letting *you* go to the show but not *me*," Sydney said, brushing the hell out of her hair the way she did when she was pissed. By then, most adults—Gram, Poppy, Mrs. Sherman—were confounded by my living situation and what, if any, rules still applied to me.

"Sucks," I shrugged, then grabbed Sydney's leather jacket from a hanger and headed out.

⏪ ⏸ ⏩

Nothing soothes a broken heart like a Shrapnel show. And for those few hours, I was my old self again. Back with Frankie, Annie, Peter Reefer, Mark, Matt, and Winkie—even Kuts and Bert—all buzzing with holiday cheer and offers of kamikaze shots. And Viv was back from rehab! It was a true Christmas miracle.

At one point, I found myself standing next to a beefy punk rocker named Ratt. Ratt was a regular at Shrapnel shows, but we had never actually spoken, so I was surprised when he turned and said, "Hey, Alisyn. What's up?"

I was visible again.

At that moment, my affection for Ratt was so deep that I was tempted to tell him how in the past year I'd moved to Olympia, how Mom and Walter had broken up, how we had moved to Bellingham with Mac and moved next door to the Hennesseys. How I made friends at a new high school. How Jake and I fell in love. Then Jake left for college. How Mom moved to Pittsburgh. How I cheated on Jake. And how Jake left me...

"Not much," I said.

"Cool," he said.

That's when Dave Vogt found me in the crowd.

"Hey!" His face lit up. He kissed my cheek. "You're back!"

"Just for Christmas."

"How's it going out there? California, right?"

Something about Vogt's confusion comforted me. In New Jersey, nobody knew the difference between California and Washington State. No one knew of Bellingham. Or Jake Hennessey.

"We should hang out while you're here."

"Yeah, definitely," I said, but I didn't mean it. I couldn't bear his steady gaze on my face. I told Vogt I had to go find Viv and walked away, but when I glanced back, I saw him standing alone under a sprig of mistletoe, still looking at me.

The show was starting. I slid between bodies to get a clear shot of the stage, my nerve endings tingling, a rush of pins and needles after months of being numb. Vogt ran up on stage, then Wyndorf marched on, raised his fist, and yelled, "Underdog is here!" The guitars cranked up, and I soared above the crush, levitating back to life.

Somehow after that first set, I was blissed-out enough to think that Jake might talk to me. He'd ignored my calls for a month, but the togetherness of the Shrapnel show inspired me to hand the bartender a dollar to convert to dimes, then to run to the pay phone in the corner of the club. Jake picked up. His deep voice was right there.

"Oh, my God, Jake. I've been dying to talk to you."

Joan Jett was cranked over the speakers, and people were shouting out orders for shots. On the phone, only silence. "I just wanted to hear your voice," I continued, "And to tell you how much I miss you."

He said something that I couldn't make out. "I *hmmmmm* you," was what I heard. Had he said he missed me or hated me? The recorded operator told me to insert another ten cents. Viv pounded her fist on the phone booth. The next set was starting.

"Merry Christmas, Al," was all I heard.

Then the call went dead.

I woke up in Sydney's trundle bed. It was a bitterly cold morning, but the Shrewsbury sun forced its lemon ice through the blinds even before I lifted the slats to look. It had been forever since I'd seen bright sunshine and spiky frost decorating windowpanes. I knew I could wake Sydney just by staring at the back of her head, so that's what I did, and sure enough, she rolled over, eyes open.

"Tell me everything."

Sydney was unfazed by my cheating drama. Cheating was common in our Jersey crowd. "Jake shouldn't break up with you *permanently* over it," she declared. I wished I could lay in the warmth of my dear friend's compassion forever. At some point, I went into her bathroom and was overcome. The same circular toothbrush holder sat on the same blue-tiled sink. The same brand of toothpaste and deodorant were in the same mirrored medicine cabinet. The cabinet below the sink still held the same orderly row of blue bottles of body lotion. I rubbed some on my skin and floated off on the scent of sleepovers and Band-Aids and childhood. By the time Sydney opened the door, I was sitting on the rug cradling a bottle of Nivea.

"What are you doing?"

"I love your bathroom."

"Ugh. I find it oppressively blue. My dad just got back with fresh bagels, if you can tear yourself away from the lotion."

◄◄ ❚❚ ►►

I flew back to Bellingham alone, the place where I had no family, no real home, and only the remotest hope that Jake still loved me. The second I got to the Eriksens, I called him. His roommate said he wasn't home. He wasn't home the next night either. Or the next.

Jake never called back.

Every day the unrelenting sky spit steel gray drops. Every morning I drove to school through lead mist and home in wet darkness. Every song on the car radio reminded me of Jake. At every bend in the road, I remembered Jake at the wheel. At night I sat in my room, trying to concentrate on history homework, but the darkness was winning. I began thinking of ways to stop the pain of abandonment, which I believed was as intrinsic to my being as my blood type. I fastened on an idea of staging a near-fatal car crash so Jake would have to rush to my hospital bed. I did not share my despair with Mom. The last thing I needed was her insisting I move to Pittsburgh. Instead,

I composed breezy letters of fluff in which I focused on a different immediate problem: how broke I was.

Dear Mom and Mac, (1/9/83)

Hi guys! What's up? Today is Sunday and I'm bored, bored, bored. Bellingham is very, very depressing lately. It is constantly dark and rainy and miserable. Cynthia says, "It's ghastly." On the flight back from New Jersey, I got a free coupon for giving up my seat. So now I have a ticket to come visit Pittsburgh.

Anyway, school is going fine. I love Psychology. I got my handwriting analyzed on Friday. It said: I'm an extrovert, know where I'm going, I'm sensitive and emotional. (Like that's a new one, ha!)

No reply yet from Dad. Can you send me my white coat? I really need it. Also, send money!!! I got the car fixed. I added transmission fluid. I'm also sending you a handwritten bill for $7.07. I needed pens and a notebook for school. I've lost the receipt but please send it soon. I also need $15 for a class trip to Canada and $8 for Ballet Folklortica. I have no money. I need some. Write back.

Love, Al

⏪ ⏸ ⏩

A group of four college guys lived next door to the Eriksens. They had a hot tub and a keg on tap. One of the guys, Nathan, befriended me, a decision he often regretted, like the mornings I ran out of gas on my way to school. There was no point in getting towed to a station; I didn't have any money to fill the tank anyway.

The guys slept late, and all was quiet as I marched down to the basement and pushed open Nathan's bedroom door, stepping into the dark. It smelled like a distillery.

"Nathan," I whispered.

"Who's there?" He said, like I was a ghost.

"I ran out of gas. I'm late for school."

"Go home," he groaned.

"I can't. Hal and Cynthia hate when I do things like this."

He emitted a guttural noise, then flung off his blanket and stood up in his boxers. "Turns out, I have A LOT in common with Hal and Cynthia. Now go get the gas can and meet me outside."

Some nights Nathan made me dinner and tried to save my life. He stood at the stove frying ground beef for tacos as I drank his beer, smoked his cigarettes, and wept.

"You've got to snap out of it," he told me.

"I can't," I whispered, shutting my eyes. I never understood people who thought you could turn off crushing depression with the snap of a finger.

"What do you want to do with your life?"

I breathed a hopeless sigh. "I want to be a TV reporter." I'd figured that out at fifteen. Back in Shrewsbury, I was on the sofa after school one day watching the *Phil Donahue Show* when I became transfixed. Donahue was running around his studio, all eyes on him, like a maestro with a mic. That's his *job*? They *pay* him to do *that*? I loved his command of the crowd and the audience's applause. The roar of validation. I loved how he made us want to stick around. *Stay tuned...* I didn't know how to get a job like that. I just wanted it.

"I have an idea," Nathan said. "You know I'm majoring in Communications?"

"Uh, yeah..." Truth was, my own pain was so acute, I hadn't paid any attention to Nathan's life.

"So, I work at the campus radio station, and the guy who read the news last semester, his schedule changed. We don't have anybody. Want to do it?"

◄◄ ❙❙ ►►

The next night I showed up at the radio station shaking. Nathan took me into a small booth, fitted some headphones over my ears, and adjusted the microphone down to my level. He handed me a stack of 8x10 sheets of white paper with black lettering in all caps. I watched the second-hand tick forward, waiting for my cue, my palms clammy, my throat closing. And when the red light came on, I started reading, my heart pounding like a Shrapnel drum solo. Two minutes later, when the red light went off, I was light-headed and drunk on adrenaline. I knew right then I was born to be a broadcaster. In fact, I couldn't believe how good I already was.

"That was amazing!" I told Nathan.

"Meh," he frowned. "It wasn't great. You were pretty flat. I think you need to read faster."

I did it again and again, and each time I imagined radio waves squiggling out over the sky into car radios and people hearing *my* voice and turning up the volume.

All at once, I was heard. I was valuable. I had power.

And maybe somehow, someday, Jake would hear my voice over the airwaves. And on that day, he would love me again.

Change of Heart

I was asleep when it happened. Yet I still wondered, as so many women do, if I'd done something wrong. Perhaps I'd been too friendly or flirtatious in previous interactions with him. Waking up with someone's head between your legs, his tongue all over you, is shocking. I gasped, bolted up, and clamped my knees together tight as a vice. I could smell the hard liquor leaking from his mouth and pores. Even in the dark, I knew him as an older friend of Brent's, who I'd always considered pitiful—his greasy grin too forced, his laugh too sharp. His girlfriend stuck to his side like a hostage.

Just a week earlier, a couple of Brent's friends had snuck into my room, short-sheeted my bed, and left a slimy unwrapped condom on my pillow, a drunken prank that sent me into a white-hot rage. I saw it as a scorching violation of the twelve-square feet of the world that was supposed to be mine. It was obvious the guys considered me a sitting duck for their frat-boy boredom. I didn't know the next violation would be worse. After all the precarious situations I'd put myself in, the assault happened in the place I was supposed to be safest, in my own so-called home. By then, the list of ways I felt wronged was so long that the assault didn't even rank in the top five. It did not become a defining event in my life. In fact, years go by without it ever crossing my mind. When it does, I feel neither shame nor humiliation. I feel about it the way I do about all sexual assaults: They reveal only the perpetrator's depravity and the survivors' grit.

I got out of bed the next morning and called Hera. I told her I was raped. I didn't think that was quite the right word, but I didn't yet know the term "sexual assault." She was sympathetic but not surprised. Things like that occasionally happened to girls we knew. I told her I was fine. I got dressed, went to school, and handed in my history paper.

The next Friday night, Hera and I got pulled over in my Chevette on the way to a party. The cop said he clocked me going forty in a school zone. I was sure my signature sass would get me out of it. "Doesn't look like many kids are heading to school at this hour," I smiled. Then he handed me a sixty-dollar ticket, and I beat the steering wheel so violently and wailed so inconsolably that the cop stood frozen at my car window. I couldn't stop. Other kids had parents who bailed them out of tickets, parents who let their kids finish high school before moving three thousand miles away, parents who gave them an allowance and gas money. Other kids had a *fucking door* on their bedroom. Other kids had someone who took care of them. But I was completely on my own. By then, Hera was crying, too. She stroked my back over and over and over.

◀◀ ❙❙ ▶▶

It had been snowing nonstop over Stevens Pass. Travel advisories warned drivers not to attempt the treacherous crossing without chains on their tires. The Chevette didn't even have snow tires. But I wasn't going to let an icy mountain pass stop me from driving across the Cascades to find Jake and plead my case. I set out after school on a Friday with no overnight bag, no money, and no plan except to find Jake. I made it fifty-seven miles to Marysville before my car ran out of gas on an overpass, and I had to abandon it and sob my way to the closest gas station, where I convinced the attendant to use his own money to fill my tank.

My last resort had failed. On the way back to Bellingham, I tracked each set of headlights speeding toward me and imagined jerking the wheel into them and ending my pain. Then a song started. A song I'd never heard before but knew it was sent by a cosmic messenger as a roadmap through my misery. Someone had broken Tom Petty's heart, but he was going to survive. The song ended before I learned the secret. I scanned the dial, frantic, until it came back on, then I pulled over and stared at the speakers, straining to absorb how someone was once his moon and sun but had become a loaded gun. And how he got over a love like that.

I got home and wrote Jake a letter. I told him his silence was killing me, and I had to find a way to live.

I was in my nightgown, math homework slipping around my mind on a Sunday night, when there was a knock at the door. Cynthia went to see who was there. Jake's silhouette appeared.

I rose, steadying myself on the sofa, then ran to him. He lifted me off the ground. Quivering, I led him down the stairs out to the boathouse.

"I got your letter, Al," he said. "I forgive you."

He pulled me onto his lap, into his chest.

I wrapped my arms around his neck, hanging on for dear life.

◄◄ ❙❙ ►►

Spring in Bellingham brought the first sunny mornings in months and big blue skies. I skipped into Hera's house, excited about our friendship and shared futures with Jake and Chad.

I began spending every afternoon at Hera's bohemian house with her quirky stepfather and slightly warped, wonderful mother, who, like Hera, had a twisted take on everyday items. She likened eating a soft-shell crab sandwich to "eating a dried mummy hand" and told us she wished "teenage food" came in a big dry bag that she could scoop into bowls like dog food. Hera's parents owned a beat-up blue milk truck that sat in their driveway, which, for reasons never fully explained to me, they called "The Fuck Truck" and a beat-up brown station wagon called "The Gonad Mobile."

Within days of my reconciliation with Jake, Hera, Chad, and I made plans for a road trip to visit Jake at school. The Chevette still didn't have snow tires, but it was better than Chad's motorcycle or the Gonad Mobile. So off we went, skidding and sliding across Stevens Pass. I cranked the radio and belted out, "I'm So Excited," while Hera and Chad pretended not to be petrified.

Jake and I barely left his room. I remember the weekend as a fever dream: in and out of sleep, tangled in sheets, hot, thirsty, delirious with reunion. When it was time to go, Jake stood at the Chevette, leaning through the window. He said he'd call but didn't offer any details on date or time. I left anxious as ever.

Hera and I fluctuated between being furious when we thought the guys were taking us for granted and terrified when we thought they might move on. We consoled ourselves by jumping on her mom's bed and singing heartbreak songs into our hairbrushes, as if we would ever have the guts to leave them. A few weeks later, Hera, Chad, and I made another trip to see Jake, this time to Chad's family's rustic cabin in a remote town also over the mountains. A couple hours in, the guys got antsy.

"Hey, Al," Jake started. "Chad and I are going to run to the store to get some supplies for dinner."

"Okay. Let me grab my jacket."

"How 'bout you gals stay here and get a fire started?" Jake said. "We'll be back just like that." He snapped his fingers.

Hera and I sat on the sofa. We drank a couple beers. We smoked a cigarette or two and watched the sky darken. Hours passed.

"Where are the lights in this place?" I asked.

"The cabin doesn't have any electricity," Hera said.

"Are you fucking kidding me?"

They had left us again—those assholes—this time without any food, money, car, or phone in an unheated cabin in the dark woods.

"I hope by the time they come back, we haven't been chopped up into little pieces," Hera said. But I would have gladly accepted a ride home from a homicidal maniac to end the all-too-familiar feeling of being left behind.

Jake and Chad eventually returned, buzzed and guilty. They'd found a bar with a pool table, and, well, some guys wanted to play for money, and it was so funny, they kicked the guys' asses in the fifth game and, hey, won forty bucks! Hera took it in stride, the price of having an in-demand boyfriend. But I was a one-girl conflagration, lighting up the whole cabin. I hated being abandoned, hated feeling so helpless and dependent on Jake. I didn't want to live like this, but I'd proven I couldn't live without him.

Alone back at the Eriksens, I opened my diary and landed on an entry exactly two years earlier. The night of the RBR school musical. I'd recorded the joy of being in the cast, the laughs and camaraderie. I had forgotten that

Dave Vogt kissed me on the cheek that night. Tears streamed down my face. I missed my old self, the one I remembered as ambitious and confident, whether she truly was or not. I missed talking about classes and colleges, rather than sitting on the sidelines watching Jake windsurf. I wanted my old life back. I wanted my future self back.

Hey, Ho, Let's Go!

The Ramones were playing a show in Vancouver, Canada. The only kid I knew in Bellingham who liked the Ramones was Jake's friend Tom. Tom had a leather jacket and a Flock of Seagulls haircut that made him look edgier than the rest of the fleecey crowd. As always, a big part of me hoped Jake would hear that I was doing something cool without him and race home. It never happened.

A long line formed outside the Commodore club. Vancouver punk rockers resembled New York punks: mohawks, safety pins, combat boots. But to me, they looked like they were playing dress-up with consignment shop clothes.

Tom spotted a reporter from the *Vancouver Sun.* I watched the reporter, notebook in hand, talking to a couple in line and felt a stab of envy. "That's what I'm going to be," I told Tom.

We made our way into the club and to the bar. That's when I heard it. Over the din of the crowd, I heard the voice I knew, the song I loved. "*She was my Combat Love, the one I'm thinking of!*" Shrapnel was blasting from the speakers.

I became unglued, thinking Shrapnel was *in the building*, opening for the Ramones, which they often did. If Shrapnel was there, they could save me. They could take me back to New Jersey in their van. They could be my superheroes one more time. *Hey! Ho! Let's Go!*

The lights dimmed, and I held my breath. *Please, please let Shrapnel be here.*

A band called The Actionauts strutted out.

I was sick. I didn't want to see the Ramones anymore. I stewed through the entire show. By the time the Ramones left the stage, I'd hatched a plan.

I pulled Tom by the sleeve to the door at the side of the stage. The bouncer's meaty arms were folded across his butterball chest. His eyes stared over my head.

"We really need to see the Ramones," I told him.

"You just saw them," he said.

"Funny. No. I need to talk to them."

He didn't move a muscle.

From the recesses of my brain, I unearthed a nugget of gossip in Sydney's recent letter. She claimed that Dave Wyndorf's little sister, Sally, was dating Dee Dee Ramone. It had seemed completely implausible...until the second I heard it come out of my mouth.

"Tell Dee Dee that Sally Wyndorf is here."

The bouncer glanced down at me for the first time.

"What'd you say your name was?"

"Sally Wyndorf. He knows me."

"Who's that?" the bouncer asked, jutting his chin toward Tom.

"That? Oh, that's Erin Reilly," I said, invoking the name of Sally's best friend from RBR. This was a bigger gamble. Back in New Jersey, Erin Reilly was a girl. The bouncer narrowed his eyes on me.

"Listen, you're gonna be in big trouble," I warned, "if you *don't* tell them we're here."

The bouncer whistled to a roadie on stage, gesturing with his head for him to come over. The bouncer whispered something in his ear. The roadie disappeared.

A few minutes later, the roadie was back, nodding to the bouncer who opened the door just wide enough for us to squeeze through. "Wait here," the roadie said, depositing us at a folding table between two closed doors.

"*Oh. My. God,*" Tom mouthed. I hoisted myself onto the table, my heart racing. A minute later, the door ripped open, and the roadie burst through, followed by a black-haired guy in skinny ripped jeans and a leather jacket. Before that instant, I wouldn't have been able to pick Dee Dee out of a Ramones line-up. But standing before me, he was as recognizable as if he were my real boyfriend. The roadie pointed at me.

Dee Dee stopped cold. His face fell.

"That's not her," he said. "Get them out of here." He turned on his heels.

"I know," I shouted to his back. "I'm not Sally. But I am *friends* with Sally. And Dave. And *Shrapnel!*" I jumped off the table. "And see, I'm from New Jersey. And I thought if I saw you, you could tell me where Shrapnel is and maybe if they're opening for you somewhere out here. Really, I was just hoping to talk to you."

Dee Dee stopped walking and shook his head back and forth in disgust. He gave the roadie a resigned look and sighed. "Let 'em back," he said.

The roadie swung open the door. I grabbed Tom's arm and hustled us fast down the hallway. Dee Dee vanished through a door on the right, and by the time the roadie pushed it open, Dee Dee, Johnny, and Richie were right there, in the flesh, in folding chairs. Three Ramones sitting in a row.

Johnny turned to Dee Dee. "Who's that?"

"I don't know," Dee Dee said. "She says she knows Wyndorf."

"I do!" I said. "And I was just wondering if any of you know if Shrapnel is playing anywhere around here anytime soon?"

The Ramones stared at me.

"No, man." Dee Dee finally said. "I think they're in Jersey."

"That's where I'm from!" Then it hit me—our biggest connection. "I went to Red Bank Regional! You know, 'Rock 'n' Roll High School!'"

The Ramones stared blanks at me. Rip-roaring silence. Either they'd never heard of their own song or RBR wasn't it. After a few long beats, Richie said, "You want a beer?"

I moved to the middle of the room to accept the bottle and slipped into what I hoped resembled cub reporter mode, filing away factoids for some imagined future assignment. I noted the Ramones drank Miller beer but, strangely, were not touching a tantalizing fruit plate that sat wrapped in plastic on a long folding table.

Just then, the door opened and in plodded Joey Ramone. On album covers, Joey looked tall, but in real life, he was space-alien-sized, as if he were made of Play-Doh stretched to the point of almost tearing. Behind Joey, a refrigerator of a man with a shaved head ambled in. He wore a spiked dog collar and chains across his black leather vest. Joey nodded at us without asking who we were, then stood alone against the folding table with the fruit. I went over.

"Do you want some fruit?" I asked him. I was trying to make conversation, but I also felt Joey might be anemic. He was that pale.

"You can have some," he said.

I peeled back the plastic wrap and began loading up a small paper plate with mounds of melon, strawberries, and pineapple. The Ramones were just going to let this go to waste!

"How's the tour going?" I asked between bites.

"Not bad," Joey said.

I turned to the group, figuring now was as good a time as any to hone some talk show skills. "Which would you say has been your favorite venue thus far?"

Silence.

"Who the fuck is this?" Johnny asked again.

The guys went back to talking amongst themselves, and I signaled to Tom to come get some fruit, then I took a seat in a folding chair next to the huge shaved-head guy.

He nodded at me. "You live in Vancouver?"

"Oh, no," I said. "I'm from New Jersey."

He seemed interested. "Yeah? You know any of the H.A.s back there?"

The ha's? I almost asked. "Oh, the Hells Angels? No. No, I don't." I tried to think of some other commonality but drew a blank and went back to my fruit plate. Tom was still standing next to the door, deciding what to do with his arms. He used his head to point toward the exit, then shot me a stare so penetrating I put the fruit down. I stood up.

"So, um, anyway, like I said, we're big fans, and it was a great show, and please be sure to tell Shrapnel that Alisyn says hi…if you see them soon. So, I guess we…should probably just…be…heading out…now…" I was speaking extra slowly in case the Ramones wanted us to get on their tour bus and head to their next show with them. We were almost at the door when I heard Joey say, "Wait."

It was so soft, I almost missed it.

Reaching down in the corner of the room, Joey brought up a three-foot-long cylinder of rolled-up brown paper. He held it out to me. "You can have this."

"Don't give her that," Johnny said.

"Take it," Joey said. "It got a little ripped during the show."

I snatched it from his hands before he could change his mind. "Thanks! OK, I guess we'll see you guys later."

I walked as calmly as possible behind Tom, step by deliberate step. Tom calmly opened the door, and I calmly shut it behind us. Then, we tore down the corridor, past the rectangular table, bursting through the double doors into the empty auditorium littered with cups and cigarette butts. We tore up the aisle, out the door, and all the way to the parking garage.

We ran past a group of drunk kids struggling with their car's bucket seats and didn't stop until we got to Tom's car. On his hood, I rolled the rubber band off the cylinder and started to unroll the curled paper. It was probably fifteen feet long, but two feet in, I saw the painted red Y and gasped. "It's the Gabba Gabba Hey poster!"

"We got the Gabba Gabba Hey poster!" Tom yelled.

"Well, rock out with your cock out!" one of the drunk kids yelled back.

I climbed into the passenger side, clutching the poster to my chest. That poster seemed to possess the power of Dorothy's ruby slippers. "I need to go home," I said.

"I know. It's late. We can probably make it in an hour."

"No, I have to go *home*-home," I said. "New Jersey. I want to go home."

Home is Where I Want to Be

I wrote a letter. In it, I described all the things I missed. My friends, my high school, the beach, the sun. I said I wanted to come back to New Jersey for my senior year. I stuck the letter in an envelope addressed to my old grade school, then shut my eyes for a silent prayer.

Dear Alisyn,

Remember me and my family? Well, The New School put your letter in the bulletin and my family and I would love to have you stay in my house. You would have your own bedroom and share a bathroom with my little brother and me. We also have a 7-month old standard poodle named Muffin.

Hope to hear from you!

Jane Babich

◄◄ II ►►

It was the last day of school in Bellingham. My junior year was over. I was walking up the Eriksen's outdoor cedar stairs when suddenly Jake was at the top of the steps.

"Hey, Al."

It had been almost two months since we'd seen each other at Chad's cabin. In that time, Jake hadn't called much, and I'd surrendered to his absence, sometimes trying to soothe it with a Saturday night 'shroom-fest or by kissing other boys.

"I wanted to come right over and see you as soon as I rolled in." He bounded down and wrapped me in his arms. I took his hand and led him to the boathouse. We sat on the edge of the bed. He pulled me onto his lap. He said his dad would be barbequing some salmon that night in the backyard. He hoped I could come.

"I have something to tell you," I said, sitting up. "I'm leaving."

"What do you mean?"

"I'm moving. Back to New Jersey. There's a family that says they'll take me in."

Jake leaned his head back to look into my eyes. "Why?"

"I want to go home. And just think, now you'll be able to do whatever you want. Stay out as late as you want, with whoever you want. Without me in the way." I wasn't sad or angry. In fact, a little pilot light of satisfaction had ignited in my chest; a glowing, perverse warmth from burning someone I thought had taken me for granted. I'd felt the same satisfying heat the day I told Mom I wasn't going with her.

Alisyn Adage #2 Redux—Leave People and They Love You More.

Jake's face crumbled. "I only want to be with you, Al."

He pulled me to his chest and I shut my eyes. And if a fairy godmother had offered me a chance to stay right there, just Jake and me, without his friends calling, without him vanishing, without my insecurities, without the hollowness in my stomach, I'd have taken her up on it. But I knew that Jake was holding me so tight because I was going away. I knew that in order to get him to love me forever, I had to leave.

PART FIVE

home/hōm/ *noun—1. of, relating to, or being a place of residence,*
place of origin;
2. the place in which one's domestic affections are centered;
3. the place where one lives permanently,
especially as a member of a family or household;
4. Monmouth County, New Jersey.

What a Long, Strange Trip

I landed at Newark Airport on a blindingly sunny July day. Out the airplane window, an industrial wasteland stretched across the horizon. Enormous oil drums belched dark gray smoke, and chemical plants coughed up the putrid smell of rotten eggs mixed with ammonia. Stepping off the plane, I breathed in deeply and smiled. Ahhh, my natural habitat.

I had a lot of catching up to do after eighteen months away. I skipped to the baggage area just in time to see Peter Reefer limping through the automatic glass doors. In my absence, there'd been another car accident. This time, Reefer was at the wheel and crashed head-on into a telephone pole, almost killing three of our friends. He survived with a metal rod for a femur and a permanent limp.

"Hey!" I called.

A lit cigarette balanced on his bottom lip. He yanked my bag off the carousel.

"We gotta go bail Annie out of jail," he told me. Apparently, half an hour earlier, he and Annie had gotten stoned, driven the wrong way down a one-way ramp, and gotten pulled over by airport police. The cops searched the car, discovered a dime bag in the glove compartment, and promptly arrested Annie for possession.

I locked my arms through his. "Home again, home again, jiggity-jig."

When I arrived in Shrewsbury, Sydney was waiting at her back door, and we hugged and laughed until we cried. Sydney set right to making me an iced coffee, and I went right to work on a brown bag full of fresh bagels, still warm from the store. I plopped down at the Shermans' kitchen table, the same table where I'd been eating bagels since kindergarten and felt my roots traveling through the floorboards and into the earth, reconnecting and repairing.

"I'm happy to see you still have your appetite, Sweetie," Mrs. Sherman said, leaning over and kissing the top of my head.

That afternoon when I showed up in Viv's driveway, she flung open her bedroom window and yelled, "Skin! Get in here! Come into my room. I've prepared a This-is-Your-Life-Skin-Musical-Medley!"

I raced in, sat on the edge of her bed, and listened as she lowered the needle on song after song: the B-52s, the Sex Pistols, Generation X. On about the third Patsy Cline song, I realized it was actually a This-is-Your-Life-Vivienne-Musical-Medley. I couldn't have cared less. I was so happy to be home. I stayed with Viv the first couple weeks while I waited for the Chevette to arrive, courtesy of the next-door guys in Bellingham, whom I'd convinced to drive an un-air-conditioned tin can across the country by assuring them I had hot friends at the ready.

The weather those weeks was made-to-order Jersey Shore: humid, sunny scorchers. I woke up hours before Viv and stood in a T-shirt at her kitchen counter, polishing off every single green grape that Mrs. O'Leary had washed and put in a red porcelain bowl, leaving a jumble of stems behind.

"If you can wake up your friend, I'll drop you girls off at the beach," Mrs. O'Leary said from the sink, knowing that was a high-risk proposition.

"Could be a challenge," I warned. She shook her head at me. I shook mine back.

I opened the door to Viv's pitch black, Arctically air-conditioned room, then lay on her other twin bed staring at the dark outline of her back. Even asleep, she reeked of smoke.

"Psst, Viv," I whispered. "Do you want to go to the beach?"

"What time is it?" she croaked.

"Almost nine."

"What the fuck!" She yanked the comforter over her head.

"What time do you want to get up?" I knew better.

"Jesus, Skin. *Shut up!*"

I smiled. Skin. She still called me Skin.

The second Viv's parents left for work, I opened their refrigerator and began foraging under foil with my fingers, gobbling up last night's cold roast beef and red potatoes off a platter. That month, no matter what I was doing, even eating leftovers in a still house, I felt a current of energy coursing up my spine. The crackling sensation of triumph over loss, an electrical charge from the sheer determination to be where I wanted to be. That year I'd read *The Odyssey* and knew that Odysseus had nothing on me. I'd survived a strange journey, too. And there was no sweeter victory than the victory of coming home.

◀◀ ▐▐ ▶▶

I'd been home for a day but couldn't abide even a short lapse in attachment to a desirable guy. My first choice was Tommy Kelly. I didn't know him personally, but he was famous at Red Bank Regional in the way that handsome, shaggy-haired, pot-smoking, captains of the football team who surf at sunrise and listen to the Grateful Dead are.

That summer, Tommy could be spotted tan and shirtless, chain-sawing branches and planting perennials as part of a landscaping crew on the road to the beach. Tommy's family lived in an Italianate-style Victorian in Little Silver with a grand wrap-around porch and lots of second-floor balconies next to sturdy oak trees, which he and his four siblings shimmied down after their parents fell asleep.

In a town of abundant parties, the Kelly kids' blowouts were top tickets, filled with Dead Heads, punk rockers, prepsters, and football players— Tommy was friends with the Black and white players alike. He had an easy laugh and a detachment that drew people toward him. That detachment held big appeal for me.

I didn't want to be too demanding of God, so I merely asked him to send me a boyfriend "like Tommy Kelly." But in my experience, God can be pretty literal, so he immediately sent Tommy Kelly himself. Viv and I were cutting through some bushes into the inky darkness of another backyard party when I saw his silhouette passing.

"Hi," I said.

"Oh, hey," Tommy replied, and in that momentary brush, I could feel the spark. That summer, I had acquired a magical power, a magnet that had turned on while I was gone. Even the kids that hadn't previously paid any attention to me, like Tommy, now wanted to know my deal—not in intricate detail, of course; no one other than Sydney cared to hear my diatribes on the differences between East and West Coasters. No, the guys like Tommy were satisfied with the basics: I had vanished, and now I was back, and I'd chosen them over whatever else was out there.

In my time away, I had also missed the break-up and back-together cycles that had left the rest of the crowd burned out and bored of each other. I was new yet familiar, friendly yet mysterious, and unsullied by baggage—at least not the kind they could see. Also, and this was perhaps the biggest draw of all: I came back alone. As anyone knows, an unparented seventeen-year-old in a bikini and a Chevette can be a very shiny object. And for that sparkling summer, I stepped into the sunshine.

◄◄ ❚❚ ►►

Five of us sat in a loose circle of lounge chairs at Michelle's beach club, the sharp smell of cold chlorine clearing my nostrils. I was lying on my stomach, my head propped on bent elbows, bouncing my heels together, sending warm grains of sand down the backs of my legs, too excited to lay still.

"So, Tommy calls my house first thing this morning and says, 'Hey, your friend Alisyn. You have to introduce me.'" Viv laughed like an evil genius.

"Tommy Kelly was my first kiss," Sydney said. "In eighth grade. Yes, I know. I was a late bloomer. Goody-goody Sydney. I wasn't making out with Ethan like you were in, what, fifth grade?"

"Sixth," I said.

"Or having sex with Joey Ramone, like Viv probably did at nine years old."

"Eight," Viv said, taking a long drag of her cigarette for comedic effect.

I was back with a vengeance, back at the beach with these girls who spoke my language and shared each other's secrets. Back where I knew the rules of summer nights and station wagon back seats. Back on the terra firma of pineapple-free pizza, in the land of long vowels and Jersey accents.

That month, Sydney told a vivid story of a girl loudly interrupting a school assembly with a dirty comment. Sydney was a great storyteller. She described the teachers' shock in hilarious detail, and I was cracking up, until I stopped.

"Wait a minute," I said. "That didn't happen at RBR. That was Bellingham! A Bunny did that. That's MY story!"

"Oh, my God!" Sydney started choking on her own saliva. "I've heard your stories so much I think they're mine!"

I loved how even though I'd left, our lives had stayed braided together in the kind of connectedness that deposited each other's stories into our own memory banks.

"So, Dave Vogt stopped by my house yesterday," Sydney went on. "He rang the front doorbell. I was so excited until I realized he was looking for *you*."

I clicked my heels faster.

"Decisions, decisions," Michelle laughed.

My friends saw me. I mattered again. The sensation in my body that month was beyond bliss; it was fuel-injected euphoria vibrating through every vein, filling me with the deepest sense of belonging I'd known in my seventeen years. I'd crawled my way back to New Jersey, and now every cell was wide open with anticipation, knowing that on any given night, at any backyard party, anything was possible. Sydney would later describe that summer as tremulous.

"That's the only word for it," she said. "Everything was tremulous."

We left the beach and went to Michelle's brother's apartment to raid his fridge for beer. I only had a few bucks, but I asked Michelle if I could leave a dollar on the counter and make a long-distance call.

Mom picked up on the first ring. "So? How is it?"

I told her how happy I was, how thrilling it was to be back together with my friends. And that Shrapnel was playing later at the Fast Lane. I told her I'd gotten a job at my childhood haunt Friendly's—the same place where Frankie, Annie, and I used to leave without tipping the waitresses.

Mom laughed. "Ah, your comeuppance."

"It's just so wonderful, Mom, to be home."

"You know, of course, it was Thomas Wolfe who said, 'You can't go home again.' But you've proved him wrong. You did it. You stayed away just the right amount of time, long enough to be missed but not so long that anything changed. And who knows? Maybe our strange detour to Bellingham worked out after all."

Something about her way of describing that tumultuous time struck a chord. It was a strange detour. And now it felt fated. Of course, I was destined to move next door to Jake and to find Hera. And destined to come back home stronger than I'd left. That day with a cold beer in my hand and the Go-Go's cranked on the stereo, it seemed like maybe Mom's take was right, maybe it had all worked out, maybe no lasting harm was done, maybe the palm reader was wrong. In that heady moment, I remember thinking life was perfect: Mom and I loved each other but she was hundreds of miles away and no longer in control of my fate. Jake was thousands of miles away, yet still called and wrote love letters. And after so much loss, I felt I had reclaimed myself.

The Safety Dance

The neighbor guys from Bellingham finally showed up with my car, and I paid my debt by encouraging two friends to fool around with them. It wasn't a hard sell—the guys were cute, so the girls didn't notice I was pimping them out. Reuniting with the Chevette kicked my unbridled freedom into high gear. Now I could go anywhere, do anything. I could swing by Sydney's job at Cumberland Farms to watch her slice cold cuts. I could drive to Viv's beach club and order lunch with an unsuspecting girl's membership number.

I drove wantonly wherever my last twenty bucks would take me, cruising around Shrewsbury like I owned the joint, smiling at street signs, Sunnybank, Silverbrook, Sycamore. Since returning, my sense of belonging to those streets was so strong that I felt as though my car were traveling through the town's very arteries, which carried the lifeblood of my memories. Home had absorbed and metabolized me. Shrewsbury Liquors, the Shrewsbury Diner, the discount clothing shop, I treated like long-lost relatives. Hello, Dunkin' Donuts! Don't you look tempting…Martinizing Dry Cleaners, you used to clean Dad's shirts, right? What's up, Planned Parenthood? Remember me?

Now, in the driver's seat, I saw old landmarks anew. The engraved marble of the Rumson Country Club—once cold and off-putting—now part of my personal roadmap. Even the scenes of past car crashes were stripped of trauma and bathed only in warm nostalgia. But nothing made my heart swell like the Sea Bright Bridge; kids on banana seats pedaling across, towels spilling from their beach bags. And just beyond it, spreading its wide welcoming arms, my old friend, the Atlantic Ocean, its whitecaps winking.

◄◄ ❚❚ ►►

The family that took me in, the Babichs, lived exactly thirteen miles and twenty-three minutes from Sydney's house. They had a son and daughter several years younger than me and probably believed I could act as an au pair for the kids or at least a responsible role model. But I had other plans.

Just as with the Eriksens, I'd arranged to give the Babichs most of the money Dad sent each month for child support. The Babichs would be getting a deal, I figured, since I planned to primarily use their house as a crash pad while I spent every waking moment at Sydney and Viv's houses or the beach or a party. I suppose the Babichs and I should have talked through our expectations before I arrived so they didn't wait for me to eat dinner or expect me to come home before my customary 2:00 a.m. Truth was, had we talked when I was still in Bellingham, I would have agreed to anything. In fact, if the warden at Rahway State Prison had offered me a cement cell, three hots, and a cot, I would have said yes just to be back in New Jersey.

For the first couple of weeks, I tried to comply with the Babichs' requests. I occasionally set the table and talked to their kids. I even petted their poodle, before immediately blazing back to the beach. I guess it was bound to blow up, but I was too drunk on belonging to see that.

Tommy and I struck up a frothy summer romance, spending every night together at parties or beach bars in Sea Bright. In the mornings, he went to his landscaping job, and I went to blend up a boatload of Fribbles at Friendly's before meeting back up. On our days off, he went surfing early, then snuck me through the back of his beach club, where I spent the day dodging the darting eyes of the owner. In the late afternoons, we hit Moby's deck over the ocean for pitchers of cold beer and buckets of buttery steamers at sunset. I knew he'd be leaving soon for Villanova in September, and that was fine—as long as he didn't leave *me*.

◀◀ ⏸ ▶▶

I was ecstatic to be home but Sydney couldn't wait to leave. She was a year older than I and felt she'd outgrown Shrewsbury and her oppressively blue bathroom. She yearned to be free of a curfew and the parental monitoring of clothing choices and caloric intake. But I knew we'd never have another hot

August where I lay on her bed in my Friendly's uniform, watching her rage against the suffocating safety of her home, feeling an affection so deep for the closest thing to a sister I'd ever had.

The day Sydney was leaving, I got to her house at 8:00 a.m. and went straight to her bed. I watched her buzz around the room, darting from closet to dresser, packing pens, a flat desk calendar, pillowcases. She grabbed sweaters from a shelf, folded them into her suitcase, then yanked them out again. I lay motionless, my eyes burning.

"Do you think I should just have my mom bring up my sweaters at Parents' Weekend?" she asked.

I didn't respond. How could she focus on fall fashion when *I didn't want her to go?*

"Sydney!" Mrs. Sherman gasped at the doorway. "That's too much to fit into your suitcase. You won't be able to close it."

"I'll close it," Sydney barked. Mrs. Sherman's footsteps retreated down the hall.

Alisyn Adage #6: Only Kids Who Know Their Parents Will Never Leave Have the Luxury of Hating Them.

"Come out to the porch with me to have a cigarette," Sydney said.

"I think I'm going to throw up," I told her.

"Well, don't do it in my bed. My mom won't have time to change the sheets." Sydney stood at her mirror, stopping to brush her hair.

"Don't go!" I howled at her reflection. Sydney was speeding forward, and I wanted time to stop. I knew she would be back for Thanksgiving and Christmas, but I also knew that by then, she would have new friends and new memories that I wasn't part of.

"Don't you understand?" I said to her back. "It will never be like this again. It will never be this good."

Why was I the only person who could feel loss before someone left?

Mrs. Sherman reentered and came to me. "Sweetie, you're going to have to get up. I need to make the bed. I can't leave with it unmade." I used my palms to dam the tears draining onto Sydney's pillow.

"You and Sydney will always be friends," she said, as she started to tug the sheets, making the bed with me in it. "Now, Sweetie," she said, petting my head. "Go to the kitchen. I got fresh bagels."

Checkmate. Game over. Mrs. Sherman knew me too well.

The automatic garage door glided up, and the station wagon backed out, stickers of Sydney's Ivy League school already festooning the back bumper. I stood in the driveway next to Rachel and started waving before Dr. Sherman put the car into drive.

"I miss you!!" I yelled.

"I haven't left yet," Sydney said out the window.

The car rolled forward. I watched the brake lights flare at the end of the driveway and the right blinker flash, then the station wagon turned onto Sycamore and pulled away.

◀◀ ❚❚ ▶▶

Thank God Viv wasn't going anywhere. Being with Viv was just as thrilling and dangerous as ever. I was with her day and night that summer, chasing after her into various cars and bars, while she imitated the Safety Dance video just to make me laugh. Yet I never once saw Viv do drugs. Unlike her extravagant drunken episodes, her drug use was so covert, I sometimes naively wondered if it was real. I did not understand yet that hardcore addicts don't do their drugs at parties. They don't like to share them.

One night Viv insisted I take her to a friend's house in Eatontown, which I didn't want to do since it was 10:00 p.m. and I had to work the next morning. Her friend's name was Kenny Da Chemist, and, yes, I took that as a clue that he might dabble in drugs. Though the moniker was so over-the-top, part of me imagined being greeted by a goggle-wearing scientist in a white lab coat with steaming beakers and Bunsen burners behind him.

I parked the Chevette in a gravelly driveway and got a bad feeling even before we walked up his cracked cement stairs. Beige paint peeled from the wood door frame like dead skin after a sunburn. A TV blared. Viv rapped on his door. Nothing. She rapped again.

"Who is it?" A man's voice growled.

"Avon calling." Viv sang in a creepy lilt.

The door ripped open. A guy with stringy dishwater hair and sunken eyes stood backlit through the screen. He was probably fifteen years older than us.

"Vivienne O'Leary, as I live and breathe," he said. He licked his lips. "To what do I owe this pleasure?"

Viv pushed past him. Kenny Da Chemist's couch was vomit yellow. Foam burst from rips in the cushions, and the coffee table was littered with empty beer bottles and two ashtrays overflowing in gray volcanoes. In the middle of the table was the top of a battered board game, Candyland, turned upside down and holding a pack of Marlboro Reds, a lighter, a razor, and a baggie of pills. Pink pills, black and white pills. A Good-n-Plenty collection of pills.

Kenny eyeballed me. "Who's your friend?"

"Oh, please. Don't even think about it," Viv said. "She's much too good for you."

"Is that right?" Kenny cocked his head and leered at me. "I don't suppose this is a courtesy call to check on my health."

"You don't offer your guests a drink?" Viv said.

"Oh, where are my manners?" he said with mock graciousness. "And while I'm fetching you a refreshment, you get out the money you owe me."

"Whatever." Viv took a drag off a cigarette and held up her left middle finger. She sat down. Kenny went into his kitchen. A refrigerator door shut. A bottle cap clicked on a counter. I sat on the edge of the sofa.

"I don't want a beer," I whispered to Viv. "I gotta get home."

Viv stabbed out her cigarette and stood up. Relief washed over me. Then she bent over the table and, in one quick swoop, swiped the bag of pills out of the Candyland box and dropped them down her shirt. My throat closed.

"Whoa, whoa, whoa," Kenny said, coming out with a beer bottle in each hand. "Not so fast, ladies." He blocked Viv's path to the door. "I appreciate the visit, but I'd appreciate the money more." He pressed his forearm against Viv's chest and backed her up, pushing her back down on the sofa. Kenny put the beers down and reached for the Marlboros in the box. His head shot up.

"Hey! Where's the bag?"

"What bag?" Viv said too quickly.

"The fucking bag of pills I had right here." He picked up the Candyland box and looked around the table. "They were right here." He started pulling up the cushions. "What did you do with them?"

"I don't know," Viv shrugged. "But we gotta head out."

From behind, it looked like Kenny had fallen to the floor to look under the sofa, but then he sprang up like a jack-in-box with a small black object in his right hand. He pointed a gun at Viv's head.

"Give me the fucking pills!" he yelled. The gun was four inches from her frozen face. I screamed, and Kenny wheeled around, the round black hole of the barrel pointing at my chest.

"You got 'em?" he yelled.

"Give him the pills!" I screamed.

Kenny spun back toward Viv just as she lifted the bottom of her sweater. The baggie fell to the floor with a soft slap.

Viv made her eyes wide. "How did *those* get in there?"

"Get the fuck out of here," Kenny said. I started moving, not knowing whether to run or walk, but certain he was going to shoot us both in the back. Viv grabbed her pocketbook. I fumbled with the door handle, then didn't take a breath until I was gunning it in reverse out of his driveway. I looked to Viv for some explanation, apology, anything.

"He's such an asshole," she said. She struck a match, lit her cigarette, and we drove off into the night.

This Must Be the Place

I got kicked out of the Babichs on one of the tamest nights that summer. No party. No Shrapnel show. Viv, Peter Reefer, Tommy, and I had gone to Barnacle Bills for a drink, then down to Sea Bright to hang out on the dark sand, drinking beer, talking, and laughing. It was the end of the night, time to wrap it up. That's when we realized we had nowhere to sleep.

The Babichs were on a family vacation. Before leaving they had given me explicit instructions not to enter their home while they were gone. I had agreed, assuming I could stay at Viv's or with other friends. But Viv had lied to her parents that she'd be babysitting the Babich kids with me that night. We couldn't show back up now. We couldn't sleep at Tommy's house. His mom had flipped out a week earlier when she caught me sleeping there. Reefer had a million siblings and no spare beds.

What harm could there be in going to the home where I actually paid rent? I assumed the Babichs' strict instructions not to enter were meant to keep me from *partying* in their home, not sleeping. I warned the gang that we could *not* disturb anything and *had* to leave the instant we woke up. There could be no beer drinking or loitering.

Everyone complied with my rules, though once inside, I couldn't resist a quick tour of their suburban oddities, such as the stationary bike in front of the widescreen TV, with an ashtray on the handlebars so Mr. Babich could chain smoke *while exercising*. We all slept in my room, Tommy and me on top of my twin bed, Reefer and Viv on the floor with pillows. At 7:00 a.m., the guys had to leave for landscaping. We exited without eating and quietly shut the door.

On Monday morning at the appointed hour, while Viv slept, I stood in her kitchen and called the Babichs to determine what time I should return to their home. Mr. Babich took the call. He told me he knew I'd been in the house. A neighbor had seen my car in the driveway and reported it to them.

They wanted me out immediately. No if, ands, or buts. I tried to plead my case, begging him to listen. He wouldn't. He told me to come collect my stuff right away. He was adamant. It was over.

I hung up and stared at the phone on the wall. Then the floor dropped out from under me, and I fell into an empty elevator shaft, the only cable tethering me to New Jersey suddenly severed.

That night I slept in my car in the A&P parking lot. I woke up on the surface of the sun, my mouth as dry as sandpaper, sunbeams broiling me through the windshield. Delivery men were unloading produce two feet from my window—and I was startled and embarrassed that they'd seen me.

The next night, I slept on the beach. Tommy and I found a stretch of sand on the ocean side of an abandoned house in Long Branch. I woke up alone, covered in dew and salt and sand. Tommy's T-shirt, which I'd used as a sheet, was balled up beside me. The sun was rising fast, as if on a pulley over the Atlantic, shining a spotlight directly on me. I sat up and saw surfers in wetsuits already bobbing on swells and an old man in swim trunks striding along the sand. A scratchy self-consciousness crawled across my shoulders. The shame of being seen with no shelter. I stared out at the waves and racked my brain. In times of despair, I often imagined a stranger coming to my rescue, but I didn't know which road to drive down to meet that rescuer. Maybe the old guy in swim trunks had a spare room.

I had to tell Mom not to call me at the Babichs anymore. I had to admit that they'd kicked me out. I heard her suck in her breath.

"So, you'll come to Pittsburgh."

The thought was unbearable. "I can't, Mom. I can't leave again."

"Well, if you don't find a place by Saturday, Mac and I will come get you, and you'll do senior year here."

The Babichs weren't the only parents who were sick of my antics. I'd already tested the patience of the Shermans and O'Learys and Kellys by flouting their curfews, tracking sand through their living rooms, and standing in their kitchens eating them out of house and home. I was too ashamed to tell any of them that I'd been kicked out of the Babichs. I knew no one else wanted to take me in.

That afternoon, I showed up at Friendly's with sand stuck to my skin. I didn't have anywhere to shower or wash my white ruffled apron, still smeared with strawberry syrup from my last shift. And when my shift ended, I was too sticky and tired to find Tommy or Viv. I planned to sleep on the beach again. But just as I went out Friendly's back door, fat raindrops started to fall. I ran for the Chevette, sliding in as the sky opened and crashed. A classic Jersey thunderstorm.

I drove up and down Route 35, my old street, until a secluded corner of the ShopRite parking lot summoned me. Funny how familiar that parking lot felt after all the times Mom and I strolled across it for groceries, our pinkies intertwined on the cart. I didn't want to risk waking up in the middle of morning deliveries again, so I pulled the Chevette around back against a line of dark trees and reclined the seat. In a minute, I was out cold.

Even with my eyes closed, I sensed a shift in the rhythm of the taps, something different from the raindrops on the roof. A persistent rapping. A man's face at the window. I was a heavy sleeper, so it took a moment for the pieces to pixelate into place. I pulled the lever and raised my seat. I rolled the glass down an inch.

"What are you doing here, Miss?" The cop looked past me into the passenger seat, shining his flashlight over it, then onto the empty back seat, then into my face.

"Oh, sorry, Officer. I was just resting for a minute."

He narrowed his eyes. "Where do you live?"

Well, that's a long story. I didn't know that strange cars in dark parking lots attract police attention, and for a second, I thought this might be the rescue I was waiting for. That night the idea of a locked cell, a hard cot, and a hot meal sounded like something akin to a home. But one look at this cop's baby face told me he wouldn't be my savior. He didn't know what to do. He wasn't even asking for my license. He shined his flashlight into the back seat again.

"I live right over there," I lied. "In Little Silver."

"Why are you sleeping here?"

"Oh. I work at Friendly's." I gestured to my modern-day milkmaid uniform, now doubling as a nightgown, as though that would explain all my recent life choices. "I got off late. I was worried about driving in the storm. I decided to wait it out here."

"You should go home," he said.

If only.

"Okay, will do, Officer. Thanks so much!" I rolled up the window. I slowly adjusted the rearview mirror, fiddled around as if looking for my keys, adjusted the rearview mirror again, then had no choice but to start the ignition. He stayed in his car, watching me until I backed up and pulled away.

Nothing to Do, Nowhere to Go

The rain had stopped but the streets were still wet as I drove up and down them, searching for somewhere else to sleep. I knew these streets so well—Ridge, River, Prospect—but in the quiet of that dark night, I was lost and couldn't see which way led to shelter. For the rest of my life, I would never forget the feeling of being utterly alone and exhausted, searching the dark for some hidden shelter.

You should go home, the cop said.

Yes, of course. Home. Why hadn't I thought of that? I could see my house. The snow-white cement and shiny black shutters set on the upward slope of the front yard, as if on a pedestal, behind our white picket fence. I'd driven by it a dozen times in the past month and noticed the giant sunflowers back in their August bloom.

When I got there, the driveway was empty. I swung into the dirt patch under the Norway maples, where Mom and Dad used to park side by side. Even in the darkness, I knew I was home, and it felt so good to be back. Technically it *was* still my house. The renters were deadbeats. Maybe they'd moved out. Good riddance.

I walked up the old cement steps to the screen door as I'd done a thousand times and gave a gentle tug. Unlocked. It had been almost two years since I'd been inside and walking in felt triumphant. I'd come home. Look, the laundry room! That cramped walk-through where the hulking Maytags used to shake violently. God, I *knew* that smell. That mix of damp concrete and detergent.

I entered the hub of our old life, the kitchen, and though dark, got an instant rush from the familiar parquet floor and the cherry wood cabinet where I used to stash my babysitting cash. Then I turned toward the sink, and the sight straightened my spine like a record scratching. Our clean countertop was buried under stacks of dirty dishes. The spot where Mom's cutting board sat every night—with its neat piles of chopped herbs—lost in someone's filth. I was stunned but too tired to turn back or see any warning signs. Being in survival mode can apply some sturdy blinders to your field of vision. I padded up the staircase, ready to collapse in the comfort of my old bed.

When I got to the door of my room, I stopped cold. The window shades were up, moonlight pouring in. My mattress lay naked and exposed, splotched with stains. A twisted white bed sheet, the kind an inmate might use to escape out a prison window, was knotted on top. There was no pillowcase or comforter. A strip of wallpaper next to my bed— where my Shrapnel poster once hung—was torn off, leaving two open wounds in the paint.

Just then, I heard a long low groan, followed by a thud. It came from the TV room right down the hallway. Next, hard footsteps. I'd traveled that path a thousand times and knew that in a matter of seconds, the monster would be at my bedroom door. There was no time to get out. I dove into the closet. Curling into a ball, I covered my mouth, my heart pounding over the heavy footfalls.

A presence entered and collapsed on the mattress, the springs squealing under his weight. From the back of the closet, I wanted to call the police. *There's an intruder in my house!* But which one of us was it? I waited for his labored breathing to shift to snoring, then crawled out on all fours, arms shaking, down the stairs. I ran out the back door, threw myself in the car, and peeled out with no headlights.

I let the Earth's eastward gravitational pull steer the Chevette seven miles back to the ocean, back to the abandoned beach house that was starting to feel like home. I killed the engine and rested my head on the wheel, crying and searching for a plan, but nothing came. Out the windshield, I watched the gray horizon slowly brighten to a pale blue over the water. The hypnotic waves rolled in, churning the water white in violent crashes, always another swell building behind the last, another chance at the perfect lift, the perfect ride into shore amid the turbulence. The Atlantic Ocean possessed a lot of power, but even it couldn't solve this problem. I clicked on the radio and got clobbered with the incoming message. The Cosmic DJ in the Sky having a laugh at my expense. The Ramones. Of course.

Nothing to do

Nowhere to go-oh…

I let out a snort. There *was* nothing to do. There was nowhere to go. No other place I wanted to be, nowhere else with the same salty air and early morning lemony light. At seventeen, I already knew that geography was destiny. I knew I was who I was because I was born in Monmouth County, New Jersey, where the beach always beckoned and the radio played the Ramones, even at 6:00 a.m.

The sky had turned a cloudless electric blue. Warm air poured through the top of my window. It was already getting hot, the start of another perfect beach day. I rolled down the window and started to sing out to the ocean.

Get me to the show

Hurry, hurry, hurry, before I go loco!

I turned the key. I still had a few hours of aimless loops around Little Silver before I could show up at Viv's for breakfast without arousing suspicion. Passing an Exxon station, my eyes grazed my gas gauge, the needle still stuck on E as it had been for days. Three more days until I could collect my first paycheck. If I didn't find somewhere to live by then, I'd have to leave again.

◀◀ ❚❚ ▶▶

I sat on the black vinyl couch in Viv's basement and finally admitted the truth: I was homeless. Mrs. O'Leary looked pained. "You can stay here a few nights. But I can't have you live here. I would if I could." I understood. She had her hands full. "Can't you go live with your mom?"

Tears spilled down my cheeks. "I can't move again," I told her. "This is where I belong."

Mrs. O'Leary's eyes welled up, and she reached for my hand. And then something extraordinary happened, something I never thought I'd see. Viv started crying, too.

"Oh, Skin," she said, leaning over and embracing me. Then Mrs. O'Leary hugged both of us and we all dabbed at tears.

"What does your mom say?" Mrs. O'Leary asked.

"She said I should ask you if you know anyone who might take in a boarder."

"A boarder." Mrs. O'Leary repeated, straightening up. "Hmm. Let me think about that. Actually, I think I heard that Audrey Maxwell might have a boarder."

"Not our drama teacher!" Viv exclaimed.

Amazingly, Mrs. Maxwell answered when I called. It was true. She did indeed have a boarder. Even better, she told me she wanted her current boarder to move out. Astonishingly, she said I could live with her. Mrs. Maxwell delivered all this news matter-of-factly, as if she hadn't just saved me from a life in the Shop-Rite parking lot. The only issue, she said, was that she'd have to give her current tenant a couple weeks to get out before I could move in.

"I kind of need a place *now*."

◀◀ ❚❚ ▶▶

Mom and Mac drove from Pittsburgh that Saturday to move my belongings out of the Babichs'. Mr. Babich opened the front door, face tight, cigarette smoldering, and Mac met that glare with his own burning cigarette. No one apologized to anyone. I don't even remember Mac extinguishing his cigarette before running a vacuum across the rug in the room that had been mine. I was impressed by Mac's angry asshole act. It felt good to have an asshole on my side, too.

We drove my stuff over to Mrs. Maxwell's, where her boarder was still in the bedroom. My new roommate, this thirty-something-year-old man, did not appear to be as excited about our arrangement as I was, which I deduced from his harrumphing as I stacked my boxes in the corner of our small, shared space, before plopping down on my empty twin bed, six feet from his.

On my second night there, at about 3:00 a.m., I awoke to see my new roommate bolt upright in bed. He stared straight ahead into our silent room, like Frankenstein slowly animating. I pretended to be asleep but kept one eye cracked, my nerve endings twitching. He sat ramrod straight, not moving a muscle for a solid spooky minute, then suddenly collapsed back down onto the mattress. *Oh, great*, I said to my aerial cameraman, *I'm sharing a bedroom with a narcoleptic nut job. Oh, well, whatever.* I exhaled and rolled over. It was just so good to have a home.

◀◀ ❚❚ ▶▶

"She's back, Motherfuckeys!" Frankie said, as I marched through the glass doors of Red Bank Regional for my triumphant return.

I stopped to take a deep breath, filling my lungs with RBR. Sloppy Joes, it seemed, would be served for lunch. I must be in heaven.

Rachel Sherman sidled up to me.

"Is it as glorious as you remembered? Ha! Do you regret coming back yet?"

"Never!" I said, flinging an arm in the air and spinning, à la Vivienne, all the way down the hall into my glorious senior year at the Shangri-La I'd crawled my way back to.

College Bound

One year after we fled Olympia, Walter wrote Mom a letter.

> *Dear Catherine,*
>
> *I don't know if this will reach you. I'm counting on an old address. It's a letter that has to be written for my own peace of mind. It is a letter of apology and appreciation. Apology from one human being who knows now he hurt another for whom he cared very much. For all that I did to hurt you, dear friend, I am sorry...*

Mom read the letter aloud to me as she sat with Mac at their kitchen table in Pittsburgh during one of my visits. In it, Walter described how karma had indeed caught up to him, how his girlfriend had left him, and he'd become estranged from his three daughters.

"He's looking for closure from you," Mac said to Mom.

"I don't feel I need to give him that," Mom replied. She wanted to know what I thought.

I shrugged. "Tell him, I told him so."

As happy as I was to have returned to New Jersey, I still carried seething anger and self-righteous outrage about being uprooted to begin with. If there were a Girl Scout badge for grudges, I'd have sewn it to my chest.

Somehow, from Shrewsbury to Olympia, Olympia to Bellingham, from Mac's cabin to the Eriksens' lake house, from the Babichs' to Mrs. Maxwell's, I managed to hang onto an old aluminum popcorn tin; a rusted barrel, filled with concert stubs, love notes, and report cards, ephemera of past chapters, including stacks of handwritten letters from Mom, starting the day after she left Bellingham. Most of them were records of her daily doings, recipes she thought I should try, articles she thought I would like.

Some of the envelopes remained sealed. I'd tucked them away unopened after I decided I no longer had time to incorporate her into my life. Only years later would I see that she was trying to connect with me. Trying to do it the way she knew how—her personal love language—words on a page in thoughtful, precise prose.

Dear Al: (11/25/83)

I've just finished writing my paper for work and treated myself by reading a few pages of a book that Nancy gave me, The Road Less Traveled. Some of the lines I type now for you seem to be part of the answer, at least for me, of why we took our journey two years ago this weekend when there seemed not to be any immediate material gains.

> *"As we negotiate the curves and corners of our lives, we must continually give up parts of ourselves. The only alternative to this giving up is not to travel at all on the journey of life. It may seem strange, but most people choose this alternative and elect not to continue with their life journeys—to stop short by some distance—in order to avoid the pain of giving up parts of themselves. If it does seem strange, it is because you do not understand the depth of the pain that may be involved. In its major forms, giving up is the most painful of human experiences."*

Perhaps you can use some of this material in writing your Boston Univ. scholarship essay. I'll include the bibliographical info on this book in case you want to quote it and need to cite sources. Mrs. Sherman told me Rachel mailed away all her applications. Please finish and mail yours quickly. Mrs. Sherman also wondered when you are going to study for your achievement tests. It's a good question. Talk soon.

Love, Mom

I filled out my college applications alone at Mrs. Maxwell's kitchen table. I picked schools out of a giant directory that Rachel loaned me and only applied to colleges that had campus TV stations. That was one constant in my life: I was going to find a way to become a TV reporter. I can't remember if I read my essays to Mom or anyone else or even proofread them myself before mailing them off.

When the acceptance letters came back, I felt nothing, neither excitement nor apprehension. As much as I wanted to be a TV reporter, I didn't want to go to college. I couldn't bear to leave home again. I didn't care about "the college experience," and I suspected it could never hold a candle to my high school experience.

But I couldn't stay in Monmouth County either. Mrs. Maxwell's generosity could only mask the truth for so long: I didn't have a home here. Then, another letter arrived. American University was offering me a full four-year scholarship. The die was cast. I was college bound.

The day I left New Jersey was excruciating. In my mind, I'd made it home, only to leave again. The drive to campus took four hours. Mom drove me. I cried the whole way.

◄◄ ❚❚ ►►

The second we pulled onto the campus, I saw Hera. She was standing at the top of the stairs outside the student center. Right where she said she'd be. Before I left Bellingham, she and I hatched a scheme to go to college together. Throughout my senior year, anytime I visited a school, be it Harvard or BU, I wrote Hera an after-action report on whether we should attend (oh, I'm pretty sure Harvard would have taken us if we'd *tried*). On the day I visited American, I called Hera from a payphone at the Tombs (a bar actually on *Georgetown's* campus, but I didn't fully grasp the difference). I told her we should go to American, based on my scholarship and the fact that they played good music at the Tombs. And now here she was, as promised. I ran up the steps of the student center and locked my arm tight through hers.

Hera was excited to get to orientation, look for cute guys, and see what adventures awaited us. But I wanted to call Tommy at Villanova and go back to New Jersey. I didn't want any new friends. I wanted to stay superglued to my high school friends. And if I couldn't go backward, I wanted to jump forward to being a reporter.

On the first day of freshman orientation, two hundred wannabe broadcast journalists crowded into the School of Communications auditorium to hear from our dean for the first time. Her goal was to give us a reality check.

"I know you all want to be network anchors," she said, "but look around this room. Only two of you will ever make it to the network level."

I sat up and craned my head to see who the other person was.

◄◄ ❚❚ ►►

I found the door marked WAVE-TV, the campus TV station, and entered the cramped space, filled with folding tables holding Beta tape machines and typewriters. I announced I wanted to be a TV reporter. The station's general manager, a well-dressed senior, and I'd later learn, daughter of a bigshot network executive, told me that was nice, but I would have to audition along with the other two hundred students who wanted that very same thing. In the meantime, she said, I could sell ad space on the station airwaves to local merchants. That sounded "professional" to me, so a couple afternoons a week, I sat in that cramped space dialing for dollars.

On the night of the on-camera auditions, I showed up without a clue about what to do, then stood in a line of eager anchor-wannabes already clad in jewel tones. As the hours ticked by, I moved to sit on the cement steps next to a mini-Bryant Gumbel, who had clearly devoted his youth to studying Gumbel's delivery and mannerisms. He wore the same round-rimmed glasses as Gumbel and appeared to use the same tailor. Somehow, other kids knew that success required methodical steps. All I knew was that I wanted it.

I blew the audition. I had no idea how to read a teleprompter or write a script or perform a stand-up. So, I kept selling ad space, and as is sometimes the case in life, if you hang around long enough, people start to associate you with a place. Then, one night, someone calls in sick, and you end up being the only person in that zipcode with a pulse interested in anchoring the evening newscast. And that's what happened.

For all my (misplaced) confidence in future career success, emotionally, I was stunted. The gray stone buildings of campus could not compare to the Technicolor intensity of my high school experience. No party felt as intense, and no new classmate seemed as special as my old friends. I had nothing but disdain for the binge drinking and sloppy dorm hookups around me. It all seemed so juvenile, so tired. I faked it by going with Hera to frat parties and orientation mixers, but it felt like manufactured fun. I half-heartedly hooked up with a frat boy for a few weeks, then a guy in my Constitutional Law class, thinking that might be the secret to belonging, but it wasn't. My new classmates didn't dress like my high school friends and didn't have the same humor. Even when they listened to the same music, it was all wrong.

One day I heard Squeeze wafting from a dorm room. I followed "Another Nail in My Heart" down the hallway, hoping it led back to Mark's smoky bedroom in Red Bank or some facsimile of that scene. But when I reached the door, strangers were inside, speaking with Long Island accents, looking nothing like Winkie or Matt or Mark. I backed away, hating them for not being my old friends.

Sometime that fall, Viv called my dorm room to tell me that Shrapnel had broken up. I sat alone on my floor crying, knowing that for me, everything always ended too soon.

Well, last night just wasn't long enough…

Same as It Ever Was

Those first couple years at college, I spent a lot of time visiting my New Jersey friends. I drove to their schools on weekends, hoping to recapture the magic and routine of our old dynamic. But my old friends had new friends. Sydney and Annie and Tommy were happy to include me in their college worlds, at their new bars and parties, but I was only interested in the old us—the way we were back home. Occasionally, I got my way. On Thanksgiving weekend, we'd return to Monmouth County like homing pigeons, winging our way back, our internal compasses set to a bar in Sea Bright, fluttering through the festive crowd of old faces. On those weekends, I stayed at Sydney's house, which I treated as my own.

One Thanksgiving weekend, Sydney and I went to visit Viv for the afternoon. Viv had never left for college. She'd recently gotten out of another rehab, which her family hoped meant she was clean and sober. She still lived at home, but she too had new friends. She was excited for us to meet her boyfriend, a guy named Ripper from a couple towns over.

Viv's house was just as it always was, her mom with a warm smile at the sink preparing lunch, her dad booming in and out of the kitchen, peppering us with questions about our classes.

"You're reading Dostoevsky, I presume."

"Oh, yes," Sydney responded. "I have a brilliant professor walking us through it right now. It's like a wonderful docent tour."

"I'm rather fond of Hemmingway," Viv chimed in.

"Me, too," Sydney continued. "With him, you can practically smell booze oozing off the page."

Was no one else seeing what I was? Ripper had come into the kitchen and promptly fallen asleep at the table. He wasn't sound asleep; rather, he was sort of nodding in and out of sleep. With each bellow from Mr. O'Leary, Ripper would snap awake and blink as though struggling to remember where he was, then his heavy lids would drop and his head would roll again. I tried to catch Sydney's eye, but she was prattling on about Jane Austen.

Out in the driveway heading back to my car, I looked at Sydney and whispered. "What was up with Rip Van Winkle?"

"I don't know what was worse!" she whispered back. "Her boyfriend having the head nods in broad daylight or your furtive side glances!"

Viv's next boyfriend would be far worse than a heroin addict. He was reportedly a sadistic crackhead who threatened to kill Viv before holding her hostage for days. When she fled to the police to get a restraining order, the cops told her it wouldn't matter, it would only set him off. She said they informed her that he'd been in Rikers for trying to kill his previous girlfriend.

Denial comes in different forms. Sometimes loved ones can't see a heroin head-nod sitting at the kitchen table. Sometimes a girlfriend can't see all the warning signs of a violent relationship. My own misty-eyed denial didn't let me see that even home wasn't the utopia I wanted it to be.

◄◄ ‖ ►►

Tommy and I stayed together through freshman year and some of sophomore, though I wasn't always faithful and he wasn't always sober, which is not a recipe for relationship success.

But even after Tommy and I broke up, I didn't embrace college life. Instead, I called Jake. He immediately flew to DC, and we picked up where we'd left off. Having Jake back in my life was like catching a killer wave: thrilling, soaring, then physically crushing as I drove him back to National Airport to fly off with no plan for when we'd be together again. I kept Jake playing on repeat in my head. Preserved in his most perfect incarnation—out of reach but always available for daydreams.

Knowing that Jake loved me most, even when he wasn't present, sustained me through college and kept me from having to invest in anyone else.

Jake stoked that flame—calling at key moments and sending airplane tickets to meet him as he hopped from ski resorts to Hawaiian islands.

Then, he let me fly away. No future plans. Just our pattern of pairing and parting. Heartbreak and reunion. Loving and leaving, our song stuck on repeat.

Gasping for Air

The summer before my junior year, I had nowhere to live. Dad was still in South Jersey, living with his girlfriend of several years, but his tiny tobacco-stained apartment held no room or appeal for me. By then, Dad was virtually housebound. For many years, he had been unable to drive over bridges and since he lived on a slip of land surrounded by the ocean and bays, this meant being confined to a ten-mile radius, unable to make my high school graduation or any other event in my life. Mom called it a phobia. I didn't doubt that, but Dad didn't seem to want to address it or work to change it. Mom told me that before their divorce, she and Dad had tried counseling, but after one visit, Dad decided he was smarter than the therapist and quit going. His fear of bridges was just another of his self-limiting oddities that I knew not to bring up for fear of exposing his failings.

With nowhere else to go, I headed to Pittsburgh to find a waitressing job and live with Mom and Mac. Being back under their roof after almost four years of not living together or seeing their relationship up close was unsettling. Mac's short temper was fraying. Mom's mood alternated between edgy and exhausted, and I'd been on my own for so long, I had no tolerance for the silly rules like a curfew Mac tried to enforce.

One day I was going down the stairs as Mom was trudging up. That's when I heard Mac say, "Fuck you, Catherine."

I stopped short. Nobody spoke to Mom that way. I grabbed her shoulder, "You can't let him talk to you like that!"

She shrugged, her eyelids drooping, then moved on, muted. When you have a mother who doesn't defend herself and a father who can't brave bridges, there's a feeling of aloneness, of hollowness, of no one having your back; a sense of having to be the hyper-capable one and having to do it by yourself.

◄◄ ❚❚ ►►

I was in the middle of the lunch shift, standing behind the cash register about to bring Table 12 their check, when my heart suddenly accelerated at warp speed and my lungs felt like they were collapsing. My peripheral vision turned into a tunnel. I crumpled behind the bar, clutching my chest, tip money spilling out of my apron. Another waitress dashed to get me a glass of water as the bartender lifted me into a chair, where I stayed gasping for breath for twenty minutes until it passed.

A few days later, I was at a bar with friends when my chest muscles constricted, and the room started spinning. I was sure I was having a heart attack. I dropped my head between my knees as my hands cramped into arthritic claws. My friends tried to help, tried to coax me to sit up and unclench my fingers, but I couldn't. When the ambulance arrived, the paramedics had to clear a path through the happy hour crowd to load me onto a gurney with two prongs of oxygen stuck up my nose.

The attacks started hitting daily. I went to a family doctor, then a cardiologist, and finally an internist, who diagnosed them as panic attacks, but that didn't stop them. I couldn't predict what would bring one on, but suddenly I was spinning, my heart pounding, unable to catch my breath. The attacks continued into my senior year. I'd be sitting calmly in journalism class when anxiety would seize my chest, squeeze the air from my lungs, and force me into a ball in a bathroom stall, praying for it to pass. I couldn't control the episodes, and they terrified me. Sudden panic can paralyze you, but I had to keep moving, had to keep my grades up to keep my scholarship, had to keep working to become a reporter. Had to reach the unreachable star.

One year after the attacks began, I recorded this in my diary:

(June 8) "I feel as though I've made a breakthrough in understanding my anxiety. I'm an incredibly emotional person who is trying to suppress intense emotions in order to make it through Jake's absence. I'm very afraid of separation and abandonment but I'm trying to ignore those feelings so I can be

more productive. In the past, the way I've done it was to promptly get a new boyfriend, someone to fill part of his void. This summer I've promised Jake that I won't date anyone else. This is not a hard promise to make. It's just a hard habit to break."

Knowing that my anxiety was connected to feelings of abandonment didn't stop the attacks. In fact, knowing that Jake was heading out on a fishing boat in Alaska only made them worse. I didn't know when I'd see or hear from him again, and every single day I worried that he would be swept overboard and never return.

Then Mac broke up with Mom. He declared her too emotionally distant. Mom didn't fight it. She told me later she'd only stayed with him out of a sense of obligation, believing that he'd been our rescuer after Walter left us stranded in Olympia.

Once Mac left, I got to see my mother unattached to a man for the first time. I was proud of her as she pinned up advertisements for roommates and changed the chlorine in her own pool. Her anxiety about being alone took its usual form: fretting about how she'd make her mortgage and car payments on her paltry salary. But I was relieved to find her more present, less preoccupied, lighter. We went out to a little neighborhood Italian joint with all-you-can-eat pasta and bonded over the pesto with pignoli nuts. I felt like I had gotten my mother back.

◄◄ ❚❚ ►►

Back at school for my senior year, I relentlessly chased the two things I believed could bring me security and stability—becoming a reporter and finding love. On any given day, I raced to my first class at 8:30 a.m., then my second at 9:55. Then I jumped on a bus to Georgetown to my internship from noon to five, then hopped on a bus back to campus to shoot and edit stories, write papers, and study for exams. On Wednesday nights, I raced to the campus TV station to write scripts before anchoring the 10:00 p.m. newscast, after which the news crew and I dashed over to the local bar to pound two-dollar gin and tonics until after midnight. I never missed a Campus Career Day or weekend brunch in case my destiny was waiting at either place. In my diary, I wrote about wanting inner peace and direction but didn't know how to find them. One night, I fell asleep on a table at a crowded bar. Hera and her date tried to rouse me but got no response. Had I been Roofied? Knocked unconscious? Alarmed, they hailed a cab and loaded my seemingly lifeless body into the back seat, then into my apartment without me ever waking up. I was exhausted by *not-enoughness*.

Love. Attention. Money. Food. Time.

The Less We Say About It

Sometime during my senior year, Mom called and asked if I could meet her at a friend's ski cabin in Somerset, PA, 180 miles away from my dorm. It was a strange request. Mom didn't ski. We didn't do girls' getaways. Her voice was low and deliberate.

"I want to tell you something, something from my childhood that happened to me, that I think is important to share with you."

Instantly, I knew. And I didn't want to hear it. I didn't want confirmation that the sinking dread I'd felt in Gram and Poppy's row house was something sinister. I didn't want that row house to be anything other than the most consistent haven I'd ever known. I loved Gram and Poppy, loved calling them once a week to feel their unconditional love beaming through the phone line.

"Oh! Hold on, Doll," Gram would say. "Let me get Poppy! Gene! Pick up! It's Alisyn!" It might as well have been Publishers Clearing House calling with the grand prize. Poppy would scramble upstairs to the phone by the bed to hang on my every word about some paper I'd written or story I'd reported for the campus station.

On weekends, I often drove to their home. There they'd be, waiting at their screen door, Gram reaching for my duffle bag of dirty laundry, Poppy tending to my favorite dish of mussels marinara simmering on the stove. I shared my grandparents with friends, too, bringing Hera and Jake with me to South Philly to gorge on Gram and Poppy's homemade macaroni and meatballs. And, like clockwork, when it was time to leave, Poppy would discretely slip twenty bucks into my palm. I believed that Gram and Poppy devoted every single day to loving me as deeply as humanly possible to repent for their sin of not allowing my mother to marry the man she wanted.

I couldn't bear to lose that safe haven to something horrible.

But Mom needed me, so I drove three hours across Pennsylvania to a dimly lit ski cabin so she could deliver what I assumed would be a sledgehammer to the last standing foundation of my family life.

I arrived late in the evening. There was no point in small talk. Mom sat on the old tweed sofa with a hand-knitted afghan draped across the back. The single table lamp was no match for the darkness in the far corners of the room. Mom steeled herself.

"I've been remembering something. Actually, I've never forgotten it. But I've been thinking about it more lately. Something that happened to me in my childhood that I want to tell you."

I braced, digging my fingernails deep into my palm to beat the pain to the punch. And then she told me. She'd suffered sexual abuse at the hands of a relative who'd died *before* I was born. Neither Gram nor Poppy knew. I shut my eyes and exhaled. Mom didn't say much more, nor did she connect the dots about what that meant for her life or mine. I don't remember asking any questions. I was simply too exhausted.

PART SIX

an.chor/ˈaNGkər/ *verb—1. to connect (something) to a solid base;*
2. to hold (something) firmly in place,
usually used as (be) anchored;
noun—1. a person or thing that provides strength and support;
2. someone who reports the news.

Broadcast News

After graduation, I felt a twitchy restlessness. By then, I'd quelled my panic attacks. The ability to name them and recognize the symptoms helped to eventually quiet them until they stopped. But I was still anxious, itching to get into the real world with paychecks and health insurance and paths to becoming Barbara Walters. I was finally free to move to any of the 210 local TV markets. I would have taken a job in #1 (New York) or #195 (Eureka) or anywhere in between. I was also looking in Yakima, Washington, and Eugene, Oregon, so I could be closer to Jake but not a single station returned my calls. The job market the summer I graduated was crappy, and my resume tape was crappier (poor production quality coupled with stilted stand-ups that screamed discomfort on camera). Still, every day I cold called a half dozen TV stations, networks, or production companies to ask if they had any entry-level openings and/or if I could come in for an informational interview. Nine out of ten said no. A few humored me by arranging a meeting, though they didn't have anything.

It was hot as holy hell that summer, and the sole air conditioning unit in my rented apartment was on its last leg, belching out intermittent puffs of cool vapor that my roommates and I crowded around before staggering back into the oven of other rooms. Also, that summer Gram was suffering from a strange autoimmune disease that left her blistered and frail. As often as I could, I'd travel to South Philly where Poppy and I would walk ten sticky city blocks across melting blacktop to get to Gram's hospital room. I'll never forget the smell of that ICU: a sickly-sweet mixture of stale urine, mushy microwaved food, and rotting bodies. I breathed that fetid stench deep into my lungs. That smell meant I was about to see my beloved grandmother.

I sat next to Gram's hospital bed, gingerly stroking her hands, splotched with purple bruises from IV tubes.

Every day she had but one message for me. "Go get a job."

"But I want to stay with you."

"You have to get a job."

I wanted to spend every second at her side, but she wouldn't hear of it. She told me to come back as soon as I'd found a job, and we both knew that meant she was saying goodbye. Before leaving her bedside, I silently transmitted a message with my eyes: *These are just our human shells. We will be together again someday.*

One week after Gram died, I scored a job interview that was almost too good to be true. Ted Koppel, the award-winning anchor of the highly acclaimed news program *Nightline*, had just started his own production company to make primetime documentaries for ABC News. Working there would launch me into the coveted upper echelon of network news. It was obvious that Gram had arrived in heaven and immediately begun pulling strings.

My first interview was with Koppel's executive producer, Leonard Loughlin, a 6'5" imposing character, who I won over by regaling with the story of my overnight stakeout for an exposé on the campus rodent problem. On the way out of the interview, I stole a glance at the notes he'd jotted on my resume and saw SMART capitalized and underlined. Leonard told me the next hurdle was to meet Ted. Ted Koppel was widely considered the country's preeminent interviewer, so I knew I'd be facing some intimidating intellectual firepower. I also knew the job was a long shot. Leonard warned that Koppel was opposed to hiring anyone from outside of ABC. He only wanted people he knew and trusted to do a stellar job. (I was twenty-two and had never done *any* TV job, much less a stellar one.)

Walking into the lobby at ABC News, I felt the way I often did on the cusp of a high-stakes meeting with a powerful, intimidating man (be it my haughty high school English teacher or, later, Bill Clinton, Roger Ailes, or Donald Trump.) I felt excited for this pas de deux. After growing up with Mom and Dad, I considered winning over a remote, imperious intellectual to be literally child's play.

Besides, I felt I already knew Ted. I'd been watching him and admiring him for years. His deep voice and commanding eloquence were *very familiar*...very Dad-like. But unlike Dad, Ted showed up, night after night. One night while watching a recap of the Iran-Contra hearings on Nightline, I even found myself thinking, *I bet Ted is a great father...*

This pseudo-familiarity led me to believe that during the interview, Ted would tip back his chair, gaze up at the ceiling, and tap his fingers, considering something, letting the moment hang...for a long time... without filling the silence. I guessed Ted would use words like "Orwellian" and "Byzantine," and phrases like "Tower of Babel" and "Socratic method." Maybe he would cite Stanley Kubrick movies or Cervantes's works. A lot of people get tripped up trying to match the mental prowess of men like this. Rookie mistake. These men don't want to match wits. They want to be the smartest. So, in the moments when I encountered the Mount Rushmore of intellectuals, I did what I did with Dad (and Mom)—I injected an irreverent zing, something I knew was not their strong suit.

Not to say I wasn't nervous. Ted Koppel was very famous. And fame still made me tongue-tied. I owned exactly one interview outfit, a black and white polka dot blouse and skirt from a fire sale at Lord & Taylor. By the time I got out of the taxi, ribbons of sweat were pouring down my ribcage, gluing the polyester to my torso.

As I entered Koppel's well-appointed corner office, I smiled. Ted did not. In case you don't know, Ted has an enormous head. And an impressive helmet of hair. It makes no sense how his shoulders can support that head. (I later learned that Big Head/Small Frame is a recipe for TV success. See: George Stephanopoulos. And me.) Ted rose from his chair and gestured to the seat across from his giant mahogany desk. I had my good ol' rodent exposé story cued up, but that's not what he wanted to hear. Instead, Ted Koppel perched his reading glasses on the tip of his nose, and asked, "Are you patient?"

Whoa. I did not see *that* coming. *Was I patient?* I'd never thought about it. More importantly, was patience a good thing or a bad thing? Did Ted want a desk assistant who could wait patiently by a fax machine forever or one who demanded that the letter be faxed over STAT? I scanned the bookshelf behind Ted's huge head for clues: a ship in a bottle completed after hours of painstaking work? A framed "Patience is a Virtue" needlepoint?

Then it clicked.

"Oh, you mean will I tire of being a desk assistant and want *more* soon?"

Koppel faintly nodded. Silence.

Yes, I assured him, I was patient. I knew I had to pay my dues. That wasn't true, but I'm not sure I knew that then. Koppel was considering a weekly bookclub for his office staff. Was I prepared to tackle Proust as required reading, followed by group discussion? I could not have produced a pithy Proust quote if my life depended on it, so I nodded soberly and said, "Jackie Collins not your cup of tea?"

I got the job and immediately proved to Ted and Leonard how wrong they'd been to hire me. I had no earthly idea what I was doing. I didn't know how to do network-level research. (I didn't even know where to find the research library.) And once I got off on the wrong foot, it was impossible to stop tripping up. Ted's first concept for a prime-time documentary was called *News From Earth*, billed as a report card on the human race. My assignment was to figure out how many TVs existed in the world (a topic you'd think I could crush, having been reared by a TV) and Leonard needed that info asap! He told me to go get the stats and hustle back. Keep in mind this was five years before the Internet was available to the public. In 1988, we still had to use something called "an encyclopedia" and a concept called "math" to figure shit like that out.

I had no idea where to begin (where the hell was *that* library?). So, Leonard assigned one of ABC News's ace production assistants to shepherd me around. This guy's name was Richard Strong but he went by Dick (and it didn't take me long to fire up the sophomoric puns, which Dick met with weary sighs before gently suggesting I get back to work).

Dick was two years older than me and already knew the network ropes. Leonard—not a guy known for effusive praise—spoke of Dick reverently, describing him as the smartest, sharpest PA ABC News had ever seen. At first, I saw Dick as a buttoned-up, square-jawed, super-serious Ivy-League type, but he soon revealed a dry and devilish sense of humor.

Dick dropped me off at ABC's research library, and I roamed around searching for anything that resembled an answer. After about an hour hunched at a table, scribbling notes on a legal pad, adding up TV sets in Uganda and Canada, Nairobi and Rome (strangely, I couldn't find the number for Italy as a whole), I knew I had to race back. I figured I was probably missing some countries but hoped no one would notice. So, I returned with some half-baked number that I'd neither second-sourced nor double-checked. It took Leonard about five seconds to determine I was off by millions. He was infuriated and let me know that I'd never survive in the news biz with this shitty a work ethic. From that moment on, Leonard took it extremely personally that I was such a fuck up. He alternated between slamming doors in anger and frying me up with his fuming silence. In the 1980s, Leonard's behavior was called "broadcast news," and if you didn't like it, well, there was a stack of resumes with more talented people just waiting to fill your space (as Leonard liked to remind me).

After my first fuck up, I was basically only trusted to fetch Ted's lunches, and even that I managed to screw up. Ted liked Diet Coke. It's all he drank. One day an editorial meeting was underway in Ted's office with his top deputies discussing our next documentary. Suddenly the door cracked open, and a fist squeezed out, clutching a dollar. An urgent message was whispered.

"Ted needs a Diet Coke."

I sprang into action, darting to the elevator, then across the street to the nearest deli. I was back lickety-split and softly rapped on Ted's office door, proud that I could finally produce something Ted liked. Leonard opened the door and looked down at the bottle in my hand. His eyes turned to daggers, slicing me up and down. He excused himself from the meeting and quietly shut the door behind him, then laid into me.

What was I thinking?

"I thought Ted wanted a Diet Coke."

How could I not *know* that Ted only drank his Diet Coke from a can, not a bottle?

No one likes being dressed down by an imposing 6'5" man, and I was certainly viscerally scared. But I was also bemused. Was this for real? Was this adult man actually losing his mind over a Diet Coke in a bottle?

"I'm pretty sure it's the same recipe, bottle or can," I said and felt Dick wince from across the room.

"It's not the same!" Leonard hissed.

I put my coat back on, then rolled my eyes over at Dick, who pretended to be engrossed in logging tapes. After episodes like that, Dick liked to try to make me laugh. In the privacy of our little shared office, Dick referred to that moment as "The Great Coke Caper" and "CokeGate." He also created new lyrics for the song "Stormy Weather" and sang them to me.

Don't know why,
There's no sun up in the sky
Leonard Loughlin...

Around that time, Leonard told me to stop smiling. He said it made me look unserious and he mandated that I stay at work until 2:00 a.m. to show how serious I was. He said he needed me there throughout the night in case a fax came in that I had to retrieve. I suspected Leonard had no life—no girlfriend or wife or kids to go home to and believed he was forcing me to sit in an edit room hour after hour because he didn't want to be alone. But I didn't like sitting next to him, so I told him if a fax was that important, I'd better go wait in the fax room for that very important fax. By then, I'd figured out that the giant rubber garbage can in the fax room made a comfy place to sleep.

Here was another valuable lesson from my childhood that I was able to deploy with Leonard and any other narcissist I encountered (which happened daily, since TV news is lousy with people who long to see their own reflections and clamor for "face time"): I knew their Achilles' heel. I knew their fundamental need for admiration and how quickly their confidence could crumble without external validation. I also knew that they considered others inferior—and how ultimately that became an isolating island. Back then, I didn't know what had caused Dad's deep narcissistic wound, but I knew how to see through the mask into the gaping hole of shame that even external adulation could not completely fill.

Being loved and adored by a narcissistic father didn't make me weak-kneed for validation from the narcissistic bosses of my future. It made me wise to *their* weaknesses. I instinctively knew Leonard's withering words and diminishing looks directed at me were, at their core, about him.

After a few months of round-the-clock work, I concluded that this situation was stone-cold fucking crazy. Still, consider for a moment how a) confident, b) narcissistic, c) delusional, or d) all of the above a twenty-two-year-old newbie must be to believe that she knows more about how TV news should work than every big-brained, Peabody-award-winning producer around her. But that's exactly what I thought. Not that I knew more about US–Sino relations or Deng Xiaoping's reign in China or the sociopolitical undercurrents that led to massive student protests in Tiananmen Square in 1989 that we were reporting on for our next Koppel Report. But I did think I knew more about being human. I knew we shouldn't have to work seven days a week, many weeks in a row, without a day off to prove we were worthy. I knew that working a hundred hours a week (no exaggeration) was not going to make our documentary any better than if we'd settled for eighty hours a week. And I was pretty sure that you could actually have dinner occasionally with friends and still get the job done. But in 1989, the hard-charging culture of TV news dictated that *serious journalists* had to work nonstop. There was also a pervasive ethos that women had to sacrifice marriage and children to achieve career success. But I didn't believe that either. I vowed not to become a work widow

I credit my teenage survival skills with allowing me to navigate the madness of TV news. I'm certain that moving from house to house, family to family, waitressing job to waitressing job, made me less susceptible to cults of personality and powerful men's whims. By twenty-two, I'd learned to trust my own instincts more than the edicts of powerful people. Somehow having to find my own way fine-tuned my bullshit meter. I could smell it a mile away and knew that what I was experiencing in that edit room night after night was some grade-A bullshit. Watching these intelligent, talented producers sacrifice their personal lives day after day, night after night, made no sense to me.

At some point, Leonard decided that my friend Dick, too, had disappointed him and that Dick was not actually as talented as Leonard had proclaimed. Leonard acted as if Dick and I were making him look bad. Dick too was subjected to Leonard's angry criticisms but Dick put his head down and didn't fight back. He didn't say things like, "that's total bullshit," when told we had to work until 2:00 a.m. for the thirtieth day in a row. He didn't lie, as I did, and say that he had a doctor's appointment so he could sneak out and meet a date at happy hour. And he never confronted Leonard, as I had to, to say that I didn't appreciate that he wasn't standing up for me when one of the ABC anchors called me "sexed up" and "an Italian sex kitten."

I didn't like that Dick kept right on stoically working through these episodes.

"You need to speak up, Dick!" I hectored, during one of my self-righteous rants at his desk. "But you don't. And you know why? Because you're a chicken, Dick! That's why."

Dick cleared his throat. "As insults go, I prefer Pencil Dick." Then he stood up and steered my shoulders back toward my desk. "Now, on your bike. Back to work."

I desperately wanted to quit but couldn't go a week without a paycheck and never had a day off to try to find a new job. I also never had privacy in the tiny Koppel office space. So, I took to dragging the landline from the front desk into the hall closet where, in the dark, I would cold call other networks, while simultaneously answering incoming calls for Ted.

One morning, the senior producer opened the closet door to hang her coat and was startled to find me in the middle of a job interview. I darted up to Dick's desk.

"Uh-oh!" I whispered. "I think Tara has figured out I'm not happy here."

"Wow," Dick said, stone-faced. "What a sleuth."

You Can't Put Your Arms Around a Memory

It wasn't just my job causing distress. The summer after college, Jake became harder to reach. On the rare occasions that we spoke, he cheered me on, saying he knew I'd be the next Barbara Walters. What Jake didn't tell me was that he had decided that big city life was not for him, and it was time to get out of my way.

When Jake determined that the time had come—that he'd had enough of our drama, of our many years of airport greetings and goodbyes—he disappeared. Even his sister Kimberly, who I'd lured to the East Coast to live with me, didn't have a new number for him.

It was midnight on Valentine's Day and I was alone in my bedroom, unraveling. By then, I believed that my ongoing Jake heartache was not only unbearable for me but was also wearing thin on my friends, who I thought didn't understand and could never feel my depth of pain and abandonment.

After eight years on and off with Jake, my identity and self-worth were so tied to him, that when he left for good, something in me snapped. I thrashed about in bed. My skin and bones ached; I had a full-body migraine of restlessness, agitation, and racing heart. I chewed at my cuticles, ripping pieces of skin from my fingers until they bled. The fantasy foundation that, despite what I did or where I lived, Jake would always love me the most, was collapsing under me.

Just after midnight, I wrote a note, trying to reach some benevolent presence above the thrashing animal.

God help me. I can't take the pain anymore.

Writing usually helped summon my saner self but not that night. I looked toward the window and noticed a roll of blue tape on the sill. The landlord had sent some guys over earlier that day to paint the frame around my windowpanes. They left behind the tape and, next to it, a pack of razor blades. I stared at the compact box, then imagined opening it and using the razor's sharp edge to pierce the skin of my wrist. I noted with interest that something was off with my perception. My brain didn't register the thought of a deep slice as pain but rather, as long-awaited relief. I reached for the phone. I dialed 411. I spoke softly so as not to wake Hera and Kimberly through the thin walls.

"*Can I get...the number for...a suicide hotline?*"

"Would you like me to connect you?"

"Yes...please."

"Hello. Are you having an emergency?"

I could only manage short gasps. "I just need...to talk to someone. I'm... struggling. I'm—in so much pain. And...it...*doesn't...stop.*"

"Are you considering harming yourself?"

"I just...want it to *stop.*"

"Are there any weapons in your home?"

"No. No. Except. A box. Of razor blades. But really. I just need someone—"

Dial tone.

"Hello?" No. "*Hello?*" *Not possible. The suicide hotline did not just hang up on me.* "Hello..." I curled into the fetal position and rocked. Even the suicide hotline had abandoned me. I was that worthless.

The phone rang.

"Hello?"

"This is the operator. Please stay on the line. Reconnecting you now."

A different voice. "Miss, stay right there. Please don't hang up again."

"You hung up on me!"

"Miss, I need you to stay on the phone until the police arrive."

"Police? Oh, no, no. I don't want the police. I only want to talk to someone."

"Miss, I'm on with the dispatcher. The police should be there momentarily."

The sound of distant sirens, then louder, then piercing. Then outside.

"No. *No!*"

"Miss, I need you to go let the police in. I'm staying on the line with you."

Pounding downstairs.

"*Oh, Jesus.*"

"Stay on the phone."

"I have to put the phone down to answer the door!"

I tripped down two stairs at a time. Two uniformed officers.

"We received a 5150 call, danger to oneself."

"Listen, officers, it's all a huge mistake. I just wanted to talk to someone. And then the call got disconnected. I'm fine."

It was cold. I saw their eyes study my Minnie Mouse T-shirt and bare legs. My red-streaked face. "We're going to have to take you in now."

"No. No. No."

"Alisyn? Is everything okay?" Kimberly and Hera were at the top of the stairs, their faces soft with sleep and confusion.

"Guys, I'm fine. *Honestly.*"

"Miss, we can't leave the scene of a 5150. It's the law. We need to take you to the hospital now. We'll give you one minute to get some clothes on. Don't shut your door."

On the ride to the hospital, part of me was relieved. Maybe some doctor could save me, some compassionate counselor would have a cure for my pain. Instead, I was greeted by an ice-cold intake coordinator straight out of the Ratched School of Nursing.

I told her I just needed to talk to someone.

She told me no one was available.

I asked her when someone might become available.

She said she didn't know. Probably not for several days.

I told her I had to be at work at 9:00 a.m.

"You're not going anywhere," she snapped. "You're here until the psychiatric board can evaluate you. They're back on Monday." It was Thursday night.

That's when I started screaming. I screamed that I was leaving. I screamed that I worked for an important and famous person and when I didn't show up in the morning, he was going to be very angry. I screamed at the medics as they forced me down onto a bed. I screamed at the officer stationed outside my door that this place was the Cuckoo's Nest. I screamed that it was Kafkaesque. I screamed and kicked as the medics held my arms down and tied my legs with leather straps, then I stared into the nurse's eyes, pleading with her to let me go home. That's when she dropped her bomb.

"You do know that trying to kill yourself is a *crime*, don't you?"

Of all the shocks to my system that night, learning that my anguish made me a criminal was the biggest. A few years earlier, probably during one of my dramatic meltdowns, Jake had told me that "killing yourself was the most selfish thing anyone could ever do." I never understood that. As anyone who's ever contemplated suicide knows, it's about ending the agony—for everyone. Ending one's life means ending the pain. It's the opposite of selfish; we think we'll be sparing our loved ones more anguish. We think their lives will be better without us.

What I didn't understand that night in the psych ward was that the pain *does* end. Astonishingly, with time you can fight your way out and feel joy again. But that night, I couldn't stop screaming.

At some point, my screams morphed into high-pitched animal wails. By morning, I was delirious. Kimberly and Hera appeared at my bedside, tear tracks staining their faces. Kim wiped the wetness from my cheeks. Hera stroked my strapped arms. They said they were trying to get me home. Day blurred into night blurred into day. I don't know how long I was there. I stared into the garish ceiling light, searching for lyrics to self-soothe but couldn't find a song that fit.

At some point, I talked to some case manager and convinced him it was all a big mistake. I was becoming more unhinged with each passing hour. He let me go with a referral for a therapist I couldn't afford.

I was pretty sure that being strapped down in a mental hospital was rock bottom. By then, I had enough friends struggling with drugs to spot the tell-tale signs: the dependence at the cost of dignity, the endless cravings for more, the desire for self-destruction. I had become an addict. But my drug of choice was unavailable people, and they were harder to control than any substance I could melt into my veins.

After hanging onto Jake for so many years to avoid being alone, here I was alone, unloved, and easy to leave, which I suppose I'd known all along. And still, *still*, that morning my taxi drove away from the hospital, I believed if only I could find the right hard-to-get guy and get one more dopamine hit, I'd prove I could handle the high, and the next time would be different. The next time, I'd find a way to get him to stay.

I didn't know what my roommates had told my coworkers, but when I returned to the office that Monday morning, Dick pulled me aside and quietly cautioned me to get my personal life in order so I could perform better at work. I considered his advice curious. How was I supposed to control my personal life? I couldn't control who loved me or left me. And anyway, easy for him to say. Dick spent his summers playing tennis and boating at his family's beautiful home on a bluff atop Maine's rocky coastline overlooking the ocean. He could never know pain like mine.

In the end, it was Dick who, without warning, up and quit one day. Leonard demanded that Dick give up his umpteenth weekend to do some thankless task that would be neither rewarded nor recognized, and that was it. Dick silently and stoically decided that he'd be going to a Boston Red Sox game that day instead. At the time, I didn't know how much of the criticism Dick had internalized, while telling jokes to crack me up.

For many years after that, Dick and I reconvened for long summer weekends at his beautiful Maine home. I brought Kimberly and Hera up with me, and various boyfriends, and Dick hosted all of us for tennis playing, power boat rides, and decadent lobster dinners. And every summer, he and I would reenact a litany of Leonard's worst offenses and howl with laughter at the absurdity of it all, now from a safe distance. I wanted what Dick had—a lovely summer house with a wine cellar and what I thought was a settled life of stability. But of course, none of us really knows what's inside someone else's darkest moments.

I never imagined that years later, one late spring night, my dear friend would take his own life in that beautiful home on a bluff.

Not a week goes by that I don't wish I could have helped with his pain.

Not a week goes by that I don't miss laughing with him.

You Better Run

After two years at Koppel, one of Ted's top producers pitched me what she claimed would be a great job. I thought she was kidding.

"You should go work at America's Most Wanted."

"Excuse me?" I responded. "You want me to go from the ivory tower of journalism to a schlocky TV show that blurs the lines of news and entertainment with cheesy reenactments?" (We capital-J *Journalists* took ourselves very seriously back then.)

"Trust me," she said. "I know the producers who run that show. If you meet them, you'll want to work there. Call them."

So I did. And the second I walked into their newsroom, I got it. The producers and reporters were *smiling*. Some were even *laughing*. The place had a buzzy energy. There was camaraderie. It felt like one big crime-fighting family. The executive producer told me they had an opening for a production assistant. I'd just turned twenty-five. And though I was unhappy and desperate for a job change, I didn't want to settle.

"Call me when you have a reporter opening," I said.

Six months later, they did.

Granted, I would be an *off-air reporter*, meaning my face wasn't seen on-screen, but *my interviews* would be broadcast on national TV, and I would travel around the country with a *real live* cameraman, in addition to my imaginary one. My secret plan was to parlay all that into being on camera.

My first day at *America's Most Wanted*, I was nervous. My job would be to dig up new and gripping crime stories every week, though I didn't know how to do that. So, I showed up bright-eyed, with my reporter's notebook wide-open, ready to absorb the expert advice of my seasoned coworkers.

Instead, they immediately issued a grave warning. A senior producer pulled me into her office, lowered her voice, and told me to brace myself.

"Just wait until the nightmares start."

"Nightmares?"

"Oh, yeah," a male production manager agreed. "The stories are terrifying. All the violence. I haven't been able to sleep in a year."

I was so eager to be a reporter, it hadn't occurred to me that diving into the details of murders, rapes, and abductions every day might take a psychological toll. So, I braced and waited for the stories of blood and gore to seep into my subconscious; for the images of butcher knives and claw hammers to hack at my nerves, and the backstories of murderous revenge plots to exact payment from my sleep.

I waited. And while waiting, I kept skipping into work, digging up my next cold case in Cleveland, schmoozing a new FBI agent in Detroit, and planning my next shoot at the cop shop in Kansas City. While waiting, I wined and dined my detective sources with my new expense account, and then I waited more as the fugitives I profiled every Friday night kept getting captured.

After about three months of waiting, I realized that reporting on grizzly crimes was actually making me feel *safer*. Before I worked at *AMW* (as we called it), most of my ideas about violent crime came from movies. So, I thought it was entirely possible that a group of teenagers could be partying at a lake house on Halloween night when a psychopath in a hockey mask broke in and managed to stab every single one of them while they tried to call for help on a *cut phone line!* I also thought it was utterly plausible that you could encounter a conniving cannibal who could convince you to enter his basement, lit by one naked bulb, before he chopped you up for dinner. Basically, before *AMW*, I thought violent crime was random and common.

But in fact, in many cases, alarm bells and red flags pop up all over the place before something violent happens. (It's also those clues and foreshadowing that create a successful crime show.) The idea that if I paid attention, I could see trouble coming from a distance deeply comforted me (as opposed to, say, blithely coming home one day to find your screen missing, your jewelry gone, and your dad arrested).

There was another interesting and unexpected side effect of chasing fugitives. Empowerment. The fugitive might have a gun, but I had a microphone, and I noticed that when I hooked that lavalier mic onto the collar of a victim, it transformed them into an emboldened survivor, ready to claw back their power. Even the youngest ones somehow knew that with a TV camera on their side, the tables had turned. Now the fugitive was the one running scared. *We're coming to get you*, our host John Walsh promised. *You can run, but you can't hide.*

"He'll probably get like a hundred and two years in jail." That's what Bobby told me about the man who molested him. When I first met Bobby, he was a cherubic, cherry-cheeked seven-year-old in Michigan who, along with two other kids on his street, had been molested by Jessie Martinez, the "neighborhood nice guy" who owned an aluminum-sided above-ground pool, the only one in the subdivision. Martinez routinely offered to babysit the boys so their exhausted parents could work night shifts. Sometimes the kids slept over. Martinez made Bobby sleep next to him in his bed, then he put his hands over Bobby's eyes and raped him. Bobby's distraught mom stood in the doorway, blotting tears as I attached the microphone to Bobby's striped shirt. I told him we could stop the interview at any time. I told him the cameraman would shoot him in shadow so his face couldn't be seen. I sat on a tiny chair. Bobby sat on his bed.

"Are you scared of Jessie?" I asked.

"I was," he said. "But not no more."

"Why's that?"

"'Cause he knows what he did is bad, and he's gonna go to jail."

Fuck, yeah, he is, Bobby! By the time I interviewed Bobby, more than a dozen criminals had been caught as a result of my reporting and the reenactments of their crimes.

Reporters love gallows humor, and my success rate became a favorite office joke. "*When they hear Camerota's on the case, criminals crack!*" my boss claimed. One child molester in Ohio caught wind of me poking around and actually drove himself to the police station and surrendered. It was at AMW that I learned the true power of TV—all those eyeballs, those armies of viewers to be deployed in the service of finding someone. I also learned not to be afraid to ask victims to tell me their painful stories. They'd come before my camera for a reason—for help or to honor their loved one who'd been murdered—so there was no point in shying away from the horror. I saw over and over how sharing a painful story can free us from carrying a painful secret.

One of my favorite things about the show was its delivery of justice. Justice, I believe, is a close cousin of joy—or at least that's the emotion I felt when I called Bobby's family (and dozens more) to tell them that the criminal who had tormented them had been captured. Jessie Martinez was caught three hours after my interview with Bobby aired. Martinez would finally be held accountable. He would pay for the pain he'd caused. The sight of a criminal in handcuffs, surrounded by cops hauling him to the squad car, fired up my brain's pleasure centers. When I decided I wanted to be a reporter at fifteen, I thought it might bring me fame and fortune, worth and validation. But at AMW, I began to see that reporting could deliver justice—and justice is as basic a human desire as happiness. Back then, I felt a kinship with the victims who'd been wronged, though I wasn't completely clear on who the criminal was I was searching for.

◀◀ ❙❙ ▶▶

It wasn't just victims who offered me life lessons. Those came from fugitives, too. If ever there were a criminal I thought might try to hurt me, it was John Kravec. Kravec had a long rap sheet and a lust for violence. A year before I met him, Kravec had tried to kill an out-of-work truck driver named Dan, who'd had too much to drink at a bar in Syracuse, New York, then made the mistake of flashing around his freshly cashed disability check.

At first, Kravec had only planned to rob Dan, but after beating him to a pulp in the bar parking lot, Kravec decided to take it further. Kravec loaded Dan, now semi-conscious, into his van and drove him to some nearby woods, where he tied a belt around Dan's neck, stabbed him in the stomach with a switchblade, and almost severed his thumb. Then he tried to hang Dan from a tree and left him to die. But Dan didn't die.

Eleven months later, *America's Most Wanted* interviewed Dan while the police were still searching for Kravec.

"John Kravec does not need a reason to kill," Dan told us. "When he stabbed me in my stomach and I looked at his face, he was enjoying it as much as a bowler getting a strike. And to this day, I still feel that I am dead."

Kravec was captured fifteen minutes after *America's Most Wanted* aired his gruesome crime. The next day, I did what I routinely did: I called the jail and tried to convince Kravec to do an on-camera interview with me. The criminal (or their lawyer) usually refused my request, but Kravec agreed—with one condition. He said he would talk about himself but not the crime because he didn't want to ruin his chances at trial.

I knew that getting video of Kravec in an orange jumpsuit was the money shot for viewers. So, I told Kravec that I would ask him about the crime, and if he didn't want to answer, he could tell me that on-camera. As I flew off to the county jail in Florida, I imagined I could persuade this violent thirty-four-year-old to answer my questions. (Hadn't I escaped a drug dealer's gun in my teens? Kravec couldn't be *that* scary.)

One of my strange disappointments at *America's Most Wanted* was how few psychopaths I encountered. I thought that grilling a Hannibal Lecter-type on-camera could only enhance my resume tape, and that some future news director would be wowed by how I outfoxed a terrifying lunatic during an interview.

Instead, after sitting across from roughly a dozen murderers and rapists, I discovered that the vast majority were just deeply broken people—men, mostly, often with alcohol or drug problems, hair-trigger anger issues, no impulse control, and zero coping skills. A surprising number had parents who themselves had been criminals. These were guys for whom a lost pool game became an instant barroom brawl. It didn't feel satisfying to outfox them. It felt sad. And familiar. Too much alcohol and drugs? I knew a few people like that myself. Repeating bad patterns? Lacking coping skills to process pain? Those rang some personal bells.

As soon as the deputy deposited Kravec, uncuffed, in front of me in the visitor room, I got an edgy feeling that something was up. It didn't help that the guard immediately left the room to attend to some other issue. Kravec looked jumpy. His hands were visibly shaking. He was having a hard time keeping eye contact. I had a mental flash of him lunging across the table and taking me hostage. I looked to my cameraman for protection, but his head was buried in his bag, searching for a battery.

"Do you want a soda or something?" I offered Kravec, trying to feel him out and steady him.

"No," he said. "I want to get this over with."

Suddenly I did, too. "OK," I started. "So, what is your version of events on July twenty-second, 1993?"

He took a breath and stared right at me. "I'm going to be honest with you, Alisyn. What happened that night was pretty much a blur. But I am guilty of it."

Wait, what did he just say?

"You know what I did," he continued, his face flat. "And I'm admitting to it right now. I have no excuse for what I did. I was not really in sound mind, you know? But I did it, and it bothers me."

I turned ever-so-subtly to my cameraman. *ARE YOU ROLLING?*

He nodded, mouth agape.

No criminal had ever confessed to me before. I hadn't even prepared for the possibility.

"Do you know what made you do the crime?" I ineptly pressed.

"I don't know why. The guy was innocent. He was brutally beaten and hurt by me."

"The crime that we showed was very brutal. That's what the police have told us. That's what the victim says." I wanted to keep Kravec talking.

"Anytime you leave somebody to die, it is brutal, especially somebody who didn't do nothing. It is bad. I left a man to die. In my heart, I killed him." Kravec stopped to take a breath. "And I want to say something else. To the person I hurt, I think his name is Daniel. I am sorry. He didn't deserve this."

I was stunned. Here was Kravec, a man capable of brutal violence, facing twenty years in prison, but at the same time, demonstrating unheard of accountability, honesty, and compassion.

Right after the interview, I flew to Syracuse to tell Dan in person that Kravec had confessed. Dan was still in pain, struggling through physical therapy, trying to recover the use of his hand. He went silent for a few moments as he absorbed the news of Kravec's apology.

"That's beautiful," he finally said. "I feel a lot better now that you told me that. There's not that much hatred anymore." Dan welled up. "I accept his apology."

Again, I was floored. I already knew that no one fits into a tidy box of predictability. I knew that good people could do bad things. Some of my wonderful friends had done "bad things" to feed their drug habits. Some had done jail time. But I was still astonished by this outcome because I didn't know yet how to do the things these two broken men could—reveal raw vulnerability, apologize for my bad behavior, or forgive someone who had hurt me.

The Freedom to Flee

While hunting for fugitives, I was also searching for love. From the outside, my love life looked great. I was a serial dater, going to cool restaurants and concerts with various handsome, fun-loving boyfriends, straight from one to the next. But when it came time to truly commit, I hit a wall. Then, at twenty-six, I fell in love with a tall, dark, and handsome network news producer. From the instant we met, he and I were thunderstruck by a feeling that *something intense is happening here*, which was awkward because I was sitting next to a different boyfriend at the time.

For a month, I secretly flitted between both guys until I came down with a debilitating case of double-vision that I didn't need a shrink to diagnose. (It resolved the second I broke up with the first guy.) The network producer and I agreed that we were pawns of fate and meant to be together. For months, we finished each other's sentences as we jetted off to Spain or a Caribbean island for fun. But at the witching hour of six months, he grew jealous and accusatory and complained I wasn't giving enough emotionally (well, that was one of his myriad complaints). He was highly mercurial. We'd be laughing over a plate of pasta and some Chianti one minute, and the next, he'd need to know why a cop was calling me at night or if I was attracted to a certain editor. He demanded I tell my platonic guy friends to "back off" and began insisting I was "emotionally dysfunctional," "had shit for character," and "could never accept blame" for our issues. It was horribly destabilizing, not knowing when he'd be set off or if our relationship was moving forward or falling apart. As he withdrew, I turned into a whirling dervish, trying to prove I was worthy of his love and emotional return. We'd fight and reunite. A vicious, exhausting cycle. My old intimacy/distance dance was never-ending.

The conference room walls at *AMW* were covered in funny quotes written in magic marker. Usually, the quote was something one of us reporters or a producer had said in a pitch meeting (i.e., *"There's nothing quite like toying with the minds of violent criminals,"* A.C. 5/13/94). Sometimes the quote came from a criminal. My favorite was from a fugitive who uttered this pearl of wisdom to his cellmate just before climbing out an unlocked window and escaping the county jail: *"The last freedom is the freedom to flee."*

By my late twenties, much of my life had been devoted to this felonious philosophy. I often found bailing out of a tough situation to be the best solution. I particularly liked the element of surprise, sometimes leaving so fast, as I'd done in high school to Robbie and Jake, and with such little explanation, it left someone's head spinning. Fleeing a problem was so much easier than fixing it. But with my mercurial boyfriend, I was determined to do something different. I was determined to stop running.

◀◀ ❚❚ ▶▶

I was twenty-eight years old. In the space of one month, one college roommate got married, then another. My officemate announced her engagement, and another friend told me she was pregnant. Even Mom had gotten remarried. A couple years after she broke up with Mac, she met a steady, loving man named Steven, a political science professor, whom she wed in a backyard ceremony with me as her maid of honor. Even Dad had remarried again, to his longtime girlfriend Carolyn, another high school teacher, a wonderful woman who loved him unconditionally, despite his drinking and spotty employment. I served as his "best man" at their wedding, all of us giggling as the justice of the peace repeatedly referred to Dad as Albert, rather than Antonio, which allowed Dad to later joke that they weren't officially married.

Then Kimberly called to tell me that Jake was getting married and having a baby. He'd reconnected with a childhood friend who Kim wasn't certain he truly loved, but it didn't matter. He was going to be a father. Hearing the news, an electrical jolt zapped my heart muscle. But as soon as I hung up, I felt a freeing finality. That was it. The futile fantasy was finally over.

I desperately wanted the relationship happiness I saw blooming around me, as I continued soldiering through battle with the disparaging producer. I was going to have to learn somehow, some way to stay in a relationship, and here was my chance to prove I could handle a Herculean challenge (Don Quixote had nothing on me). I also believed his nasty critiques about me were true. I *was* dysfunctional. I *did* have a problem with emotional intimacy. Maybe by staying, I could prove us both wrong. Over the next year, I grew more miserable by the day. When the endless fighting and reuniting became unbearable, I suggested we take a three-week break. I feared I would be devastatingly lonely but found myself accidentally having fun with friends and dancing with cute guys at beach bars. Still, when the three weeks were up, I asked him to take me back. Thank God, he didn't.

I'd been at *America's Most Wanted* for five years and in Washington, DC, for more than ten. I wanted a new job. I wanted a loving relationship. I wanted the freedom to flee.

Real Life

I'd sent my resume tape to several local stations and gotten offers in Houston and Orlando. But then I got stuck. Which would be better? Where would my future husband be waiting? I wished I could go to Boston, a place I'd felt a deep affinity for from the first time I visited at thirteen, but I knew that was too competitive a TV market for someone with no local news experience.

I called a psychic. Apparently, neither Houston nor Orlando were in the Tarot cards. She said I was on the cusp of a thrilling new job on a "national" morning show, "something like *Good Morning America*," she said.

Oh, brother, I thought. She has no idea how TV news works.

"I've only sent my tape to local stations," I explained. "A national show is not possible."

She was insistent. This job would be national. Also, I would be "headed north," she said. She saw "a lot of snow" where I was going, but not to worry—I would love the job so much, I wouldn't mind the cold. She sensed I "would be close to Montreal."

Would I find love? I asked.

On this, she was noncommittal yet oddly specific.

"You'll have a relationship. I see him walking through the snow."

Ugh. This lady's a crackpot. Can I get my money back?

A few days later, my phone rang. It was the Miami office of the TV news impresario Joel Cheatwood. He had seen my resume tape. No one knew this yet, his producer told me, but Cheatwood was about to launch "a new national morning show on NBC." Cheatwood wanted to hire me as a correspondent. The show would be based in Boston. He'd just hired a super talented host named Lu from…wait for it…Montreal. The show would be called REALlife.

Could I start in three weeks? I put down the phone and wandered around for hours in a fugue state, stunned and shaken by how fate had found me.

(Nov 22, 1995)—I am one of the luckiest people on earth. I can't believe that I'm going to be able to live in Boston, the city where I've always wanted to be! Ever since I first visited all those years ago, I've felt a huge sense of belonging there. But it's more than that—I feel as though I'm heading in the direction of my destiny. I truly think my life will be divided into two parts: Before Boston and In Boston. I know good things await me there.

I moved to Boston at the beginning of what would be its snowiest winter in a century. Fifty of us were hired at REALlife, most in our twenties, most unmarried, some from Boston, some from elsewhere, but all of us instantly gobsmacked by the kismet. We knew fate had brought us together. At our first staff meeting, we sat scattered across the floor of a big, carpeted room with no conference table and not enough chairs, already leaning against one another, already laughing at inside jokes.

I rented a cozy one-bedroom in the basement of a Beacon Hill brownstone on the most enchanted street I'd ever seen. But entering my apartment was no easy feat. It required turning my body sideways to squeeze through a miniature door the size of an ironing board four steps below street level. One date, picking me up for dinner, asked if I had just climbed out my window. When Hera visited, she exclaimed, "Alisyn! You live in a Hobbit Hole!"

It was immediately apparent that everyone on the show's staff brought some special sauce to our merry mix. It was also clear that many of us had been hired at deeply discounted rates for roles that far exceeded our credentials. But who cared? When our lead booker entered every room with an elaborately staged pratfall for our amusement, what did it matter that he didn't have a golden Rolodex? Did it matter that our head writer's skill set was creative writing, not news copy, when she wore mismatched stockings and a baroque hat covered in silk flowers for no reason at all? What did it matter that two of our top "producers" had yet to graduate college and were too young to drink booze?

My friends back in DC joked that I'd accepted the job before seeing a single camera cable or mic cord. But with chemistry like this, I knew the show would be a surefire smash. The stars had finally aligned.

Soon we were eating every meal together. Many nights, after countless hours spent in dark edit rooms, we'd take over a local bar, and I'd sit in dazed bliss, gazing at all my new friends, feeling completely connected. It's not a stretch to say we fell in collective love. We referred to ourselves as REALlifers.

For me, this group love potion contained extra zest because of a particularly funny, flirty production assistant named Jamie. Jamie was tall with the triangular build of a swimmer and the cocky confidence that comes with washboard abs. We started palling around, going to lunch together and after-work parties. All that time, I kept wondering where my "relationship" was that the psychic saw—as Jamie walked to my house through the snow. But Jamie was three years younger than me and a few rungs lower on the career ladder. So, I continued going on date after date with guys I considered more appropriate suitors. And I was crystal clear with Jamie. We could *never* have a romantic relationship. I told him that over and over…every single time he slept over.

He wantonly flouted my rule.

Our secret office romance dance of restraint made every day more exciting; sneaking around, trying not to stand too close, catching each other's eyes, pretending not to. I insisted that Jamie keep our relationship secret. I believed that I, a network correspondent, could not be openly involved with a PA. I also believed that Jamie liked that I played hard-to-get, and I still considered love a dish best served from a distance.

My Boston brand of belonging felt even sturdier than the one I'd had in New Jersey because this time around, I had a tight-knit tribe *and* a salary. And my job? It was everything I'd dreamed of. I was a national correspondent on a morning show. I was traveling the country with a camera crew, producing creative pieces, and having the time of my life. Cheatwood wanted heavy reporter-involvement stories, and I relished that type of storytelling. For one piece, I shot an on-camera stand-up while being pecked by a gaggle of ostriches. For another, I conducted an interview while driving at 100 mph. I did another interview on horseback. I found a ten-year-old college student in California with an astronomical IQ and a woman in Minnesota who'd spent years researching whether she was the "ugliest" person in the country. Cheatwood loved what I was bringing back from the field. I loved hearing him chuckle as he screened my pieces.

I was working my ass off but doing it in grand style, flying First Class and staying in the penthouse suite at the Chateau Marmont. It was a far cry from the mobile homes and prison cells of *AMW*, but the storytelling was the same: find interesting people and get them to show me a slice of themselves.

Then REALlife was canceled.

The news of the show's demise came down in a crushingly curt email and sent our fifty-person posse spinning. We grabbed tissues and cigarettes—somebody had a spare bottle of vodka. We went out to the fire escape, some crying, others shell-shocked. I was sobbing the hardest because I just knew. I knew we'd never find this chemistry and connection again. I was crying so hard, one of the senior producers was moved to say, "Don't worry, Alisyn! You're talented. You'll be able to get another job!"

Job? REALlife wasn't a job. It was my family. It was my home. My tribe. I could have cried on that sorrowful fire escape all night. But the senior producer had to get home to dinner with his wife and kids. One of the bookers had to head to her weekend place on the Cape. Another had to get to a party in Southie that night with his college pals. One writer had already gotten a new job at CBS in New York and had to go home and pack up her place. But me? I had no spouse, no place on the Cape, no escape from the loss.

Then Jamie dumped me. He'd grown tired of our late-night sleepwalk dance. And, like the tango I'd done for years, only when he left did I realize how much I valued him. Only then was I desperate to get him back. My tortured pattern was ever-present. And I had no idea how to stop it.

Friends were moving on. I was stuck in a Hobbit Hole. I needed money for rent, so I worked a pupu platter of freelance TV jobs: reporting on time travel for a syndicated show called *Strange Universe*; planting hostas for *Better Homes and Gardens TV*; covering three-alarm fires and water-main breaks for the local station; and the cruelest joke of all, hosting a cable fitness show called *Body By Jake*. Those jobs were the only thing holding me upright for ten hours a day, before I fell back down on my couch for a feverish night of fractured sleep.

One of my most startling dreams happened when I was wide awake. A few months after the show was canceled, I ventured back up to the now-vacant REALlife offices one morning and saw actual apparitions of our old staff. Vivid flashes of my friends. There was our producer Steve carrying a box of tapes, Jamie behind him laughing. I was familiar with the phenomenon of phantom limbs that soldiers feel, but these were phantom friends still haunting the hallways. I remember wondering if my deep depression was triggering some kind of psychosis. And why my psyche could not process the loss.

◀◀ ❚❚ ▶▶

A few months into my despair, Maria, my best friend in Boston, told me she was having a baby. Another gut punch. I tried to rally and throw her a shower. In home videos from that day, I'm standing against the backdrop of yellow bunting and a table of baby bottles filled with champagne. My arms are rail thin and clinging to the wall. I hadn't been able to eat for weeks, and that day, the scale dipped to 100—a number I hadn't weighed since I was eleven. On the tape, when asked to offer wisdom for the soon-to-be mom, I force a flat smile and shrug, "What do I know? I can't keep a plant alive."

Viv once told me that one big takeaway from her years of addiction was that every drug will eventually turn on you, no matter how much it romances you at first. She wasn't even talking about that seductress heroin. Even more common companions, like tobacco and red wine, will at some point betray you and leave you feeling shittier. As I lay bereft on my sofa, it wasn't hard to apply this Viv adage to my love life: My habit of keeping guys at an emotional arm's length and only being attracted to ones who liked distance wasn't keeping me safe any more. It was killing me. But I had no idea how to stop it. Maria tried to give me love advice.

"Guys think you don't like them," she said. "You act like you don't care."

But I really like them, I told her.

"Then show them how you feel," she said. "Bake them cookies."

Cookies? Oh, dear God, no. I could never do anything *that* vulnerable, something that *giving*, without a guarantee.

My dark thoughts of death returned. The demise of my show and relationship brought to the surface all my fossilized feelings of worthlessness: that my needs never mattered, that I wasn't worth sticking around for, that my cries for help weren't heard, that Mom and Dad chose other people and places over me, and that I'd never been able to count on them. That missing safe harbor kept me spinning in a cycle of self-preservation.

I believed I wanted to get married, so I went on date after date with "marrying types" and returned home hating all of them. Let me be clear, these were good guys: attractive, nice, and generous. That may sound lucky. But it's a cold day in Boston when you realize that no relationship will work, no guy will do, you don't like anyone. And the problem is you.

◄◄ ▐▐ ►►

I entered a cluttered Cambridge office and saw a Sphinx-like woman sitting in a beat-up leather chair. I had gotten the name of this psychiatrist from a woman at my monthly book club who was concerned when I showed up red-eyed and sullen. She claimed this shrink had unrivaled powers of healing. If so, she kept those powers hidden in her desk drawer. The therapist was inscrutable, not even cracking a sympathy smile as I described my depression. I told her I was desperate to find lasting love but didn't know how. Then I stopped, awaiting her compassion and expert advice. Silence. I went on to explain some of my cat-and-mouse games and how I was forced to hedge my bets against loss by juggling a couple guys at once. Still no sympathy. In fact, she acted like that was a strange love strategy.

"It sounds like you're being hurtful and selfish," she said.

"No, no," I clarified. "See, guys don't like it if you make it too easy for them. They get bored and leave. They need a challenge."

She stared directly at me. "Where did you learn that?"

Jesus, lady, look around. "Uh, it's everywhere," I said.

She didn't break eye contact. "The happy couples I know are present for each other and make a commitment to be together."

I shook my head. "I don't even know what that looks like."

"That's what you need to learn."

"But I can't get anyone to do that for me," I told her. Tears flooded my eyes.

She didn't blink. "Have you ever done that for them?"

Seoul Searching

I hadn't seen Mom in months, and our practice of talking once a week had fallen off with the time zone shifts and expense of international calls. Just as REALlife ended, Mom and Steven moved halfway around the world to Seoul, South Korea, so Steven could fulfill a six-month teaching fellowship.

The same month Mom moved to Seoul, Dad was diagnosed with bladder cancer. Though I was accustomed to his absence, the possibility of it becoming permanent was different. His looming death felt inevitable, overdue even, yet it also felt like a sad surrender to his demons that didn't have to happen. His cancerous mass was quickly removed, but I still heard the clock ticking.

My depression wasn't going anywhere. The psychiatrist prescribed Prozac, but some part of me resisted. I didn't want to mask my symptoms without getting to the root of my problem. So, I carried the pills in my purse, waiting. Mom wanted me to spend a couple weeks with her in Korea, and I thought if I could tell her what I was struggling through, it might bring some closure. Maybe she'd be able to help.

I embarked on a twenty-four-hour journey of flights and layovers, in and out of tortured airplane sleep. I landed bleary-eyed but hopeful for connection. But almost as soon as Mom met me at the airport gate, I realized the trip had been a mistake. Mom was preoccupied. She hadn't thought to get me a subway token, so we were forced to wait in an endless line as she fiddled for change in her purse. She couldn't figure out her own transportation card and got caught in the turnstile. She led us in the wrong direction, then became anxious about getting home to meet Steven at the arranged time. She seemed to be squeezing me into their schedule.

Back at their apartment, I waited while Mom and Steven got dressed behind their bedroom door and dithered over dinner plans. Old feelings flooded back. Again I was an afterthought, behind Robert and Walter and Mac and Steven, and her dissertation, and night classes. Again, I'd have to fend for myself in another foreign land. I was ten years old again, vying for her attention, becoming surly and annoyed when she didn't carve out time for me alone. I immediately moved my return flight up by three days and sunk deeper into despair at having flown all this way for nothing.

On my last full day, Mom signed us up for a twelve-hour bus tour to Mount Seorak, one of the tallest peaks in the country. We set off surrounded by rows of Korean and German tourists. I was too despondent to pay attention to the tour guide, who didn't speak a word of English anyway, and Mom busied herself balancing her checkbook and consulting her to-do list.

An hour into the tour, I couldn't take another second of her distance. A lifetime of resentment and hurt bubbled up and spewed out like lava. I started crying and laying into her, letting her have it for all the damage I felt she'd done during my youth. All the times she chose a man over me. All the times she left me. All the times I waited for her to come home or say she loved me the most.

"Now, I constantly *protect* myself and keep people at an arm's distance," I told her. "I make guys think they're not important. Like I felt with *you*!"

I wasn't through, and there was no turning back.

"I don't let anyone *know* I love them! I can't give anyone that power." I sobbed. "I only like people who are emotionally out of reach like *you were*. You *crippled* me!"

Mom kept her head down, absorbing the verbal body blows. Tears leaked from her eyes as I recounted story after story and the bus loudspeakers crackled in Korean. Out the windows, dizzying valleys and jagged peaks passed by. At various lookouts, Mom and I disembarked from the bus, our faces wet and raw, the other passengers sneaking concerned stares.

Halfway through the tour, still heaving, I took a break to catch my breath. Mom looked to the roof of the bus and inhaled sharply, then finally spoke. She said she didn't remember all of the moments I was describing, but she did remember some of them. She said she wished there was something she could do about it all now to make my pain go away.

Then she fell silent as if she were out of ideas. I boiled over.

"You could take some *responsibility*!"

"And what would that sound like?" she asked, clinically, like my therapist.

Jesus. Why did I have to spoon-feed her a compassionate response?

"Why can't you just say what I need to hear?"

"I want to get it *right*," she explained.

That's when the dam broke.

"You could say, '*I'm sorry*! *I'm sorry* that I didn't value you when you were growing up and that I always put boyfriends ahead of you!'"

She steeled herself, then turned to face me. "I'm sorry that you didn't feel special or valuable because you were the most important person in the world to me."

"Then *why* didn't you act that way?" I reminded her of how she put Robert before me. How she uprooted me for Walter, then left me behind for Mac.

Mom stared at the floor, gathering her composure. She told me that after the divorce, she didn't have a roadmap for how to function as a single mother. She said she had always felt it was important to find a man to help us, to complete our family, and have some semblance of a normal life for me. "But," she said, "I didn't succeed."

She said it had taken her a long time to realize how that secret piece of her past, the sexual abuse in her childhood, had left her with impaired judgment and blurred boundaries. She said it wasn't until she and Mac broke up, and she was finally alone, that she realized how much her early trauma had warped her relationships. Slowly, the pieces started falling into place— how her self-worth was linked to a man's desire, how she, too, had been in survival mode for years, and how she'd used her intellectual armor as a shield against people coming too close. Detachment was her defense.

I looked out the window, through our reflections, at the breathtaking rock formations created over millennia and thought of how the depraved hands of a man who died before I was born had reached through the decades to destroy my relationships as well.

Mom looked up and drew a breath. The tissue balled in her fist was soaked and disintegrating.

"I am *so sorry*," she said. "You were so good, *such* a good child. I could never have asked for a better daughter."

Tears streamed down my face.

"I didn't know that, Mom. I thought I was too demanding for you. Too needy."

She shook her head. "No, that's not true. Having you has been the highlight of my life. You were perfect for me. I wish I'd been better for you."

At the next pit stop, we were quite a sight: a punch-drunk pair of red-eyed mucus balls. Our bus mates fiddled with the cameras around their necks, trying not to stare. I found myself smiling at them. I was done crying. After years of feeling unseen and overlooked, my pain was finally glaringly visible to my mother. I felt both lighter and fuller than I could remember. The next morning, I took the Prozac out of my purse and swallowed one. I felt better immediately. Mom said it couldn't have worked that fast; perhaps a placebo effect? But I knew it was something else. With the help of the therapist and that little blue tablet, for the first time in my life, I thought I might not need to be rescued. I thought I might have the power to save myself.

Who Will Save Your Soul

Immediately after my pilgrimage to South Korea, I set out on another mission—to South Jersey to tie up more unfinished business. Over the years, Dad had drifted between teaching positions and other odd jobs but never found satisfaction. His wife Carolyn reported to me in hushed phone calls whenever he was depressed and drinking to oblivion, which became nightly. When she couldn't take another second, she and I staged an intervention and got him into rehab.

Given his lifetime of heavy drinking, I held out little hope that a rehabilitation center could change Dad's habits. My suspicion was only reinforced on family weekend when Dad spent the entire group therapy session ostentatiously checking his watch, then shooting me extravagant eye rolls as other residents shared their sad stories. But as always, Antonio Camerota had a surprise up his sleeve. After three weeks in rehab, he never touched alcohol again.

Sobriety did not make Dad a new man. He was still just as delighted to see me on my occasional visits, still waiting at the top of his apartment stairs with outstretched arms and a bear hug, before settling back into his chair to light another cigarette. He still posed only basic questions about my life and avoided sharing anything about his own. He could still only sustain conversation for a few minutes before reverting to the anesthetizing effects of the TV.

Before I arrived for my come-to-Jesus conversation, Carolyn alerted him that I had something serious to discuss. As I drove them to dinner, Dad broached the subject himself.

"So, what's the problem?" he asked. "Having boy trouble?"

I snorted at his simplicity.

"It's more than that, Dad. I've been thinking about all that went wrong in my childhood."

Dad nodded. "Is this about the divorce?"

Again, too simple.

"Dad, the divorce was the least of my problems. After that, Mom was not very available, and she made some choices that took a big toll on me."

"Don't be so hard on Mom, sweetheart," he said. "You know, Mom didn't have it easy either. Don't blame her."

This set me off. Heaven forbid I cast blame. "Oh, trust me," I snapped, "You were no prize parent either."

Dad took a drag of his Parliament and turned to look out the passenger window. I'd wounded him.

"You know, sweetheart," he said, trying again, "I was mad at my parents for a long time, too."

I looked at him. "Really?" He'd never shared anything about his childhood.

"Yes, really. They did a lot of things that hurt me, too."

OK, this was big. *Finally*, I was going to learn the root of Dad's distance and unreliability. Finally, I would hear what was behind his silence and mask-making and self-medicating.

"I was angry for a long time," Dad continued, staring out the windshield, before taking another long drag and looking at me. "But at some point, you just have to say, 'Fuck it.' And that's it."

With that, he flicked his cigarette out the window. End of story.

I let out an unexpected whoop of laughter, as did Carolyn in the backseat. Quintessential Antonio Camerota: avoidant and mysterious, pithy yet wise. His philosophy also struck me as profoundly punk rock. *Yeah, fuck the parents, man!*

After all my dark nights of the soul, my journey to Seoul, my many months in therapy trying to expand my emotional capacity and unlearn unconscious familial patterns, at the end of the day, sometimes you just have to say, "Fuck It."

Time to Say Goodbye

In the final month of Dad's life, his heart, lungs, and kidneys were giving out. His lifetime of drinking and smoking was catching up to him. The doctor said he would have to go on dialysis if he wanted to live. Dad took a pass.

"I can't be trapped," he told me.

I tried to cajole him, telling him the dialysis would give him more time to meet his grandchildren, the children I hoped to have someday.

No, he said, then added, oddly, "I can't be tied down to a table."

Figures, I thought. Just another weird, self-destructive personality quirk that would cut Dad's life short. He and I were alone in the dark of his living room on a cold January night, his hospice bed in place of his TV chair, when just before midnight, Andrea Bocelli appeared on TV singing "*Con te partirò.*" *With you I will leave.* For two practiced escape artists, in the end, Dad and I stayed right there, together in the dark of that room as death crept closer. I knew he heard the music and felt my presence, and I was proud that for the first time in my life, I was a fully present caregiver. Dad's breathing slowed to shallow wisps, then stopped. I called out to Carolyn asleep in the bedroom and she rushed out to sit by his other side, but by then we couldn't detect any more breathing.

"I think he's gone," she said.

"I think he's faking it," I said, because Dad could be tricky like that.

She was right. Dad lived sixty-seven years, long enough for me to say what I had to, and long enough to have a deathbed reunion with his son, my long-lost brother, whom I'd lost touch with at thirteen but who had, twenty years later, seen me on TV, recognized my name, then called my office in time to reconnect and say goodbye to our father.

Just before I gave the eulogy at Dad's funeral, I had a revelation. I realized that death doesn't really care if you love someone fully or at an arm's distance. Somehow death, with its unfailing GPS system, comes calling anyway, and even emotional distance can't protect us from it. People leave. And that's life. So, you might as well love them fully while you have them.

That day, I decided maybe it was time to amend the vow I'd made at ten years old. Maybe it was time to take a risk on unconditional love. Maybe it was even okay to love someone more than they loved me. Maybe that wasn't a weakness after all. Maybe it was courage.

◄◄ ❚❚ ►►

One month after Dad died, the women in my book club set me up on a blind date. I'd been hearing about this guy Nick for years. He was their friend from college. Sometimes they'd mention that he was flying in from Chicago to visit or that they were meeting him in Nantucket. From time to time, they also discussed setting me up with him. They used an unusual selling point.

"He's a professional dater. Just like you!"

I had to admit, that did sound good. Even therapy couldn't completely cure me of liking the idea of a tough catch. I had an upcoming job interview in Chicago, and my book club decided the moment had come. Arrangements were made. Nick and I would meet at a Southside bar for happy hour, then have dinner with a couple of my friends.

"After that," he said during our first phone call, "we can go catch some live music at a blues bar."

"If we can stand each other," I responded. Nick laughed, but I wasn't kidding. I was open but not optimistic. The women in my book club were kind, down-to-earth intellectuals, married to do-gooder environmentalists. Their husbands were handsome and funny—but not a single one had a substance abuse problem, or disappeared without explanation, or picked fights when people got too close. And while I longed to be attracted to healthy, available guys, I wasn't sure I could be. I was so unconvinced of my own capacity for stability that I didn't bother getting dressed up for the date. I stayed in the interview outfit, showing up at happy hour in a blue pinstripe pantsuit and red turtleneck, not a sliver of skin showing from chin to toes. I might as well have worn a nun's habit.

I was thirty-three years old. By that time, I'd been on a lot of first dates. I'd dined al fresco with a date on a Greek Island and done shots with another at a beach bar outside of Lisbon. I'd danced with the first mate of a sailboat under the stars at Halicarnassus, an open-air disco in Bodrum, Turkey, and with an ad exec at a dive bar in Dewey Beach, Delaware. I'd been on first dates at Michelin-starred restaurants and candlelit homemade dinners. I'd kissed a suave network correspondent after a first date while on assignment at a plane crash in Newport and a hot young actor at a TV convention in New Orleans. I liked first dates. I was good at first dates.

But I never had a first date better than the one with Nick. We clicked, we talked, we laughed, we did a couple of tequila shots and played a couple games of pool. Turns out, my friends had buried the lead. They neglected to mention that Nick was dashingly handsome, refreshingly insightful, funny—and not at all intimidated by my history. He admitted that he'd heard of my reputation for being "fickle," as our friends described it, but that didn't scare him.

Nick and I did go listen to some live music, then went back to his place and made out until four in the morning, at which point I told him I had to go. He walked me out to hail a taxi. We kissed goodbye, and I got in the cab tingling with infatuation. The driver asked if that was my boyfriend.

"No, just a first date."

"That was a GOOD first date!" the driver said.

Something else remarkable happened that night. About half an hour into the date, Nick figured out that we'd met before, at a party in Washington, DC, six years earlier. Apparently, he'd given me his number and told me to call him when I came to Chicago on assignment. But I never did. I remembered that party. At the time, I was stuck in storm clouds surrounding the mercurial TV producer, which were obscuring my love horizon. They say timing is everything. This time around, I could see the future clearly. My eyes…and heart were open. This time I was ready. And so was Nick.

From that very first date, we never parted without another plan to be together. And just like that, my long hellish pattern of separation anxiety and defensive games was over. My friend (the one who suggested I bake cookies) told me she knew this one was different because I never once called her for advice. I no longer had to. I knew what to do. It was easy.

In a phone call after our third date, Nick predicted, "Alisyn, I think you may have just met your match."

His confidence was contagious.

"I think you might be right," I smiled.

Nine months after meeting, Nick and I celebrated New Year's Eve with a romantic dinner in his apartment. At the stroke of midnight, just as the ball dropped in Times Square, Nick surprised me by proposing marriage, and we cried tears of joy. The next morning, I called Mom to share the news. She was giddy, repeating, "Oh, I'm *so* happy. I'm *so* happy!" She said it so many times, I felt compelled to say, "I'm *so* happy for *you*!"

For our wedding, I chose "In My Life" by the Beatles to be sung right after our vows by my dear friend Lu from REALlife, the one from Montreal. I picked the song for its beautiful ode to friends from the past while fully celebrating love in the present. At my wedding, Sydney told me that she and Viv were relieved, as if *I* had been *their* biggest worry. By my wedding, Viv, against all odds, had pulled herself out of two decades of hard drug and alcohol abuse, with a handy assist from law enforcement and a judge's promise of prison if she broke probation. Once clean, Viv was transformed into a rescuer of stray animals and a devoted friend who bestowed gifts without waiting for birthdays. She ended every phone call to me with "I love you." She became the sturdiest of sounding boards, even on subjects like infertility or TV news scandals, which she hadn't experienced. But Viv had a PhD in life. The one department that Sober Viv fell short in was memory. She claimed not to remember her formerly frightening self.

"I've always loved the underdog," she told Sydney and me one day.

"You hated the underdog." I reminded her.

"No," she argued, "I always had a soft spot for the downtrodden."

Sydney and I traded quick glances. "You *don't* remember terrorizing loners in the lunchroom?" I asked.

Viv looked baffled. "No. What am I missing?"

"Um…the eighties," Sydney said.

One day Viv was trying to describe to me how bad her addiction had gotten, and why counselors at rehabs had labeled her a "lost cause" and "garbage-head junkie."

"There was one time," she said, "that I was held at gunpoint."

"Really," I said.

"Oh, yeah. There was a drug dealer in Eatontown, and he wanted my bag of pills, and he put a gun to my head."

I stared at her. "Hmm. That rings a bell. BECAUSE I WAS THERE! I WAS WITH YOU!"

"Oh, my God. Really?"

"YES. And he didn't want *your* drugs. You stole *his* drugs!"

Viv burst into a waterfall of laughter. "OK, that makes *a lot* more sense!"

Make Someone Stay

Marriage grounded me in ways that were unfamiliar and not entirely comfortable. If Nick and I had a disagreement, I could no longer immediately look for an escape. Leaving was no longer an option.

New Alisyn Adage: Marriage Means You Stay.

Nick routinely seized on my discomfort, taking delight in saying, "Don't worry, you're just stuck with me *for the rest of your life*." Another one of his sayings, any time I would lay into him with some grievance, was to smile and say, "*I don't see you complaining*." It cracked me up.

For the first time in my life, I had a partner to help with tough decisions. I didn't like that. I wanted to do what I wanted to do. I desperately wanted to leave my job. Nick didn't think that was a good idea.

I was working as a reporter and anchor at FOX. I'd gotten the job a year after REALlife ended, when an old college friend—actually my coanchor from the campus TV station—told me about his cool new job as a correspondent for an exciting upstart network called the FOX News Channel. He sang the praises of the place: high salary, great perks, exciting assignments with his own designated producer/photog team. At his urging, I mailed off a resume tape to the network's vice president. About a month later, my agent called to tell me that FOX wanted to hire me as a national correspondent based in Boston. I was thrilled and surprised. I hadn't had so much as a phone interview.

For a couple of years, FOX was a great gig, everything my friend promised. My producer, photographer, and I traveled around New England, covering stories from medical breakthroughs at Harvard to leaf peeping in Vermont.

In 2002, I scored the coveted assignment of covering the ten-day Ceremonial Funeral for England's Queen Mum. This required that I spend a couple hours a day strolling along the Thames outside of Westminster Abbey, conducting man-on-the-street interviews with a long line of apparent octogenarians about what the Queen Mum meant to them. But good reporters never stop searching for new angles. They enterprise original story ideas. That's why the London Bureau Chief and I put our heads together to research which London restaurant served the best vodka gimlets. We took this assignment very seriously—not allowing ourselves even one night off from research. Those gimlets weren't going to drink themselves, and we had our work cut out for us. By the end of my trip, the bureau chief and I concluded that the biggest headline of the entire week was Britain's shocking dearth of good gimlets.

FOX was all fun and games...until it wasn't. It began morphing into a different experience. The assignments started taking a conservative slant, and editors started trying to inject snarky comments—about the ACLU or Hilary Clinton or Muslims—into my scripts. One morning, I was assigned to do a story on a lesbian couple with two young children in Massachusetts who were fighting for marriage rights. I started working the phones, trying to cajole the couple to go on camera. They agreed, but only if it didn't interfere with their baby's naptime. My crew and I raced out, hitting the timing perfectly and scoring the sweet money shot of the moms putting their baby and toddler down for their naps. Then we raced back to edit the package for the 6:00 p.m. show.

But as soon as we fed my story into New York, one of the executives called my bureau chief. I watched his face tighten. The executive demanded to know what my "agenda" was. Why did my script refer to the women and their children as "a family"? Apparently, Roger Ailes did not want those women to be called a family. The piece was immediately pulled off the air.

My crew and I sat shell-shocked and I started looking for a way out.

Nick thought I should stay at FOX until I found another job. He argued that my salary helped pay our mortgage and that my Massachusetts health insurance paid for infertility treatments, which we were in the middle of. I wanted to flee and figure the rest out later.

Before long, the CEO of FOX, Roger Ailes, was spending an irrational amount of time trying to bully me into embracing and broadcasting his narrow worldview filled with Islamophobia, racist tropes, and conservative boosterism. I've already written about this in various places, and I don't want to go over plowed ground, except to say that Roger's now infamous sexual harassment, for me, wasn't even the half of it. (In 2016, Ailes resigned from FOX after several women accused him of sexual harassment and inappropriate behavior, which he always denied.)

"You'll never be successful," he told me repeatedly during my years at FOX, "until you learn to think like a conservative."

Roger liked to control how his anchors spoke, dressed, and even thought.

I assured Roger I was well-versed in conservative thinking since I interviewed dozens of right-wing Republicans, day in and day out. I also told him that I would prefer to broadcast in a nonpartisan way, giving both sides their due and asking both sides tough questions.

"How 'bout you let me be a rational voice in the middle?" I proposed. "Doesn't it get a little tedious to hear the same conservative viewpoints segment after segment? What if I presented a counterpoint?"

At that moment, we were seated catty-corner from each other at the coffee table in his large office, and he brought his fist down on the arm of his chair and thundered, "You CANNOT do that! You will LOSE the audience! I will not let you do that!"

Roger hated to "lose." Ratings were all that mattered.

I tried to escape. Not once. Many, many times. I drummed up exciting job offers from networks where I longed to work. And without fail, Roger Ailes sabotaged every single one. He called local news directors who were interested in hiring me and bellowed at them to back off. He called network executives, threatening to sue them for "poaching his talent." Those executives would then call my agent, livid that I'd put them in such a dicey position. My agent told me that word on the street was that I had become "radioactive."

It was a vexing bind. For Roger, too. He repeatedly told me that he couldn't promote me because I "couldn't be trusted," though he also shared focus group analytics showing that I was a viewer favorite. Compounding his frustration was the fact that I got great ratings.

So, he wouldn't promote me, but he wouldn't fire me. I was a prisoner in Roger's personal purgatory, destined for career death from lack of air and sunlight. I was also acutely aware of what happened to some other talented anchors who deigned to leave FOX. They never worked in news again.

Marrying Nick had shown me that there were options other than leaving. But my escapist tendencies were still strong. I was still that prisoner who would never stop trying to squeeze through a jail cell window.

I began writing down every tortured interaction with Roger. On the days I felt trapped, I'd come home and scribble my frustration into a journal. The writing was cathartic and instructive: capturing Roger's patterns and absurd lines of logic helped prepare me for the next round of them. At some point, the pages formed themselves into a novel. A publisher became interested. But no sooner did they buy the book, than the publisher's legal team kiboshed the idea. The lawyer said that in order to publish it, I would have to delete *all the Roger chapters.* They were afraid of his litigious streak. They knew he'd sue.

Roger's long dark shadow was now blocking my future success *outside* of television, too.

Still, the act of writing emboldened me. It helped me see a path out of FOX, even if that path never led to another TV job. Maybe I could make money from writing. Maybe I could go back to waiting tables. I had to leave. Somehow, I'd survive. That's when I decided to try an approach I'd never used before with Roger, one I'd never heard of anyone even attempting: radical honesty.

I tried appealing to his sense of decency (whatever existed) by telling him that he knew it was time for me to leave. FOX *wasn't* the right fit for me—even *he'd* told me that. It was better that I go. But Roger was a fighter. Every exchange was a zero-sum game. If I left, he lost. If I stayed, he could keep me on a shelf as part of his doll collection that no one else could play with. A win.

Over the next few months, I watched Roger go through every one of the five stages of grief about my desire to leave, from bargaining to anger, sometimes in rapid-fire succession. His own version of a cable news "lightning round":

He told me he'd never let me go. He'd sue me for breaking my contract.

He told me no one else would ever want me; that by keeping me on the payroll, he was *"protecting me."*

He told me I couldn't leave because he "loved me too much" (I don't think he meant romantically, though it was hard to tell with him).

He told me it wasn't up to him; he had a "fiduciary duty" to Rupert Murdoch.

He told me he'd give me my own new and exciting show; just name my terms.

I admit, part of me found this amusing. Watching Roger wrestle with his demons to avoid losing was sort of entertaining. But it got old fast. It was also painfully transparent. I guess he'd forgotten that I was once a crime reporter. I guess he wasn't aware that I'd already heard every line abusive men use to stop a woman from leaving. I guess he didn't know that he sounded a lot like one of the quotes on the *America's Most Wanted* conference room wall, uttered by too many fugitives to count: *"If I can't have you, no one will."*

"I can tell you hate authority," Roger sneered at me during one meeting. "You must have had a horrible childhood."

Sometimes Roger took so many swings, he ended up in the right ballpark. But he didn't know that my challenging childhood made me stronger in this situation, not weaker. I sat expressionless in his office, telepathically transmitting a message. *I see you, Roger. I know about your hardscrabble past that left you with a chip on your shoulder and made you an angry man. Let me guess, you never got the girl in high school, and you've made women pay ever since, right? But see, my past has made me grateful for all I have now. And on some deep level, we both know that makes me better than you. You may sign my paycheck and have unchecked power, but I think we both know, on the scorecard of life, I win.*

The leaving dance went on for months. All I wanted was for Roger to sign a separation agreement letting me go, no severance, no nothing. I knew his lieutenants had spent weeks trying to get the crazy general to comply, I assume by telling him that the last thing he needed was a renegade subordinate spouting disgruntlement in the halls (which I'd begun doing).

But on the day he was supposed to sign the documents, word came down that Roger wanted to see me…"one last time."

I said no. I knew he was up to his old tricks. I knew once I was alone in his office, he would hector me into staying.

"Don't you see it's a trap?" I told his team.

No, no, they assured me. He just wants to *say goodbye*, that's all.

Of course, as soon as I entered his office, he told me the deal was off. He'd decided not to let me go.

"So, you'll stay, and we'll work it out," he said.

For a few long beats, my spirit left my body and hovered above us in those chairs. But in that free-floating space, I had an epiphany, a pure crystalline realization that I should have known all along. *You can't make someone stay.* Even someone as powerful and intimidating as Roger Ailes cannot force you to stay somewhere you don't want to be. The truth was that, in my head, I'd long since left the building. Yes, he could prevent me from going somewhere else, but he couldn't make me stay.

Suddenly my pattern of pulling up stakes and flying away wasn't a shortcoming. It was a superpower. "See, Roger," I told him, "you say you won't let me leave, but you don't realize, I'm already gone."

He signed the papers that afternoon.

Punk Rock Girl

Somewhere along the way, I lost Shrapnel's "Combat Love" 45, and then had no evidence of them ever existing. Over the years, I tried searching online for "Shrapnel," but only strange links popped up with words like "blast," "wounds," and "injuries." My popcorn tin contained no fragments of them. At times, I wondered if it had really been as incandescent as I remembered.

For a long time, my brain could not stop searching for missing pieces, trying to access old Shrapnel songs, getting stuck in a fruitless loop of trying to remember lyrics I'd never heard enough times to begin with. An unending earworm.

I saw Dave Vogt a few times over the years. After the band broke up, he became a bartender at the Brighton. On one visit home, I went with Viv to Hardcore Night, and there he was, hustling behind the bar. His hair wasn't Shrapnel-short anymore; it was Tommy Lee-long, crew cut vanquished by Mötley Crüe. He was still handsome, still thin and muscular. The last time I went in, the place was packed. At the end of the bar sat two girls who looked like they'd fallen out of a ZZ Top video: big hair, tight jeans, unnaturally round breasts. The rocker-chicks flirted with Vogt, and I stood watching in a crush of patrons. Somehow his radar was still fine-tuned for spotting me in a crowd. His face lit up, and I still felt special to be singled out. He gave a quick head bob and held up one finger for me to stay right there. He wiped his hands on a dishtowel, then yelled something in the ear of the other crazed bartender, who looked confused as Vogt squeezed past and ducked under the wooden hatch. He came to me, wearing that same crooked smile he'd always had, and kissed me on the cheek.

"Hey!" He reached for my hand.

"Hey!" I said. The music was loud, so we stood close.

"What are you doing here?" he yelled.

"I'm here with Viv." My lips were against his ear, before pulling back to see his face.

He moved close to my ear. "You look great."

I smiled and leaned in. "You, too."

"So, you're on TV now?"

I nodded.

"I saw you. And I was like, 'Damn, look at her. I know someone famous.'"

I laughed, then felt the twist, that moment when the dynamic shifts. Being on TV has a way of doing that, of making people starry-eyed, making them think you hover above them. I'd longed for that lofty stature my whole life, that day when I would be the star people wanted to reach. It turns out stardom is a paradox; the bright light of stars shines from above, only seen from beneath And the day that shift happens doesn't feel like a victory. It feels heartbreaking.

"I gotta get back," he said, looking at the throng at the bar.

He leaned in and kissed me again.

"I'm happy to see you," he said.

"Me, too."

He squeezed my hand, then let go.

That was the last I saw him. He died a year later. The official cause was diabetes, but I suspect it was the result of a life lived too hard—or not lived fully enough. One month later, Tommy Kelly died, too, from virtually those same maladies of the spirit. In writing this, I've thought of them both so often. They would have gotten a kick out of helping me remember it all.

I think about my teenage self, desperate to attach to friends and boyfriends, their families and their homes. Who would I be if I hadn't been so hungry? I would have given anything to stay in New Jersey for the rest of my life, but who would I be if I'd never left?

◄◄ ❚❚ ►►

It's morning, and I hear laughter in the kitchen. The kids are on the iPad, watching videos of a water-skiing squirrel.

"You can find anything on YouTube," my son says, and it sparks an idea.

When the school bus pulls away, I sit down at the computer and type "Shrapnel CBGB" into the search window. A few seconds later, they roar to life. My breath catches. It's all there: posters, photos, the album cover. The guys look different than I remembered—somehow more beautiful. I lean in to study their faces, each one a Raphael portrait. I'd always considered them cute, but how had I missed their staggering beauty?

Then, it hits me.

The fullness of their faces, their smiles winking with optimism and playfulness.

The lushness of youth, frozen in the frame.

Funny, I'd always thought of them as so much older, but I see now they were young.

We were all so young.

On the computer screen, the familiar list of song titles and audio clips from live shows: CBGB's 1979, Dirt Club 1981. Only a couple of months earlier, someone had posted a 1982 link to "Sleepover." I move the mouse slowly, shakily, certain the link is a vanishing mirage. I click, and before I can brace myself, the first beats hit like thunderclaps. I grip the top of the desk as the music pours into a parched groove in my brain.

Well, last night just wasn't long enough,
the cops had to wake us up on the beach...

I shut my eyes and feel the riptide of memory sucking me away from the safe shore of my suburban home back to the sun and salt and sand of that loud electric time that ended too soon.

Epilogue

Two years after her husband Steven died, Mom moved to the town next to mine to be closer to me. It was sometimes strange to see her at my house, sitting among toys, schoolbooks, and backpacks, the flotsam and jetsam of my family life. Funny how *she* now followed *me* and *my* husband to other states and homes.

Every Sunday, she visits, taking her perch on the end of the sofa and reading her latest book, sharing passages she thinks I'll like. On many school nights, I'm pleasantly surprised to catch her image on the other end of a Facetime, helping one of my daughters muddle through a history or English paper. Some of my mother's conversation has shifted from operatic librettos to doctor's visits and daily computer frustrations. Now in her eighties, she is smaller in stature, but her long slender fingers look the same as those on the elegant woman to whom, despite our separations, I will always be attached.

Mom leaves my house before it gets dark. She doesn't like to drive at night, and I still get an unsettled feeling watching her drive away, though now I trust I'll see her again and know if she were gone, I will survive.

◄◄ ❚❚ ►►

More than two decades after receiving the first apology letter from Walter, Mom received another one. In it, he described how he'd gotten remarried, worked to repair his relationships with his daughters, and tried to become a better person. Once again, he expressed guilt for what he'd put us through.

This time she was ready to write back.

Dear Walter,

Yesterday, I spent all day in Dayton, Ohio at the funeral of a coworker I've known and loved for ten years. It was the second funeral I've been to since retiring three months ago. Every member of my parents' generation is gone now, and I'm the oldest member of my generation. As a slacker retiree, there's plenty of time to reflect. Twenty-five years is enough time for guilt, what Erma Bombeck called, "The gift that keeps on giving." I accept your apologies. Forgiveness and redemption have become important to me.

I'm happy you have a rich, full life. So have I. I try to stay in the present. Looking back at that time is terribly sad and painful. Alisyn and I were emotionally and financially devastated. She especially deserved better than to be uprooted and derailed during her teenage years. Our relationship was affected, too. When I left Washington, Alisyn stayed to finish her junior year. We lived separate lives from then on. It took a long time to regain her trust.

Mac was truly our rescuer. He and I stayed together 6 years, long enough to realize that loyalty and a shared crisis were not sufficient reasons to spend the rest of our lives together. In 1989, I met Steven through a mutual friend. Five days after we married, we moved from Pittsburgh to Ohio.

Antonio died in 2000. Alisyn was with him at the end. Two months later, she met her future husband. They were married the week before 9/11 and were in Italy on their honeymoon when the Twin Towers fell. Two of Alisyn's bridesmaids, Kimberly and Hera, are her best friends from high school in Bellingham. Alisyn once said moving to the Northwest was the best worst thing that ever happened to her.

A year ago, Alisyn gave birth to twin daughters, born two months early. Watching them in the NICU for five weeks struggling to grow prompted my decision to retire. I spend a week every month with Alisyn and her family in Manhattan. The girls are beautiful and healthy as they approach their first birthday.

I feel fortunate to have my immediate and extended families, friends in places from Philadelphia to Bellingham, former students and patients. Life is short and precious. A crisis in the past has evolved into happiness in the present for all of us.

Sincerely,

Catherine

Twenty years after Dad died, a woman contacted me on Facebook. She had seen me on TV and recognized my name. She identified herself as the daughter of Dad's first wife, a wife neither Mom nor I knew existed, the very first of his five marriages. The woman said that Dad had been the love of her mother's life. She sent me photos of the day they eloped; Dad, just twenty-two, in a white suit jacket. His bride only eighteen. The woman urged me to call her mother, now in her eighties but "still sharp as a tack."

Dad's first wife was thrilled to hear from me; she had long hoped we would connect. She told me she met my father at a dance when she was fifteen. She'd never seen anyone dance so well, ooze that much charisma. It was impossible for me to imagine Dad dancing. She said that even after they divorced, Dad had been in touch over the years and had always told her I was the best thing in his life.

He told her I was magical.

She asked if I knew what had happened to him in the army. I repeated the standard story he'd told us that he was an interpreter stationed in Germany on the border to interrogate border-crossers. I heard a sharp inhale through the receiver, like she knew that one. No, she said, he was a spy, tasked with secreting dissidents and high-value targets out of Moscow. He spoke flawless Russian and had memorized a map of every street corner in the city so he could be dropped anywhere and get out. But something went wrong. Something happened that he didn't divulge. He came home changed, distant, no longer that bright light of a man out on the dance floor. He started drinking. No one knew the term PTSD back then, but she came to believe that's what he was suffering from. Their marriage quickly crumbled.

She had one question for me, one she'd always hoped to ask. She wanted to know if he had come out of it. Had he gone on to have a happy life?

It pained me to tell her no.

With her call, my blurry picture of Dad snapped into sharper focus. For the first time, I felt I understood his self-destructive risk-taking. Maybe he became a jewel thief to prove he could sneak in and out of danger without getting caught. Maybe he was bored by small-town suburbia and longed for a high-stakes gambit. Clearly, his psyche had unfinished business. I could relate. Well into my twenties, I snuck backstage at random concerts to prove I still could and to try to feel the electricity again.

After my call with Dad's first wife, Mom, too, was left to rethink all our sardonic references to Dad, the International Man of Mystery.

"You know how Dad's fingernails were gnarled?" Mom asked.

"Yes. They were sort of mutilated," I remembered. "He said a gun had backfired in his hand during basic training."

Mom nodded slowly. "I bet he was captured."

My mind instantly clicked to a snapshot of a wartime torture scene with Dad strapped to a table, his fingernails being torn out. So much made sense now: his drinking, the faraway stares, his anxiety about bridges, his primal panic the day he rejected being strapped to a dialysis machine. Mom and I cried, and for the first time in my life, I felt only deep compassion for my father, for whatever he, too, had suffered and never shared.

It's strange how many years after an explosion, we still carry pieces of shrapnel under our skin.

END

Acknowledgments

No life story is the storyteller's alone. In sharing mine, I had to share pieces of my friends' and family's lives that they would not have otherwise revealed. Most everyone had reservations, but in the end, they gave their blessings and generously helped me cobble the pieces together, even when doing so was painful. I'm grateful for the closure they've given me.

To my early readers and kind friends who suffered through the first amorphous drafts to offer incredibly wise direction: Brettne Bloom, Jen Marshall, David Black, Shannon Welch, JR Moehringer, and Jay Roach.

Deep thanks to the many brilliant friends and editors who shared their unvarnished impressions, suggestions, and guidance: Caroline Sherman, Svea Vocke, Stefanie Lemcke, Suzanne Propp, Adrienne Brodeur, Tina Bennett, Byrd Levell, Hilary Liftin, Joe Pascal, Leigh Newman, Bridie Loverro, Zibby Owens, Neil Cohen, Jay Sures, Peter Goldberg, Judy Clain, John Berman, and Jake Tapper. You made every page better.

I could not have gotten to the finish line without the amazingly keen and compassionate editing eye of Lu Hanessian. Lu, you mystical, magical maven, you. The psychic was right: our bond was written in the stars.

To Phil Caivano, Daniel Rey, and Dave Wyndorf, thank you for everything—for the music and the photos and for being my sonic superheroes. I'm grateful for your willingness to jump back in the van for this ride down memory lane. It's possible I wrote the book just to hang with you guys.

And thanks to my vast army of friends and surrogate families whose love saved me then and fills my soul now: the wonderful Kahn family—Gilly, Evie, Jen, Liz, and Mark. Debbie Buck, Barbara Cook, Cheryl Modica, Jimmy Hankins, and Jane Colville; the Hallorans—Beth, Marie, Bob, Karen, and

Mark; and the Peers—Kevin, Mollie, Jennifer, Sheila, Andy, Norm, and Joan. To the Maxwells—Renee, Michael, and Torri. To David Tanen, Maurice Stack, Phil Smith, Jessica Tursi, Jennifer Ruggiano, Sam Alberts, Kathy Klem, Kerrie Blum, Alyssa Diz. To all the Flannerys. To Jennifer Snell Klein, Trina Forest, Mickey Main. To the Leenstras. To all the Lewises. To Maria Villalobos. And, of course, the Vixens: Lori Burns, Susan Lowry, Rosalyn Porter, Amy Fanning, and Gerri Riggs.

Thanks to my fellow crime fighter, music lover, and literary agent extraordinaire, Marc Gerald, for believing in the story from the first note, and Leah Petrakis at Europa Content. To Gary Dell-Abate for great advice on memoir writing. To the amazing team at Rare Bird, especially Tyson Cornell for recognizing the enduring power of punk, and Alexandra Watts and Hailie Johnson for helping it all come together.

To the team at CNN for their thoughtful read, in particular, Mariano Castillo and Veronica Molina. And to Danielle Desser for all her guidance. To my amazing cheering section: Daniella Landau, Lisa Lori, Blyth and Charlie Lord, Alison and Tim Lord, Deirdre Lord, and Alex Wright; Kristin and Charles Bieler, Annika Pergament, and Michael O'Looney; Britt and Stephanie Szostak, Lauren Weisberger, Jane Green, Emily Liebert, Daniela Taplin Lundberg, Melissa Kondak, Emma Marshall, Phil Lerman, Jennifer Rivera, Susan White, and Jeff Zucker; and to Mike Cohen for his fabulous photos.

And to the friends we lost far too soon. Gillian Kahn, who served as my lifelong editor, partner in crime, and memory bank, how I wish you were here. Dave Vogt, Kevin Peer, Doug McLearen, Michael Coolahan, Mark Eulner, Marty McHale, Kenny Buck, Greg Montgomery, Mary Warner, Kelly Tobin, Nick Caivano. Your presence lives in these pages.

Deepest gratitude for my beloved and brave husband and our children who gave me the space and support to write this story without judgement, even when they didn't know what the pages would contain. You're my every prayer answered.

And for my mother, who repeatedly asked during my writing, "Can't you wait until I'm dead?" Thank you for staying alive and helping me process the past. Thank you for listening even when it was hard. Thank you for giving me the freedom to realize my dreams. I wouldn't change a thing.

Playlist

"Willkommen"—John Kander and Fred Ebb

"The Impossible Dream"—Mitch Leigh

"You Are My Sunshine"—Jimmie Davis

"Will You Still Love Me Tomorrow?"—Carole King

"Don't Go Breaking My Heart"—Elton John/Kiki Dee

"You're So Vain"—Carly Simon

"Shout It Out Loud"—Kiss

"Stayin' Alive"—Bee Gees

"Revolution"—The Beatles

"Combat Love"—Shrapnel

"Special Forces Boy"—Shrapnel

"Sleepover"—Shrapnel

"School's Out"—Alice Cooper

"Dreaming"—Blondie

"Rock 'n' Roll High School"—Ramones

"Born to Run"—Bruce Springsteen

"Walk on the Wild Side"—Lou Reed

"Dance This Mess Around"—The B-52's

"Another Nail in My Heart"—Squeeze

"Chop Up Your Mother"—Sic F*cks

"Sonic Reducer"—Dead Boys

"Siegfried Line"—Shrapnel

"Search and Destroy"—The Dictators

"Me and Bobby McGee"—Janis Joplin

"Take It On the Run"—REO Speedwagon

"Heartbreaker"—Pat Benatar

"Once in a Lifetime"—Talking Heads

"Hold Me Now"—Thompson Twins

"Satellite of Love"—Lou Reed

"Skidmarks on My Heart"—The Go-Go's

"On Your Radio"—Joe Jackson

"Change of Heart"—Tom Petty

"Blitzkrieg Bop"—Ramones

"This Must Be the Place"—Talking Heads

"Truckin' (What a Long Strange Trip)"—Grateful Dead

"The Safety Dance"—Men Without Hats

"I Wanna Be Sedated"—Ramones

"You Can't Put Your Arms Around a Memory"—Johnny Thunders

"Once in a Lifetime"—Talking Heads

"You Better Run"—Pat Benatar

"Who Will Save Your Soul"—Jewel

"Fox on the Run"—Sweet

"In My Life"—The Beatles

"Con te Partiro (Time to Say Goodbye)"—Andrea Bocelli

"Punk Rock Girl"—The Dead Milkmen